DEDICATION

To all who marvel at nature and feel themselves to be a part of her splendour.

To all who look up in awe and wonder at a twinkling night sky.

To all who know instinctively that the creation is of Grand Design.

To all who acknowledge the questions that arise within and in sincerity, seek answers.

SALUMET...

HIS MISSION TO PLANET EARTH

Dialogues with the 21ˢᵗ Century Source Teacher

Co-author and Editor: George E Moss

Presented on behalf of the Kingsclere Group who receive from spirit

Salumet is a Master in spirit from the 'far soul integrations'. He comes to a spirit communication group, on Monday evenings, that meets in Kingsclere, Hampshire, UK. He speaks with a wonderful clarity through the full trance medium Eileen Roper, teaching the ways of spirit and answering questions on a wide range of subjects. There is a striking parallel with the Master known as White Eagle who came through Grace Cooke in the mid-20ᵗʰ century. The Salumet mission to Earth began in June 1994 and continues. The objectives have been twofold: to steer the world away from a course that had been taking us steadily towards nuclear oblivion and then to raise spiritual awareness as we proceed into this New Millennium. His teaching is of that same Divine Source as Jesus, Krishna, Buddha, the one who 'revealed' to St John in Revelation, he who came to Thoth in more ancient times and other Masters ... but the difference is that Salumet's words are for world-consciousness as it stands today. His mission is for 21ˢᵗ century humanity.

Printed in Victoria, BC, Canada

Note for Librarians: a cataloguing record for this book that includes Dewey Decimal Classification and US Library of Congress numbers is available from the Library and Archives of Canada. The complete cataloguing record can be obtained from their online database at:
www.collectionscanada.ca/amicus/index-e.html
ISBN 1-4120-2661-X

TRAFFORD

This book was published *on-demand* in cooperation with Trafford Publishing. On-demand publishing is a unique process and service of making a book available for retail sale to the public taking advantage of on-demand manufacturing and Internet marketing. On-demand publishing includes promotions, retail sales, manufacturing, order fulfilment, accounting and collecting royalties on behalf of the author.

Offices in Canada, USA, UK, Ireland, and Spain
book sales for North America and international:
Trafford Publishing, 6E–2333 Government St.
Victoria, BC V8T 4P4 CANADA
phone 250 383 6864   toll-free 1 888 232 4444
fax 250 383 6804   email to orders@trafford.com
book sales in Europe:
Trafford Publishing (UK) Ltd., Enterprise House, Wistaston Road Business Centre
Crewe, Cheshire CW2 7RP UNITED KINGDOM
phone 01270 251 396   local rate 0845 230 9601
facsimile 01270 254 983   orders.uk@trafford.com
order online at:
www.trafford.com/robots/04-0489.html

10   9   8   7   6   5   4   3   2

FOREWORD

The Earth was created about four and a half billion years ago. If the various stages of creation from the beginning when it was too hot to sustain physical life, to the Jurassic period, to Homo erectus when man first learned to stand upright and on to Homo sapiens (the hunter-gatherer with a brain large enough to write poetry, build a violin or a personal computer). If that four and a half billion years were to be compressed into one hundred, then this ability to compose, paint and build cathedrals, skyscrapers and *manned* spacecraft would all have happened in the last eight months!

These are not my thoughts, although I echo them, but those of astrophysicists Fred Hoyle and his poetic colleague Chandra Wickramasinge.

Salumet is not a scientist and yet he is. He is not the wisest being that ever was created and yet he is. He is not the greatest philosopher that ever lived and yet he is. He is not an expert on any given subject yet he is. That is the point he is trying to make! WE ALL HAVE THE POTENTIAL, we have it 'here and now', especially in the NOW!

For NOW is the starting point, not yesterday, not tomorrow, but TODAY! We all have the ability to LOVE and CREATE and this is his message to us all.

This Earth of ours is about to undergo vast changes, not only physically but spiritually. **Salumet** is not teaching anything new. Oh no. But if you think you are going along for a 'free ride' without putting any work into this project FORGET IT! You can start the change NOW, TODAY. However, *nothing* is ever lost. If you get lost along the way just *ask* and you will be answered. Death is a continuum, an illusion. There *is* no DEATH; that is also a small part of what **Salumet** is teaching. But above all – and I am sure many of you are sick and tired of the phrase: 'Love Conquers All' – but it's a truism. 90% of the songs written are about love, love lost, love found again, unrequited love; even rock and roll and jazz lyrics are based on love. So are all the great religions, including the so-called pagans. It is woven into the very fabric of this Earth's culture. This is what **Salumet** is about and what he's come to teach. But he is not unique in this; many have come and more and more are *getting through this Earthly vale of tears*. He – **Salumet** – comes from a light where a million suns are but a mere candle flame.

This book is full to bursting with his love, with his teaching, with his soul, and drips off the pages like honey: sweet and pure and clear, like truth *is*. However, truth can be *tough* but never changes. It is only our perception of truth that changes ... but I have come to the conclusion that even the *Creative Principle / God / Infinite* (whatever label you care to use) is still evolving, the truth is ever evolving. LOVE is ever evolving.

Love does not, CANNOT ... stand still!

PAUL BURA
Author and poet
www.paulbura.co.uk

CONTENTS

~ *"Go back to your biblical times that you are all familiar with: was not the voice heard in the wilderness? Was not the voice of those great spirits heard upon the mountains? What is new about it?"*

Salumet.

ACKNOWLEDGEMENTS

The Kingsclere Group functions as a team, part of which is on the physical Earth and part in spirit. It is an extensive team and all have contributed in their various ways towards assembling the data for this book. All are thanked for their valuable contributions. The one I would single out for particular mention is Leslie. It was under Leslie's presidency and guidance that the lengthy (Earthly) preparations for Salumet's visits were made. There have followed wonderful years of the teachings with but a small interruption around the time of Leslie's passing to spirit in the autumn of 1999. But his work is still evident on the other side and we continue to receive word from him, as will in due course become evident to the reader.

Salumet, whose words are presented here, has made it clear on several occasions that he does not seek our thanks, yet we are much indebted. He has also made it clear that he is from the far soul integrations, where that spiritual realm merges into Divinity, and he is not the single entity that we would better understand. He has suggested that, to aid our understanding, we visualise him as one facet of a much larger diamond. He, the one facet, comes to us with the knowledge of the whole diamond. It is therefore appropriate that we respectfully acknowledge 'the whole diamond' in regard to the wondrous information received and presented here.

In editing and presenting what follows, I have felt it appropriate to make occasional reference to our literature. It is as well that we see clearly the connections between the teaching that comes to us direct from spirit and the products of our advancing science and intellect. It all helps to illustrate the fact that science, mysticism and spirituality are at last merging together as they should in the 21st century. I therefore acknowledge with sincere thanks the authors of 37 reference works listed at the end of this book. The patterns of connection to our Earthly thinking also help to establish some degree of credibility, for the words that come to us direct from that domain of spirit, for any who may seek further assurance.

PREFACE

The author of the teachings that follow resides in spirit. As pure energy he is without form, as we would understand it, yet his presence is felt and the voice conveys so much love and richness of being. He regularly visits and teaches the dedicated group who meet weekly. In these pages, all the words that have been received from spirit are presented in quoted italic script and preceded by '~' to denote that they are indeed the words 'received', as opposed to our own physical dialogue and commentary printed in standard font. All communications have been recorded during the séance meetings then carefully transcribed. In compiling this work superscript reference numbers have been inserted to indicate connections with our literature; also a word has occasionally been inserted in brackets to make a sentence flow better. It is wonderful that a consciousness that would normally communicate through telepathic process is able to piece together our clumsy word language. Despite the awkward limitations imposed by language for describing details of formless spirit, the author manages to convey a description of his own essence. Suffice to say here that he is pure energy from afar in spirit, where the soul integrations merge into Divinity.

The mission to Earth has long been foreseen and its timing carefully planned. Across the millennia there have been other missions to uplift this planet and there has been reference to these. All such teaching has centred upon love and peace. But this one is for our time, the teaching honed to our needs, to our awareness as that awareness stands at present and to the ways of 21st century humanity. Many contemporary topics are embraced and they include such items as space travel, extraterrestrial life, crop circles, smoking, drinking and how the disease of cancer should never be. There are also interesting references to civilisations of our ancient past. We live in a wonderful time of advancement and our way forward is becoming clearer by the minute.

It has occurred to me both at the outset as well as since, that there is one big question concerning the mission. How can ordinary, mundane people such as ourselves … address, receive from, question and discuss with one of all-knowledge and endowed with the infinite wisdom of Divine Source? How dare we, with all our Earthly imperfection and inadequacy, confront one of such advancement that it simply places him beyond our perception? Surely we can only make complete asses of ourselves? Leslie, who will be properly introduced in due course, had once used the 'pack of cards' analogy, suggesting that in the cosmic cultural order, we come 'at the bottom of the pile'. That has to be seen as a realistic view. But Salumet puts it differently when he says:

~ *"This planet is so very young that souls who come to inhabit it, come to learn. That is what you must always remember about this Earthly planet."*

The statement is profound. We may know little of the vast universal truth, but this does not matter just so long as we are open to learn from the planetary experience.

Spiritual advancement embraces boundless love, compassion and understanding, and these qualities seem to be embodied in the very tenor and vibration of the voice that issues forth. The meetings are it seems, not just for receiving words. Those present, leave enriched with love, healing and a certain spiritual connection. The gulf between teacher and those who receive gets somehow dimmed through that connection, and a oneness prevails. So perhaps this is in part at least, an answer to the above question, and of course love and humility always remain paramount where matters of spirit are concerned. And it might be said that, when you know you are at the bottom of the pile, humility comes easy!

IT IS TIME for us to look to wider horizons. One has to see a creation that extends throughout the cosmos, and Earth as a small speck within. Christianity, Hinduism, Buddhism, Islam and other enlightenments that have arisen from the teaching of Masters in earlier times are but local planetary expressions of a greater cosmic truth. The separate sect divisions that have sprung up within these enlightenments are even more localised and transient. Although the religions have been blessed with Divine teaching for communities in particular time and place, each has become flawed in various ways … through human misinterpretation, jihad, crusade, inquisition, religious conquest and the dogmatic input of historic councils. Nevertheless, the world's religions, on account of their central cores of inspired input, have been 'springboards' to an ever-widening awareness. The cosmos has a multiplicity of beings, all of the same spiritual essence, to be acknowledged as we progress. In grasping that ever-increasing awareness it is a blessing that help for us is always to hand.

PART I - INTRODUCTIONS

1. A PATHWAY OF LIGHT

The twelve of us would meet each Monday evening at Leslie's place … that is, at the home of Leslie Bone in a quiet, residential part of Kingsclere. Our shared interest being 'spirit communication', presided over by Leslie who had pursued such matters for almost fifty years of his life. He was now into his eighties and to the casual observer, what he did not know about the ways of spirit was not worth knowing. He was a between-worlds expert and a healer; the two so often go together. He also made the tea at the close of a session. That was always the cue for review of the evening's events and a good old chat. And a message had been received some months earlier that something special was in preparation and we would become aware in due course at a time when the roses would be in bloom.

Much always happened during the course of an evening. Several entranced mediums were usually present and 'controls' would drop by with messages from loved ones who had passed on. Those in spirit who had mastered the use of a physical medium/instrument could speak direct of course but not all in the near astral planes are able to do this. It is something that has to be learnt whilst in spirit and requires patience. There were also evenings when interesting ones came through who had achieved much in their Earth lives; sometimes public figures, sometimes royalty, sometimes criminals. Occasionally there was unfinished business or a detail of recorded history that required correction. And there were some that were having a problem in their transition to spirit so that a 'rescue' was in order to help them on their way. Such had thus far been the nature of our many evenings together.

This particular evening was that of 27th June 1994. At first it was much the same as any previous Monday until the wonderful voice, so richly imbued with a vibration of deep love and compassion … came through Eileen. There was some faltering at first as the voice articulated:

~ *"I … am … Salumet. I have waited a long … long time to come to you."*

Leslie warmly welcomed our guest and a few details were sorted that would assist further communication. Our visitor then continued:

~ *"We are reaching the point where your world will… **will** be a better place. Do not doubt these words. It may seem that (this) cannot be so. I am here to say … it will be … **will be**! … We have much to teach you."*

Leslie replied that everything would be recorded to pass on to others and our visitor replied that they in spirit already know this will happen.

That is how the Salumet evenings began. The following Monday he returned and reminded us:

~ *"We have told you in the past that there would be 'happenings' … when your flower the rose was in bloom."* And he continued: *"My mission here is to extend our love and to bring you knowledge. I want to say to you all … you are already in the pathway of light."*

Indeed, the roses in Leslie's garden had been at their best in the month of June, as they have been each year since. Salumet's 'mission' (for that is clearly what it has been and still is), continued through the remaining years of the twentieth century and on into the twenty-first. Now, as I write this record in the year 2003/4, the words of our Source teacher Salumet continue into their tenth … ten years of A PATHWAY OF LIGHT. As will become evident, that is apt description for the progressing journey of his mission … a mission to be shared with as many who may care to read his words.

At the outset our teacher saw that we had many questions lodged in our minds and invited these. So our early meetings were very much question-and-answer sessions. The exchange was good. It helped to acclimatise. We needed time to adjust to the idea of conversing with a 'supreme intelligence'. And with hindsight, certain subjects were really best avoided … at first … for example, all those questions involving 'time', due to it having such different connotation in spirit. It was Leslie who delivered the first question in that typically lucid, cavalier way of his:

"Well, I'm going to ask a question relating to something we were discussing earlier. Often we are told ... when I say 'we are told' ... let me clarify that ... Often one can be told what is going to happen in the future. Am I right in presuming that, if that is possible, then the event has already happened? Otherwise it cannot be known..."

~"*Your presumption is partly correct.*"

"Partly?"

~"*Yes ... all things are known. All things have been. But do not forget you are on a cycle of time. Therefore, without being too complicated in my explanations, I will say only this: What is to come is past. What is past is the future. We are on a never-ending cycle of events. Can you follow? It is difficult for you Earthlings to understand this. Time ... time is a complicated matter. But I will say ... there are those of you who can see what is ahead, not because it is the future but because it is there. It is past. It is the present. It is the future. It is 'one whole' ... a never-ending cycle of events.*"

And Salumet then added: ~"*It is possible for you to understand only once you have been enjoined into that ... how shall I say ... 'time capsule'. It is always the problem of explaining to you, in understandable terms, what we know.*"

So our very first question to our teacher happened to be one of those questions that was really best avoided ... at first! We felt a little confused. But it got things under way. The subject has been returned to on several occasions since. 'Time' still remains difficult, but now, ten years on, we can accept that time is linear here on the physical Earth (with events happening in sequence as they do) while it is 'all as one' in spirit. That oneness of past, present and future can only be perceived whilst in spirit. It follows as a natural consequence that those on Earth who accurately prophesy, can only do so by going into trance and seeing as in the way of spirit. It also follows that true prophecy ... that is, by those who have the true gift (examples that immediately spring to mind being Saint John, Jesus and Nostradamus), is a reality that issues from the nature of the Grand Design of Heaven and Earth.

It seems impossible for the physical mind to grasp exactly how conditions are in spirit. But it may help to visualise past and present events in spirit ... interlocking such that future events are instantly created to coexist with that past and present. It is a clumsy way of wording it. And that is the other difficulty with between-worlds communication ... the words. We use physical world language to describe spirit world phenomena. You may think on this picture of spirit world and say, 'Ha! So the future is fixed!' Well ... not quite. I have learned from Salumet's further teaching that the future is very largely determined (by past and present) but not quite fully fixed. Our free-will factor influences that which is pre-determined by the system ... just a little bit. That future events are not *entirely* fixed also means that the fulfilment of 'genuine' prophecy will be not quite 100%. It will be very nearly so ... perhaps 98-99%. That then, is the nature of true prophecy. There are cosmic laws that power our progression in the general sense but free will also has a fractional influence.

Having described the very first steps in receiving our teacher, I am tempted to go straight into the nature of the question-and-answer sessions and the teaching evenings that followed. There also have been some truly astonishing visits from ones in spirit, *arranged* by Salumet. But maybe just a little restraint is in order. Perhaps it would be to some advantage, if I next attempt to describe who Salumet is, where he comes from and then to provide a few details as to the general nature of the realms of spirit and their connection to us. I also propose to give brief description of the Kingsclere group who receive Salumet and to mention the reason for the worldwide programme of which our teacher's mission is a part. Then we shall be equipped to see things more clearly on treading the pathway of light that stretches invitingly before us.

2. WHO IS SALUMET?

Every so often through history, the world has been blessed with an inspired teaching of peace and love delivered by a great one from spirit. Sometimes religions have been constructed based on the words received. Thus, five thousand years ago, Krishna incarnated on the Earth and two thousand years ago it was Jesus the Christ.

Not all Masters from spirit choose to incarnate through the birth process followed by the childhood years. There are those who choose to remain in their natural habitat. There are several ways in which an enlightened one may influence our planet whilst remaining in spirit. One way is to establish a link with a group of people on Earth that regularly meet, and speak to them through a spirit medium/instrument who is in trance. The trance state is rather like a gateway between worlds. Examples of Masters or Source Teachers who have used this method are known by names such as Silver Birch and White Eagle. Silver Birch came through the medium Maurice Barbanell and White Eagle came through the medium Grace Cooke. These are well-noted mid-twentieth century examples and books have been published on those teachings received.

Such an arrangement is in no way new. Two thousand years ago there was the one who revealed elements of mankind's future to Saint John whilst he was on the island of Patmos. That is the one who declared he had the keys to death and to the spirit land. That has been accounted in the Bible Book of Revelation. In the more distant past, it was the Divine Pymander ... Shepherd of Men ... from spirit, who instructed Thoth of Egypt, whose wisdom was so revered by the Greeks that they called him 'Thrice Great Hermes' [1,2]. The mode of communication then, is not new ... neither is the message. Always the teaching received by mankind has centred on love and peace. It has differed only in 'a fine tuning' sense, adjusting to suit the stage of awareness of those living on the physical Earth at the time.

Salumet likewise continues to reside in spirit. He speaks through Eileen Roper, a full-trance medium. 'Full-trance' means that Eileen's mental being is placed to one side during the séance so that she is completely unaware of what transpires. At the conclusion of a session we generally chat and bring her up to date so to speak. Then she takes the tape-recording home and listens to the words of the one who has 'borrowed' her voice box for that evening. I think I would be correct in saying that Salumet comes from afar in spirit ... from beyond the Astral Planes and is from that region (if one dare visualise regions), where individuality is lost and soul-body merges into the Divinity. Accordingly, there is rather more than just 'a world of difference' between such a teacher and our planetary selves.

There is a gulf between all-knowing, all-loving, compassionate Source and we physical beings of limited knowledge and meagre mentality. Masters from Source know the extent of our awareness and are able to use phraseology appropriate to our time, place and individual development. But of course the gulf remains, and in accord with that gulf, the most difficult question that can be put to a Master is: "Who are you?"

(It might also be worth the mention at this stage that such Masters are in reality pure energy so that such things as names and syntax are not the norm for them. They will give us a name to know them by and speak un-telepathically, using word-language because that is our way ... the only way we know. Accordingly, the names used are generally pseudonymous and apt. In fact, it was not until 5ᵗʰ May 2003 that I thought to ask Salumet about his chosen name. It is a name of 'salutation' derived from our language. Where Source teachers come from, lies well beyond the realms of individuality and any connection with our particular planet in the past may have been nebulous or even non-existent).

I well remember the salient phrases of the reply that followed when the question: "Who are you?" was put on 4ᵗʰ July 1994:

"I will try to explain to you ... 'I' come to you as a single entity because it is easier that way to communicate ... I am not 'I' as you would know it ... I am a conglomerate of beings ... We spoke earlier of a diamond ... I am one facet of a diamond, who has chosen to break from the rest to come to you at this time, to teach and to instruct you."

In other exchanges we learned that each facet would have the knowledge of the whole diamond. Just one aspect of that diamond once had an Earth life … a life of merit but apparently unknown to our recorded history. Other aspects have walked upon other planets but the vast majority of aspects are of pure energy form and have never had a material existence. This is a big statement and is in itself some indication of the sheer complexity that exists beyond our physical Earth.

In a conversation between Leslie and Salumet on 11th March 1996, our teacher was describing soul development or perhaps I should say … its refinement to a degree beyond which we are able to imagine:

~ *"… The soul becomes more refined until you come to this stage of beyond being. You all fully understand that the soul's growth is a matter of striving, that we all strive towards that true energy which you fear or love, called (spiritual) light … but which is matter so refined that to you it is invisible. It is something that, as far as I too am aware, always seems to be unattainable … and I speak only from my heart upon this matter. We are speaking of aeons of your time to reach this stage of non-existence. To reach this stage I will tell you, there would be no returning to Earthly matter under any circumstance, because the state you have reached is purity itself, where you have shed your many layers … where you have attained the power to express true love … where you have reached the point of non-existence as you would know it. Now I will answer questions in your mind: Am I one of non-existence? I would say to you: Yes I AM. When this state is reached, much can be achieved … the workings of the cosmos … the workings of the universe … the workings of that truer light."*

There followed a long pause.

~ *"Would you like to ask any questions?"*

At this point Leslie became quite emotional and overwhelmed, and I think this may have been a moment of full realisation of the enormity of Source connection and of Salumet speaking as Divine consciousness. Then it was as if he were in thought/telepathic exchange with Salumet, considering possibilities and airing gratitude. Finally he said:

"I am bound to say … that is the only other alternative isn't it?"

~ *"I hear you and understand … and I ask not for thanks … because you see my dear friend, all of you are responsible for growth within my soul too. I have accepted many tasks. I have to say to you: This one has been quite difficult for me. I don't say this lightly ... but to return to such dense matter is indeed a task that I have to say to you was not one that I took with ease."*

Leslie: "I can't tell you how much we appreciate it. We can never understand the cost involved."

~ *"It has cost me a little discomfort only ... compared to the love that abounds here within this room..."*

Our teacher went on to compare us to jewels in the night sky, which was very flattering ... but then, those in spirit do tend to see the light of our being. And the realisation together with the emotion of it was certainly a wonderful moment for Leslie, as indeed it was for us all.

Some further clarification followed at the meeting of 15th May 2000 when I was talking with Salumet about reincarnation and our selves in relation to soul connection.

Q: "I think we sometimes refer to that part of the soul which is in spirit as the 'higher self'?"

~ *"That is part of the soul."*

Q: "The higher self would be the greater part of the soul?"

~ *"Not the greater part. Remember, I have told you that there are many parts to the soul and my dear friend, the diamond ... the facets of the diamond and then you will begin to understand ... the **facet** of the diamond is perhaps the higher self of the spirit that is here in the physical body now. Do you understand? We are moving into deep matters but I hope that will clarify it for you just a little. The spirit here within the human form is but one spark or one facet or one small piece ... choose your own phraseology ... but it is one small part of the whole."*

Q: "And that small part can have several Earth lives ... may reincarnate several times?"

~ *"Different facets, yes, yes."*

Q: "I just wanted to clarify that that same facet of soul can have several lives?"

~ *"Yes, yes, I understand. That one facet of the soul may return to your world many, many times. If the failure of the spirit in the human form ... fails in its mission, then it will return or accept that another facet of the soul needs to return in its place for a certain length of time."*

Q: "It could be either way?"

~ *"Yes, we are onto complex issues here."*

Q: "I think you also said (on a previous occasion), that more than one facet could have Earth life at the same time, but this would be very rare?"

(And on a separate occasion it was made clear to us that Jesus and Mary were in this special circumstance.)

~ *"Yes, it is not ... how should I say to you ... usual in the sense you would understand, but it happens, yes; but normally one facet of the soul returns to this planet at any one given time. Is that helpful to you? Are you happy with that explanation?"*

Q: "Yes ... I was just wondering if the soul ... which is itself moving on..."

~ *"Yes, I understand..."*

Q: "I was just wondering if there was any further conglomeration of souls?"

~ *"Yes. You must also understand that as I speak of soul, there are again many facets of soul which, as we move as energy, is also moving ... will join and expand and increase. And I think this is where you are falling down in trying to understand what happens to soul.* **It is not spirit returning to one soul in one time.** *There are many facets to the soul and the soul belongs to a much ... I use the expression: larger soul ... but it is actually a joining with Divine energy. It becomes a much larger issue."*

Q: "And you yourself would come to us from that ... that further domain?"

~ *"Part of me, yes. I am but one smaller issue from that Divine soul. It is difficult is it not?"*

"But it does help to make it clearer. Thank you very much!"

~ *"Yes ... I ... as I am speaking to you now through the human form ... am part of that Divinity which has come to your planet to help mankind expand its knowledge. I do not belong to the lower-integrated-smaller-version of what you call soul. No. It is something that we will speak about further on another occasion because it is a vast subject that I feel you are not quite ready for."*

I was left at the end of that particular session with the feeling that our teacher had been extremely patient with my questioning, for which I remain humbly grateful. And I apologise to the reader for introducing a 'brainstorming' session at this early stage, but Salumet's answers provide such a valuable picture of the complexity of soul. And it simply does not matter if that picture is hazy. It is important that we have some idea, no matter how approximate, of the immensity and order of spirit beyond the near-Astral planes, so that we may appreciate sufficiently the wondrous value of such visits by Masters.

It is difficult for those of us who live on the physical planet to fully grasp the details. But it seems that here on Earth we each are an iota of soul that springs from a lower-integrated-smaller-version of soul system. And there is a system beyond that, which merges into Divinity, whence come our teacher and other Masters. Salumet has to attune to our very much slower vibration and dense matter, making necessary the involvement of a 'full trance' medium. We are fortunate indeed in having Eileen with us. Without her, this particular mission would I think be impossible or at least would need to be re-worked some other way.

3. NATURE OF THE MISSION

It is my understanding that Earth now enters a more spiritual age and many Masters are involved in 'influencing' that progression in a variety of ways. The change has been the subject of prophecies. These have been accounted elsewhere [3] and I do not propose to give account here of the many prophecies concerning this present time on our planet. I would remind however, that Saint John described in Revelation how humanity would endure a period of conquest, wars, pestilence and famine, suffering under the ravages of the four symbolic horsemen. Various contemporary factors are now rapidly bringing that period to a close. Widespread wars in the generally accepted sense are no longer possible. Our culture has moved away from the possibility of such inexcusable and senseless eclipse. It is now time to move on and in this context Salumet makes several references to the present work of Masters from spirit.

On 18th July 1994, two questions were asked of our teacher that relate. The first concerned nuclear weapons and the plausibility of nuclear power development. He replied as follows:

~ *"Nuclear energy has been misused by you people on Earth. It would not, I think, be wise to leave it be. It has been given to you, the knowledge of it, for a very good reason … for the betterment of mankind, but it has been misused. We are trying from our realms now, in a concerted effort, to influence world leaders in these matters. On that I can say no more, other than that we are trying to put the right thoughts to the right people, that these things will and can be changed."*

Our second question to him concerned the ability of Nostradamus, the sixteenth century seer and healer, to make accurate prophecy. He had this to say about the seer:

~ *"… He was influenced by the religions of his time. He was a great visionary, and of course, with his extended views and knowledge, he could predict events to come."*

Our teacher then appeared to make a link with the previous question, and indeed Nostradamus had accurately predicted difficulties for these times of threatened aggression. He went on:

~ *"You speak of nuclear disaster. Your world has been heading towards that for some considerable time. Let me say to you all: There has come the time when many of us, and I speak as, let me say, a Master …* **Many Masters have come to tread this Earth plane at this particular time. There will not be a nuclear holocaust. That is our mission at this time in your evolution! That will not occur!** *But let me tell you the Earth is changing. And now we get to deep matters again. We spoke earlier of the Earth having an etheric … an etheric body. That is the one that will be filled with love and (will) change … and that is why we have descended at this time … to bring forth the knowledge to help that transition."*

(As regards his dated prediction for these times, Nostradamus refers to July 1999 for a key move by *the Great King of Terror*, adding that war will reign 'happily' both before and after that date. It is a curious but appropriate wording and most people 'happily' continue their lives despite the war. The quatrain accurately relates to the terrorist war orchestrated by the terrorist leader Osama Bin Laden. He is the Great King of Terror. There is no doubt of that. Nostradamus compares him as a destroyer to Genghis Khan.) [4]

Prompted by further exchange, Salumet went on to say:

~ *"That is why the (nuclear) energy was made known to man … to be used for the good of mankind. We also at this time, as I have said, are trying to influence those people in power, and I think you see it as happening with nuclear disarmament. It is a stepping-stone in the right direction. We are working on this."*

At a later date … 10th March 1997 … we received an update:

~ *"… I wish to say this to you: that mankind in general on this planet Earth, has reached an awareness that brings joy to those of us in my world who are striving … who are striving to bring knowledge to this Earth. Surrounding this planet, there now prevails a stillness and peace, which you would not be aware of, but (which) brings much satisfaction to us. The stillness and peace, which over your next thousand-plus years will pervade all of mankind to such an extent, that no longer will there be the fear and … the distrust shall I say … over all things termed 'supernatural'. They will become known and 'natural' to mankind. Mankind will return to knowledge that belongs to him. Though I say to you, dear friends … although you will not exist as you do now, in these times to come, I extend this knowledge to you in order that you may carry it forward with you, to our side of life. Keep it with you. Use it wisely, and know that you have become part of it."*

There is much to absorb in this statement ... there has been a fundamental change in the planetary etheric. There have been past great civilisations that had a oneness with nature and with the creation such that what we now term 'supernatural' was then the accepted norm. We will return to knowledge of the ways of spirit, of our past lives (the result of reincarnations), of the work of angels, of the work of elementals and of the subtle energies. All will be readily accepted as part and parcel of Earthly existence. The 'invisible forms' of life will become the more readily accepted as our science reveals more; as our science reveals that we humans and the many animal and plant forms of nature are only in part visible to us. All have their invisible 'energy envelopes'. And of course, Salumet is addressing us in our immortal wholeness which includes our soul connection with its accumulated past lives, all a part of the norm to be accepted unreservedly by future generations dwelling on this planet.

A 'lucky photo' at a function: Leslie, president and founder of the Kingsclere Group and Lilian who was later to become president.

Eileen, through whom Salumet speaks whilst she is in full trance.

4. THE KINGSCLERE GROUP

One of the interesting visitors who came to us from spirit world (a visit arranged by Salumet on 30th June 1997), provided information on our most recent past lives, that had been in what we now look back on as the Tudor period. We were at that time all brothers in a small monastery not far from Myddle in Shropshire. The monastery was blessed with a good clean water supply from a river, something that not all had in those days. And we all lived beyond 50 years, which for those times was unusual. I understand that it was during our further progression in spirit that we made the decision to meet again as a kind of brotherhood in this, our next incarnation. A difficulty was of course that memories of all past lives and time of sojourn in spirit are generally erased on being born anew. This means that the process of reuniting must rely upon the inner intuitive feelings plus whatever 'influences' are available from those friends who continue in spirit. Even then there would be no actual, conscious, Earthly knowledge of the conceived plan. And that I have to say was the status quo prior to the events of 1994.

Today, we happily have knowledge of that life spent together in the monastery; also the reason for our coming together now. But before going further let me draw your attention to the interesting way in which traits from the earlier life can be carried over into the next. The three of our number that were gardeners in the monastery days still very much enjoy growing vegetables and flowers. And the one who cared for the herbs had a particular liking for rosemary ... and still has today. It seems that two who worked in the kitchens had a divisive sense of humour, sometimes sneaking a handful of flour into a Franciscan hood whilst tied in the 'down' position! They have both retained a lusty sense of humour in this life, and on those occasions when laughter is with us, theirs always strikes me as the loudest and the most hearty.

During 1994 I lived with my family in an old farmhouse that for several years we had thought of as 'a monastery'. Often after a day out we would say, "Ah well, back to the monastery!"

There was no particular reason for this … it just seemed to be a comfortable expression!

Leslie excelled at woodwork, fashioning all the plates and spoons that the brothers used. And apparently there were times when he got just a little irritated if a brother dribbled gravy and failed to make best use of his handiwork! He also made oak casks and was responsible for the ox carts. Moving on to the earlier days of this life he continued to enjoy woodwork, making decorative furniture as a hobby. His main job as a monk however, apart from devotions, was preparing wines for the monastery cellar. It has suited his present life path not to drink wine, yet he has continued to make plenty and takes pleasure in giving it all away. On learning that he made wine for the monastery, Leslie immediately declared:

"So that's why I make all this wine when I don't drink! It's something that has always puzzled me!"

He who was so good at winemaking as well as providing tea, continued to preside over our evenings together for a further five years. And what wonderful evenings they were! At first the questions and their subject matter were diverse. As time moved on, the sessions were more frequently teachings that centred upon the nature of spirit and spiritual development. Some time was still allotted to question and answer, and then there were the arranged visits from those in the ethereal realms; experts in their particular vocation you might say.

At the start of the mission, Brent, over here from North Carolina, was a pillar of strength. His computer skills were both an asset as well as an influence, and he transcribed the first six months of the recorded sessions. He also made improvements with microphones and put some interesting philosophical questions during our meetings. His input was much missed when he returned to the United States.

In his earlier days, Leslie had had a career in management. It showed. He was of senior stance, clear in reason, succinct in expression and organised extremely well. We were fortunate indeed in having his presiding influence in the early Salumet years. And in the latter part of that period he seemed to get used more as a medium himself … a president who also doubled as medium! Several times he sat at the close of proceedings with cup of tea in hand, and the heavy breathing that always preceded his trance would take over. One of us would quickly dim the light while another took the cup and saucer, and the visitor would speak through Leslie. Afterwards he would declare: "I can't even have a cup of tea in peace!" That was his humour of course, with which we had become so familiar over the years.

Through 1998, although mentally continuing in unquestionably wonderful shape, he was becoming physically frail and there were recurrent breathing problems.

He was periodically helped by our friends in spirit; also by the nearby hospital who were very caring. Leslie had a well-developed clairvoyance and could see things that most of us do not. In the hospital he would inform the nurses when they had lost a patient further down the ward (having seen the spirit depart). And when the lady with the tea trolley came by, he pointed out to her that she was not alone ... always she was accompanied by one who walked the wards with her. "Well", she said, "Funny you should say that ... I never feel that I'm alone."

"I can assure you you're not", he said, "and your friend always likes to do her hair up like this..."

"That's my mother", she said, "Very particular about her hair she was and always did it like that!" And she continued on her round, happy in the confirmation that she was accompanied in her work.

Leslie made the move to the East Coast to be with family early in 1999. In the autumn of that year, it was time for our dear president of so many evenings together to return to spirit. That brought sadness, and yet we all knew that life in spirit continues, where we shall have the opportunity to meet once again before long. In this life he had achieved so much and was respected by so many as a healer. Fortunately for us all, he had realised the importance of recording all communications on tape for later transcription. That would enable a much wider audience to be reached. Our president had returned to Earth ahead of the rest of us in keeping with his fuller life plan. But in so doing he has initiated and progressed such valuable work, and paved the way for our continued meetings. He was already into his eightieth year when I first met him. I suppose one might say that I was a straggler who returned to the fold a little later than those better attuned to their inner impulses.

Following Leslie's departure, there was a period of some uncertainty during which we continued to meet as two small groups ... one at Margaret's and one at Lilian's place. Within our number, Lilian and Eileen were senior in the sense of being well versed in the ways of spirit. Both groups received word from our spirit friends that the work would continue in due process and there was assurance that the groups would reunite again as one. Accordingly, our first full meeting at Lilian's place with Lilian presiding happened on 21st June 1999. That date just happened to be on the last summer solstice of the old millennium. What better time for a new beginning! We were able to discuss with Salumet on that occasion, our joy at being reunited and our vexations concerning the war in Yugoslavia ... and the suggestion that had been put to the American President that a large transcendental meditation team should be sent in as alternative to military action. It was only a suggestion that got rejected, but ten years earlier such a suggestion would not even have been voiced. This in itself was an indication of a world in the process of change.

You will have noticed that not all of the brothers of old, are still brothers in the strictest sense. In fact, more than half have now, in this life, chosen the female configuration. Our new president was the mendicant of old. 'He' then travelled between monasteries with news and information, coming originally from an Abbey in Lincolnshire. Clearly, 'he' would have had that aura of friendliness and the comfortable conversing skill that 'she' has today. Likewise the two brothers who worked in the kitchen and who enjoyed a joke at times ... today they are Sarah and Margaret. We are indebted to Sarah for transcribing many, many tapes, sharing that task with Leslie in the earlier years, then more recently doing most of the transcribing and copying herself, with useful back-up from Paul.

Today's group is very much a mixture and we each make our different contribution. In séance, Eileen, as has been said, is a full-trance medium, several are partial-trance mediums (they have awareness of the words that are spoken through them), and several have clairvoyance. Jan often has strong and detailed images that are sometimes shared by others, and then there is the energy that we all give. And I would say that there is a shared energy factor uniting all who sit. Energy is clearly a very important matter and Sue contributes in a particular way, always sitting next to

Eileen and being 'away' in trance for much of the session. We are conscious of the energy that builds in the room as those in spirit join us. I am rather deaf these days and the energy sometimes causes a feedback that makes one of my hearing aids whistle so that I have to switch it off for a spell. (It might be said that there is scientific evidence for the energy build-up.)

Ages vary. At the time of writing, some of us are into our seventies and have the cares and joys of both children and grandchildren. The younger 'regulars' are mostly around forty, some being our own children. Several teenage grandchildren have sat in on occasions to see what we more elderly folk get up to of an evening. Likewise, acquaintances, visitors from abroad and a newspaper reporter have stopped by to see for themselves what prevails. We generally have the courtesy to seek permission from our teacher on these 'irregular' occasions. But one evening a cat walked in unannounced mid-session. While Lilian settled him in the kitchen, Salumet said, "All are welcome!" and proceeded to give some account to us of the cat's feelings.

I can just about visualise Margaret wearing military uniform … she served with the WAAF in World War II. Mark has a Pandora's Box style shop and is a tennis coach. My youngest son Paul is a teacher, but one reason for my regarding him respectfully is because he was the abbot in our old monastery days! Sue looks very chic behind the counter of a high street jeweller's. Graham has had a career as a geology teacher and has more recently developed a surprising talent as a portrait artist for which he receives commissions. Lilian has spent time behind a desk in a public library. Jan is a company director of a family-based plumbing and heating firm. Sara teaches part time, has a singing voice, composes and has made a few CDs. The formal qualifications that we have between us include one B.Sc., one B.A. and two degrees in psychology. Several of the group regularly do healing. Leslie was a member of the National Federation of Spiritual Healers, as also is Eileen. And I am a retired forensic scientist. The point that I endeavour to make is that we are a very mixed assortment indeed. But we all come together with a remarkable unity. As a group, we have a spread of mental skills and a fair mixture of spiritual gifts. Yet our energies combine so well both in session and over a cuppa afterwards.

That then is a brief description of the Kingsclere group as we are at the present time. It is an accurate statement apart from one point. I am in error in giving the impression that Leslie is no longer with us. Let me explain. On the Monday following Leslie's return to spirit, we were much saddened. Our teacher came and had wise and loving words to say. It was a short visit. A teaching session would have been inappropriate on this evening of our so many thoughts. An Amerindian friend of long standing from spirit, Moon Feather, spoke through Sue:

~ *"Moon Feather will see old friend. Moon Feather will be happy to talk face to face and talk many, many long moons ... Have come many times but will return again to speak and will one day come with friend and all will be happy..."*

Then another spoke through Eileen:

~ *"I am very old acquaintance of the friend who has come to us. I wish to tell you that he has been overawed by what he has encountered. ... I am Sister Anna who over the long years of his Earthly working have visited with him on many, many occasions. What I wish to tell you ... that he will, in time, endeavour to make contact with you but, as you will probably be aware there is much for him to do and to know."*

It was on 30th July 2001 (just 21 months later) that Leslie returned and spoke with us through Eileen. He greeted us with:

~ *"Hello everybody. I tried really hard to get the voice but I can't do it, so please accept me for who I am.* (Actually, as Sarah ventured, it wasn't a bad effort.) *I have taken quite a long time to come to you but I promised I would and here I am."*

It was an emotional and a joyous reunion and Leslie brought news. He had met Lilian's husband Roy in spirit and they had had a good chat. He follows the work we do and is pleased with the progress. Leslie explained some details of his passing and how he had been met by his father, and how he had soon got to see everyone else. His surroundings are as wonderful as we imagine them to be and better, and he is supremely happy. He also referred to the breathing difficulty. (Such things often return briefly on coming back to the physical world.) Eileen felt the emotion and the heaviness of the breathing. She also felt Leslie's little touch of annoyance when he could not get the pitch of the voice quite as he would have liked. (Leslie always did like to get things just so.) And so, our dear president of those earlier years continues to watch our progress and will doubtless make his presence known again sometime. In fact, at the end of proceedings on 7th April 2003, one came through from spirit for healing. As he left, he told us that he had been directed to visit by one whom we know as Leslie. Leslie's work continues!

Having made that small but significant amendment, I am now happy that the above is a fair description of the Kingsclere group that now continues its meetings into the twenty-first century.

(Note: Reflecting on Leslie's return 21 months after his passing to spirit, then speaking through Eileen who also channels Salumet, I was reminded of Sir Arthur Conan Doyle's similar achievement. It is well documented that Sir Arthur returned 10 months after passing to spirit, and then spoke through Grace Cooke who also at that time, channelled White Eagle. One has to see this as a parallel happening. Whilst Sir Arthur is so well known for the Sherlock Holmes stories and for The Lost World, he is probably less well remembered for his lectures to promote knowledge of life after death.) [5]

5. OUR WAY AHEAD IN THE 21ST CENTURY

It is our privilege to be living in the first century of a brand new millennium and to feel a certain newness that prevails. Already we can look back several decades and see those years as slightly old fashioned and somehow different. The fact is that we live in exciting, fast-moving times. Our awareness and consciousness grow like they know no bounds ... and indeed they have none.

In the old 20th century we survived two world wars, endured the abysmal East-West Cold War, squandered vast resources, razed rainforests, holed the ozone layer and came close to curtailing our very existence upon the planet through nuclear default. By the grace of God we have evolved beyond all that and now emerge into a time of renewed hope and fresh optimism. There will continue to be disasters and political strife because Earth remains a planet for learning and evolving. We should recognise too, that as Earth evolves, we evolve physically, we evolve spiritually and all evolution is connected. But we are now past the dangerous extremes of our wayward youth that loomed in that 'slightly old fashioned and somehow different' time that was not a part of *this* century.

Fortunately, we have received help and influence in our moments of deepest peril ... from those that might be described as 'higher beings'. I refer to the teachers from Source who have influenced through the ages, leaving our history speckled with legend, myth and religion. Whilst all Masters or Source teachers that have spread good influence upon this planet have been always consistent in their teaching of 'love' and 'peace', they have made allowances as necessary for the prevailing states of our awareness, culture and language.

Over thousands of years these factors have of course changed enormously. And even looking back just a mere fifty years the differences in both culture and awareness appear quite staggering. It is partly that in our recent past, the pace of change has accelerated so much. It follows that the current Salumet mission should be and is different from earlier missions. It remains consistent of course where love and peace are concerned because these first principles form part of inviolable cosmic truth. The differences in the teaching lie in the details that we are now able to accept due to our more advanced awareness, cultural progression and expanding knowledge.

Within our culture, it can be said that science, media systems, computer logic, communications and knowledge in general, have all progressed remarkably in just a few decades. We continue also to discover facts about past great civilisations of our planet and their achievements. It follows that now as never before, we can put questions to a Source teacher regarding both current developments in the world as well as details of our more distant past. We can ask questions and discuss such mind-bending contemporary topics as: space travel, UFOs, crop circles, the Bermuda triangle, flipping dimensions and past life regression therapy. We can also put our queries concerning the ancient world ... Noah's ark, Atlantis, the Egyptian pyramids, the Nazca Plateau markings and certain puzzling statements from traditional religions. We have in a sense 'come of age' sufficiently to have such questions within our consciousness so that we may now put them to an all-knowing, beyond-Earthly intelligence.

We cannot of course just put any old question. There is certain information that is to be withheld because the human race is simply not yet ready to receive. Progress must in general be powered by our own experience and thought process. That is important. That is the way on this planet. It has been made clear in the teachings that nuclear technology has been a 'timely' development that unfortunately has been misused by mankind. It has its proper place in our time and should improve life on Earth. But we came so close to disaster that it also serves to illustrate that it is imperative that we have sufficient wisdom and spiritual growth before we can be entrusted with such knowledge.

Neither can we ask for the solutions to all problems and expect straight answers. If we create difficulties for ourselves on Earth then we must solve them. That again is the nature of our way forward. Examples of problems of our own making are political confrontation, industrial disease, stress-related illness and repression of the spirit within. An all-knowing teacher will be loving and compassionate, can influence and be guiding in prayer or meditation and can offer good direction for our thinking. But to simply erase the problem would equally erase the learning to be had from overcoming that problem. Indeed, confronting and overcoming difficulty is a valuable road leading to our spiritual advancement. So clearly, a question-and-answer session is not an opportunity for wiping the slate clean of all life's difficulties. It would also wipe the slate clean of life's very essence. That kind of road to Utopia would turn out to be a dead end and serve no useful purpose.

There remain many questions, of course, the answers to which help us to understand both our selves and our planet. There are many valid and interesting questions that connect with legend, antiquity and folklore. Many more concern planetary factors and our progress. We have also on occasion sought answers to questions that lie at the cutting edge of advancing science. This kind of question seems acceptable if a plausible idea backed by reason is presented, in which case the idea may well get usefully embellished. All questions relating to such matters as the nature of spirit, soul and prayer have been readily accepted and I feel that in this area our Master has given as much detail as we are capable of understanding. One must accept that the creation is highly complex and the physical mind cannot grasp every detail concerning the nature of spirit.

On 23rd June 2003, Salumet had been speaking of the way ahead and I had the opportunity to make reference to his ten years of teaching. This led to an interesting reply:

"Perhaps I could observe that we have continued as a group for ten years and it is most refreshing that I notice you are looking ahead several more years in terms of the next development. That is very nice to know ... thank you!"

~ *"I know that when you speak of Earthly years, to you my friends it may seem some considerable time, but it is but one blink of your eye. There is much to know and to learn and, after all, my purpose in coming to you is not only to give you teachings but to bring you together ... as that group that has existed in many times in many forms ... but in this existence I want you to be more aware. So you see, it is a double-edged purpose that we have. What would be the purpose of giving you information if you know not what to do with the information ... if you cannot take into your hearts and souls that eternal truth?"*

The ten years of teaching, and of question-and-answer sessions may be compared to the steady growth of a tree. We ourselves grow in awareness as the exchange continues. Sometimes an answer has been given, then after a year or two, further detail has been forthcoming to suit our improved understanding capability. With this in mind, the reader may well find it an advantage to stop and reflect at times, before going on. The journey may also be compared to a magnificent ride on a roller coaster during which we must hold on tightly to our perception and credibility. The ride takes us through the realms of both Heaven and Earth. Certainly many wondrous intricacies in both Heaven and Earth are encompassed as we travel. In the pages that follow I shall endeavour to present a wide selection of material with such commentary and explanation as seems appropriate.

PART II - QUESTIONS AND ANSWERS

1. BEGINNING WITH DREAMS AND MEDITATION

It was on the evening of 30th January 1995 that Salumet asked a question of Leslie, enquiring if he was aware of how busy he had been since last time. Leslie had responded that he was aware but then Salumet made it clear that he meant ... during his sleep state. Leslie had been unaware of leaving his physical body to visit the next plane of life during sleep, night after night. Salumet continued:

~ *"Your communication skills are well known on our side of life. There are many who offer you their thanks. If only you could feel their love surround you, it would uplift you in all your daily tasks, whilst remaining in your physical body ... You have all within these last months, come to me in your spirit bodies."*

Our teacher went on to suggest that we might attempt to improve our recall of dreams so that we might see for ourselves.

Leslie: "So everyone here then must try and remember what has happened during their sleep?"

~ *"The exercise would be very worthwhile to you all ... to your development and I am here to help you with that aspect of yourselves as you well know."*

Leslie: "Yes ... true. Can you suggest any particular mental exercise that would be beneficial for remembering our visits to you?"

~ *"Yes, if you wish. I would suggest before you go into your sleep state ... and here once more we come to what I will always tell you ... the power of your thoughts. If you would mentally say to yourselves, in the state between being awake and being asleep ... you know the state I speak of? When you are ... how can I say? ... half here, half with us ... mentally make the thought **to remember** *all that occurs in your sleep state. Do this each night and eventually you will come to the state of remembrance. It must be thorough. It must be done continuously, if you wish to achieve results; also, on your awakening perhaps you would write down what you remember. Gradually you will see a formation of thought. To begin with, it may seem rather jumbled up. But no matter, it will eventually all come together. You will realise what is natural dream state and what is an occurrence in the spirit realm."*

There was some further talk about possibly confusing the natural dream (the physical mind reacting to the happenings of the day), and excursions of the spirit into other realms. Leslie then declared that perhaps he had some memory after all, because there had been a few rather strange ones that he had put down to physical dreaming.

~ *"Yes, this is what happens. Your physical brain tries to interpret what is a spiritual happening, which sometimes causes confusion. But if you endeavour to continue each evening, each morning, you will find a pattern emerge. I hope that will be helpful to you and I say to you all: Please do these things for your own unfoldment."*

Then came the assurance:

~ *"It is not an unusual event. You all leave your physical bodies while in your sleep state … all of you."*

Leslie: "So it might be helpful also then, to concentrate on coming over to you … would it?"

~ *"You need not concentrate. It will happen in any case. What you need to concentrate on is the remembrance of the visit. Do you see? Because then you can remember what has been taught to you … to the spiritual aspect of yourselves. Do not try to force yourselves … that will not work."*

Salumet confirmed on another occasion that the sleep state raises consciousness making it easier for our spiritual counterpart to leave the physical body.

A query then followed regarding the difference between sleep and meditation:

~ *"It is slightly different when you speak of meditation. When you sit for meditation, it is of course raising your consciousness … yes we know (as in sleep). When you are in your sleep state that spirit aspect of yourself returns home to be rejuvenated. Although you can sit in meditation and raise your consciousness, the spirit remains in your physical being. Can you see the difference? So you don't necessarily leave your physical body in your state of meditation … unless you are in a very deep state of raised consciousness. There is a slight difference but people assume it is the same. It is not."*

Leslie next moved onto a connecting incident that had puzzled him. A lady had on a much earlier occasion, come through to us from spirit. She had been utterly astonished to be confronting his physical self in the group because she had thought he belonged in spirit realm. And she had declared:

~ *" But I've seen you here in your pyjamas!"* (A few chuckles broke out at the thought as Leslie recounted this.)

~ *"And that confused you?"*

Leslie: "It did, yes."

~ *"Yes. It was the mirror image of you as you slept. Mainly what would be seen is your colour ... your light, in the spirit world, but for recognition purposes, your own higher self decided that you needed to be clothed. And so it was that you were seen in your pyjamas. It was that part of you that was a little unsure and needed, not protection, but assurance that you would return. You see ... things are not always as clear cut as people would expect, but that was the reason."*

Leslie expressed his delight at having that little matter cleared up. Then Mark had a question about a ringing in the ears during his meditation and pointing out that he gets a similar ringing whilst standing on a ley-line.

~ *"Let me speak on this. When you meditate, there are many degrees of meditation. One of the first things you will notice when you become used to meditation, is I believe ... some of you call it the 'audible sound'. It can take many forms. It can sound like a hum, sometimes a ringing as you have described it. All it means is that you have reached a particular level of meditation. What happens next is that the consciousness is raised even higher and all these sounds, that are within you, not without, will stop and from the 'audible sound' you go to the 'darkness within'. Yes ... don't be concerned. It is, I would say, the second step in meditation. Most people would not even be aware of it. The very fact that you are shows your own sensitivity to the audible life force. I say to you, continue. Allow these noises to happen. Be happy about it, and eventually you will be taking that one step further. When these noises stop, it does not mean that you have not meditated properly. It means that you have moved forward. You see, you are all rather like the radio waves ... the frequency of the radio waves, and you are tapping into the sound power. That is all. Is that helpful to you?"*

Mark: "Yes … thank you. I do quite like it actually. I enjoy that state."

~ *"Yes … because you are raised. You are slightly away from your physical being. It is the second stage of meditation."*

Mark: "Which is the first stage?"

~ *"The first stage of meditation is to go within and try to rid yourself of all everyday thoughts. The first stage of anyone beginning this meditative state is I think probably the most difficult."*

Leslie: "Yes, I believe you are right in that. I found it so."

~ *"But he has moved beyond that now. And you are just a power source tapping into an even greater power. It is as simple as that."*

Mark: "There are some places that are easier to meditate in than others aren't there? I wondered if being on the ley-line helped?"

~ *"There is much power within the Earth structure, as I have said before. If you find that your meditation is greater within these areas, then please do so. But I would say to you all, it really should make no difference to the progress that can be made … find your own little niche. Be happy with what you are doing for yourselves. That is what is important … that each and every one of you seeks and finds that inner spark, no matter where. The important issue is that you find that quiet time, to find … to find that stillness … to find that love that is there for all of you."*

Leslie thanked our teacher for his careful instruction and then went on to say that he could in fact recall dreams in which he had talked with people and helped them. He had mistakenly pictured himself to be in a physical situation but now realised it would have been in spirit. Salumet replied that when he first came to this life, he had set out on a planned life path (without physical mind memory of it, as with us all). He declared Leslie to be an 'old soul' and went on:

~ *"You made the decision in this lifetime, that you would return to this Earth plane to help others, but mainly your task was to teach. Part of your decision was that regularly you would return to that home of love, where you would continue to help those on the other side … our side of life. This was to be a difficult life for you at many stages. You wanted to make recompense for that which was left undone last time. So you see, from the very beginning of your Earthly life, you have returned to us to work. You can say you work on both sides of life."*

After some further exchange, Leslie added:

"It certainly has cleared a lot of points, which have been not exactly a worry, but which I couldn't quite understand. I do appreciate what you've told me."

The session had in fact clarified points for us all, about the duality of dreams as well as the way of meditation and the difference between the two. In recent years there has been much said in our world about out-of-body (OOB) phenomena in such situations as sudden accidents and the hospital operating theatre, but it is still considered by many to happen only rarely. On the contrary, all of us are OOB in our dream state most nights. Furthermore, it appears that we can train ourselves to have memory of the experience if we so wish.

There has been further reference to meditation that of course is so important in both personal as well as worldly development. Colin who sat in with us during a November 1999 meeting received a very fine answer to his question on the subject:

~ *"You mean … is there a better way to find yourself than to meditate? No. What is meditation? It is prayer, but it is prayer that is seeking that within. It is not external. It is a prayer of trying to know your self. Therefore, in meditation you are allowing the human aspect of you as you know yourself now to be forgotten and the soul to come forward. You go deep within that spiritual light, that spiritual knowledge that has the answer to all questions. Therefore I say to you, to meditate is the answer to all things, all things spiritual."*

As time moved on, it became clear to us all that Earthly spirit self (within the physical being) is but a small aspect of each 'parent' soul body that remains eternally in spirit. Aspects from the soul-bodies in spirit incarnate and reincarnate as necessary. And meditation strengthens our soul-connection that is always there. By 1ˢᵗ May 2000, I was able to put a more detailed question to our teacher concerning the 'voices' encountered within the silence that comes with regular meditation:

"Could I just recap on when we go within … we might hear the 'I' of Divinity, the ego 'I' (that needs to be subdued at times). Then there might be influence from a spirit guide, and on rare occasions there might be the voice of a 'teacher of awareness'. Is that a fair statement in connection with going within?"

Salumet was clearly pleased that his many words of several evenings had been absorbed correctly and added:

~ *"There are many degrees to what you call meditation. You can have a group of people who can speak to you of different experiences ... but true meditation in the spiritual sense ... of course you would always be guided by those friends, helpers and yes ... 'teachers of awareness' at times. You are correct in your assumption. (In order for) meditation to be true, you need to give of yourself with love, with openness and to offer yourself to the Divine Creation to be used ... to be used not as* **you** *will but as that Divinity would have you do. Do you understand? If you want to achieve meditation on the highest level, then you have to forego the physical traits of thinking..."*

It was nearly two years later during a session concerning physical brain output as opposed to spiritual thought energy (intuition), that Graham again brought meditation into the equation, as a possible means of distinguishing the two. Salumet replied:

22nd April 2002 ~ *"True meditation my dear friend excludes the human brain. If you are in meditation in the proper sense, then all human thinking should be quiet (absent) ... then comes forth the spirit, that true part of you, you understand. That is why we always encourage you to have quiet times, not only for your benefit but so that those in our world can come closer ... because what happens to you is that your energy is quickened and ours lowered so that the two can communicate. But that is where you will find your true self ... in the state of deep, deep meditation, not the meditation of the light kind, because the human thinking is still rather close. The meditation I speak of is the one where you do not exist in the sense of feeling. Do you understand? Where the human form no longer belongs to you but only that energy is left that we call spirit. That is true meditation my dear friend."*

These then are the words of a Master from Source on the important topics of dreaming during sleep state and of meditation. The latter clearly has a number of levels that are approached with practice and I would observe that this is broadly in line with the teaching of revered Indian mystics. The notion of 'thought energy' has been mentioned. I would point out that in recent years this has become a scientifically accepted reality. (The energy of events such as 'world peace meditations' has been physically recorded through a linked system of sensitive electronic devices known as 'random number generators'. These devices have also been referred to during our Salumet evenings and are reported in more detail later.) It has been necessary to make passing mention of matters such as 'immortality of soul', 'reincarnation' and 'ley-lines'. There will be more on these subjects as we move on. There is much connectedness in the huge amount of material that has been received over the years, making it difficult to present a single topic in isolation from the fuller picture. It also makes it difficult to know where best to begin and where to proceed next. But it seems appropriate enough to have begun with our spirit connection. That, one might say, is our 'life-line'. Perhaps we could next consider the very beginning of time … the creation.

2. THE CREATION…
IN THE BEGINNING WAS THE WORD

Today's science is largely based upon reason and experiment, that intellectual part of us that arises from the physical mind. Such logical process has led to theories of origin of the universe known as 'steady state' and 'big bang'. If we are to be strictly logical in our physical mind reasoning, then we should observe that it is only the physical universe that is being considered. (If there are non-physical or other-dimensional universes, as theoretical physicists have claimed, then the details of these are not being considered in the material view.)

As early in our meetings as 15th August 1994 Leslie had indicated to Salumet that our literature refers to a universe that has always existed; also to a universe that has a beginning. These two statements are of course contradictory. Salumet's reply included the statement:

~ *"I do not know of a beginning. I only know that it has always been and always will be. That is the state of the teaching as I know it. … As far as I am aware there has been no beginning as such. There always has been. … I am aware of what you are speaking. I am aware of the talk of 'big bang' and all the other things, but I can only state to you … as far as I am aware there cannot have been a beginning."*

It was a few months later that Brent posed an awkward question asking for the purpose of the universe to be explained. I think our teacher considered this to be a little ahead of time … ahead of teaching schedule and he was brief. That transcript includes:

~ *"Your Earth is a very small particle in a universal consciousness. The Earth, as far as I can explain to you, is a small area where teaching takes place. The Earth is one small part of one small galaxy. We have many 'Earths' in many galaxies, all doing and teaching different things. I don't think I can go into these things now. We need to go a little more slowly at this particular time. I say only to you: accept that which you do not understand. One day the knowledge will grow and expand and so too will the knowledge of your Earth."*

I include the statement here because it helps put both Earth and our knowledge of it into some kind of perspective. The following paragraph from 1st November 1999 adds to that perspective:

~ *"I do not wish this to sound disrespectful (you know this is never my purpose), but this planet is so young. This planet is so very young that souls who come to inhabit it come to learn. That is what you must always remember about this Earthly planet."*

These together with other statements that have been made leave me with the general impression that the universe contains countless galaxies, each having a variety of inhabited planets. Their miscellany of civilisations must be at all sorts of different stages of progression and a hypothetical league table would show Earth as a 'young planet' somewhere near the bottom.

There are other important concepts and tenets within the several folders of accumulated transcripts. These may possibly be best mentioned collectively at this point. Firstly, that small part of the *infinite* universe that our astronomers are able to observe is likened to a grain of sand within a sand dune. How can we be sure of a theory for the whole dune? And what if the wind blows? A several-times-repeated phrase is: 'Spirit has always been.' Now this has to be important. Long before the physical Earth was created and before the material universe was created ... there was spirit. Spirit has always been. Salumet often encourages us to think spiritually ... to see with spiritual eyes. After all, we are dual entities. We should endeavour to think spiritually as well as materially. And our teacher often repeats that THOUGHT is the most powerful thing there is. It lies at the cutting edge of both creation and evolution. All things are first created in spirit by thought process before they can manifest in the physical. And finally, the planet Earth has an etheric (non-material counterpart) as have all other material bodies in the universe. Now all this is deep philosophy as seen from spirit.

The above criteria are consistent with there being in the beginning an expanse of spirit, if I can put it like that. In the fullness of time and following the creation of our galaxy and our sun within that galaxy, the etheric Earth would have been formed from spiritual thought process. Following *that* creation, the physical Earth would then have come into existence. This is the picture of the creation that emerges from putting together the details that have been presented in the Salumet teachings.

How does this picture compare with that creation verse from the Christian Holy Bible that is so often quoted [6]?

'In the beginning was the Word and the Word was with God and the Word was God.' If we consider God as 'expanse of spirit' and 'word with God' as God's thought', then the picture is remarkably consistent. The term 'God' has suited many past generations. The more recent Masters in their teaching and certain spiritually perceptive cultures have preferred more descriptive alternative names ... Great Spirit, Creative Principle, Creative Force, Universal Consciousness etc. They are just words within Earthly language. But whatever term we feel comfortable with, I think we all probably feel instinctively that 'God' equates to the creation of all that is and to all the love contained within that process of creation and to all the love encapsulated within its end result. That is what is meant by the name used. That accepted then there is no conflict. But this picture of creation does raise one further issue that arises from our material/spirit duality.

Clothed within these physical bodies is a spark of the Divinity. We are each of us a small aspect of an immortal soul that remains forever in spirit. That parent-soul-in-spirit is a part of the Divinity that has always been. It follows that, as an aspect of that soul in spirit that has always existed, we ourselves must have played our part in the Earthly creation. The knowledge of that part played in the creation of the Earth is innate within that parent soul. And that being so it brings home to us the huge responsibility that we have in caring for *our* planet.

Salumet spelled out a part of this during the meeting of 19th June 2000 when Paul asked if the Earth has its own spirit body:

~ *"It has been created in the world of spirit before the physical creation. I have told you have I not, that all things are created first in the world of spirit and their counterparts are then brought into the physical existence. So do you see the connection between what you are (as soul in spirit) and what you are now in the human form? Can you begin to understand that there can be no separation from what we call the universal consciousness? Is it becoming clearer to you as I speak?"*

Paul: "It is like we are part of the universe ... and could we say that we helped in the designing of the Earth as well?"

~ *"Yes, you have that responsibility for what you have achieved ... You and each one of you and every human being, no matter what their lifetime is now ... each one of you has been responsible for the creation of this planet."*

I added: "I think I can say there have been past cultures that have understood this and expressed it more clearly than many of us today ... the Australian Aborigine called it creation in 'dreamtime'. We call it 'universal consciousness'..."

~ *"Yes, there are many names used. 'Universal Consciousness' is one that would seem to be understood by many. But yes, many of your earlier civilisations had much greater spiritual knowledge. We have discussed this on many occasions. But now is the time in the evolution of this planet for mankind to take responsibility, not only for Earthly living but for all that this planet has become ... and to take responsibility in such a way that mankind can look inwards and say: 'yes, this has been created, each one has helped to create what exists now. Is that clear for you my dear friends? What I try to tell you this time is that you need (to know) ... just how much responsibility you have. I want you to understand whilst here upon this Earth plane ... to understand the importance of your spirit and how much power each one of you has within these physical frames."*

A further question was put during our next meeting:

George: "I wonder if we could recap a little in the following way: If one goes back perhaps four or five billion years in our time, before the physical Earth and before the spirit body of Earth, we would have been spirit..."

3rd July 2000 ~ "Spirit ... let me interrupt you just a moment. Spirit has always existed, whether you call it spirit ... energy ... consciousness ... it has always been. Yes..."

George: "It probably would be incorrect to refer to us at that time as souls because that word, as we have come to know it, involves 'past life' which didn't exist then ... at least, not in the way that we know it now."

~ *"Yes ... yes! Of course, the soul in the manner that you understand it would not exist. But the soul belongs to spirit. In a sense it has always existed in other forms. But if you speak of the soul on the Earthly planet, then you would be correct ... that before the time of the birth of this planet, then the soul in the way that you speak of would not exist. As always there is never one clear answer."*

George: "So, as spirit we had thoughts and we thought. We played our part in the creative principle in thinking of the planet and the spirit body of the planet came into being and the physical planet followed. This I would suggest, is not a unique happening in the universe but a general creative happening…"

~ *"It is the pattern of all life. The power of thought is a creative force behind all things and thought belongs to spirit. There always has (been) and always will be thought. Are you happy with those replies?"*

George: "Yes … I was attempting to fit our role in the creation into the greater scheme of things and I can see that we as spirit were part of that great creative principle."

~ *"Yes, it would seem to you human beings to be like a jigsaw but each piece does eventually fit … It is unfortunate perhaps I could say, that whilst clothed in these physical garbs that the spirit is so restricted, not only in thinking, but in memory and in all-knowing. I have of course told you that all these things are innate within you. It is up to you all my dear friends, to cultivate each gift of the spirit but I know and I fully understand how restricting these bodies are and of course the physical brain interferes at times. Rather than help you to understand, it confuses the issue."*

It is as well with these more complex issues that we have the opportunity to recap or to see things from another angle. As has been said before, the knowledge is innate within us. That means that all-knowledge is with the parent soul in spirit and we are connected to it … but the connection is less than perfect! Intuition is the way we receive that knowledge. It can be useful to meditate and strengthen the soul connection and so improve clarity of intuition. That is one spiritual gift that may be cultivated and to which Salumet alludes. And, as he points out, the physical brain can on occasions work against the natural flow of intuition that ebbs from the soul.

If however, we in the first place can accept the basic teaching that Earth was created in spirit before it became physically manifest, then the physical brain might just *help* in our understanding. Another point worth making is that the soul's involvement in the creation is certainly difficult to grasp if we cannot perceive the nature of soul with any degree of clarity. So, using the physical brain, let us try to get a clearer picture of soul…

Some scientists, when they find a system difficult to imagine, refer to a simple model to assist their thinking. The model may be ridiculously simple by comparison. It does not matter. At the risk of appearing irreverent, I will compare the soul to a toilet roll. Let us call it the 'cosmic toilet roll model'. The central spool is a soul that has always been ... has existed throughout eternity. As a part of Divinity it participated in the creation of Earth and later, the life forms on Earth. In the fullness of time, the spool gathered pieces of paper to itself. Each piece of paper on the roll once had Earth life and is now a 'past life'. There are now many Earthly past lives that have become part of the roll. Unwind the roll and you will see that they follow one behind the other in 'linear time' order as they happened on Earth. Rewind, and the roll becomes as one, as it is in spirit (and in spirit, time's linear nature is no longer apparent). Each piece of paper still exists individually yet it is a part of the whole. The cosmic toilet roll resides in spirit where time is not as we know it. But the last sheet on the roll may remain unwound for a while. It can wear a material body and have Earth life. It always remains connected to its parent soul by the perforated attachment. The perforations allow only intuition, feelings and sometimes inspiration to pass through to the Earth life. Memory details of what has gone before are all held back, yet intuition and feelings can be strong because they are powered by the all-knowledge innate within the parent soul body. At death, the material body is cast off and remains with Earth, and the life ... the spirit ... returns to soul bringing with it the treasures of that life's learning and experience. These become part of soul and aid the soul's further progression. There are many, many cosmic toilet rolls that issue from the infinite forests of the eternal Divinity.

So on Earth we live the idea that has begun in spirit and the idea becomes 'sharpened' as the result of physical living.

Our Earthly lives may of course proceed in so many different directions to suit and benefit the needs of the parent soul. The extreme diversity of life on the physical planet is as it should be. Whilst helping others and knowing love are always tremendously important factors, it is my understanding that the overall purpose of our physical existence is to aid the soul's progress ... to further progress that which has always been, and that which existed before the physical Earth even became a thought.

3. ON THE POWER OF THOUGHT AND PRAYER

It is abundantly clear from the little that has been said so far that thought must have a special place in our lives. If it was thought that began the creation of Earth and thought that continues to steer evolution, then it is of fundamental status and it is indeed truly powerful. There is frequent mention in the teachings of the power that thought may have. Prayer and thought are very closely related, that too is made clear. Prayer is thought that is 'targeted'. It will have power if it comes from deeply within our being. Salumet began the meeting of 11th July 1994 with a prayer:

> ~ "O great and gracious God,
> We gather here before you
> In peace, in love and understanding.
> You have granted to me this day
> To be your emissary,
> To teach, to comfort and to instil some knowledge
> To our friends here on this Earthly plane.
> O great God, we offer ourselves to you
> This day to be used as you will.
> Amen."

Then he added:
> ~ "I want to say to you all about the power of prayer: It is only through your meditations and prayer that you begin to open up spiritually. I know some people dispute this, but it is an eternal truth. And so I say to you all: Please use the power of your prayers."

It has been explained to us how our thinking is energy and how our heartfelt prayers never fall on deaf ears. They have their effect, but prayers are not always answered in the ways we might expect. There are several possible reasons for this. And some of our prayers may be more heartfelt than others. In fact, in the general sense, our thoughts may be of a powerful nature or they may be quite trivial. I was able to ask a question to clarify this point during our 17th January 2000 meeting, pointing out that writers and actors on stage must have many inconsequential thoughts.

~ *"… Remember that although you are spirit, you are clothed in physical garb. You also have a brain that is within that physical garb. The power of thought that I speak of is the thought of the spirit. That is the POWER of thought. There is much thinking which is negligible within your lives … of course, there must be. It is when you come to the deep thought that comes from the spirit within … there lies the power … That is the power of thinking that you must be careful of because not only can it do good but you have the ability to affect many others also. You should be able to differentiate between the two and you have given a good example in speaking about the writer and the actor upon the stage. These are everyday thoughts. Remember too in your dream state, many of your thoughts are flippant but many are spirit-inspired. I know these many things confuse you human beings, but as life continues and your spiritual unfoldment (becomes) greater, many things (will) become clearer to you … so remember, the power of thinking must be developed within the spiritual nature of yourself. Do not be afraid that every feeling, every thought, is captured forever. That is not quite true and it is misunderstood by many, many people upon your Earth."*

It is made clear then, that it is the heartfelt thought or prayer from deep within the spirit that has power, while the general output of the physical mind is of a different nature and does not energise the collective consciousness in the same way; also, prayer from deep within the spirit part of us is made the more powerful when it is collective.

On that occasion when we talked of the war in Yugoslavia and how the American president had had put to him the idea of a meditation team as alternative to military combat, Salumet had this to say:

21st June 1999 ~ "… Prayer, as you know … thought … cannot be wasted. Collective prayer and thought, brings more power to it. This you know and understand. What I wish to say: of course continue with your prayers for the sake of your brothers all over the planet. Prayer is never wasted … but what is more important for you and for each one in this room is that you must rise above individual catastrophe within your world. You have the power my dear friends, to do this. You must see your world … your planet as it sits within the cosmos. It is but a small area. Know that all things are governed by the one law and that is the law of love. You wonder why prayers seem to go unanswered. They do not. But what *you seem to be unaware of are the negative thoughts of mankind who has lost that sense of spirit of progress. You cannot as individuals change things in your world in an instant. But awareness is on your planet now. It is growing. There are many such as yourselves who send good thoughts to those of us who can help to influence leaders in your world ... Mankind is becoming more aware, more spiritually aware. But until such time as all mankind has changed, there always will be strife, there will always be unkind deeds, man against man..."*

I feel these to be practical words that help to place things into a perspective. Our deeper thoughts are powerful but they sometimes have to bide their time. They should not be seen as instant magical salve. Where political thrust is already involved in a karmic process, then time must enter the equation and that is a wider picture that we cannot possibly understand. We have to accept that wider picture that has already been constructed from past deeds. But things are steadily improving in the world, so that we may look more hopefully to the future. And we are assured that our prayers will always help in some way or another.

Our teacher has on several occasions arranged for others from spirit to come and talk with us. On 13th March 2000, it was one we know as Edwin that came to further enlighten us on thought and prayer. He was able to tell us much about the relative values of our prayers. It seems that those springing from various aspects of fear are of a lesser kind than those that spring from compassion for others or love of planet. Genuine prayer must come from the spirit within and does not necessarily need words. I suggested that a peace meditation could be an example of unspoken prayer, but it could possibly arise from a fear of war or more satisfactorily arise out of compassion for the world. Edwin responded:

~ *"Yes, now you have touched upon the word ... compassion; not fear for the world, not fear for yourselves ... compassion! May I give you an example please, of unsaid prayer? If you were to come upon a person who is unknown to you but immediately your heart goes out to that person. Unspoken love goes out to that person. That is prayer. Do you understand? Because it comes instantly it is natural and there is that great spiritual blending. That is good prayer if I may use that word."*

A little further into our discussion Margaret was saying:

"In your thoughts you are asking for help for other people."

~ *"You need not ask in words. It should come from here (pointing to heart). There should be no need for repetitive words because, of course, I hope you do know or I hope you have been told and you do understand, that all that you think is known anyway. Therefore, this repetitious feeling that you have to continue to say words over and over again ... each time they are said without true feeling, they become less and less. Can you see this? (But) one true blending of prayer can create much, much good in your world."*

I then enquired how our visitor regarded collective prayer in church where all are speaking and thinking together:

~ *"Yes, it is difficult to give you one answer to this because with so many people being individual spirits, they are praying in different ways. You will have those who repeat words because it is words that they are used to saying. Those thoughts will not have great impact but there will be others within that congregation whose prayers and thoughts reach the targets that they are intended for."*

George: "It very much comes down to the individual..."

~ *"Yes, I would suggest so ... yes. It is wrong, and I have heard it said that churches today ... it matters not what denomination ... that churches have no use for these masses of people uttering so many repetitive words. Do not dismiss it so lightly. Much good does come from such people ... those who are genuine, whether they know of their spiritual self or not ... because, after all, it is the spirit within which is at work. Do you understand this?"*

George: "I have always felt that the Church is an overt spiritual happening and it can set an individual on a particular course..."

~ *"Yes, you cannot dismiss out of hand all churches. Many of your great ... I believe you call them cathedrals ... and mosques ... all these places, it matters not ... it is what is in the hearts of the people. It is the blending of spirit that counts. So again I would say this to you ... and I know this has been told you many times ...do not judge others. Do not suppose that your prayers are any better than another human being's, because in judging thus, you are erroneous in your thinking."*

It was a good message to hear, and will no doubt be reassuring to many who choose the formal place of worship, that their prayer can have such value. It has been so clearly stated. It quite simply comes down to what is in the hearts of the people. It really is that simple and denomination counts for nothing. The formal religions have steadily presented their versions of spiritual knowledge across hundreds and thousands of years. Perhaps it is now time, in the 21st century, to know oneness and go forward together.

The results of an experiment had been reported in the press. It referred to an American hospital where a number of patients were suffering from heart problems. Some patients, amounting to 50%, were prayed for, while the other 50% were not. It was found that the group prayed for fared statistically better than the group that was not. It was during the meeting of 7th August 2000 that Salumet was asked if he would comment on this:

~ *"Yes … if only one were helped, even by Earthly experiment, then I can only say to you this is good. You of course may not be surprised by these results. It is just a pity that so many were excluded. Of course, again we return to the power of thought which is indeed the beginning of prayer. We have discussed prayer to some degree in past times and each one of you I hope by now fully understands that your thoughts for another person are never disregarded. But of course collective prayer is a little more powerful, shall we say to use your everyday words; but the same effect is achieved by many of those within your world who you call 'healers'. Their prayers are sent to us so often for the safety and well being of others. But prayer is there for each and everyone to use. I did tell you did I not, that many changes would happen within your world and these things are taking place as I speak to you. All within this planet are slowly, slowly becoming more spiritually aware."*

We agreed that things appear to be coming out into the open more and are being reported in the media as never before.

~ *"That is what is good, that a wider audience of people are now aware that those things can happen … that non-judgemental people have the opportunity to make up their own minds … that there is no dogmatic teaching which holds them back. This can only be good for mankind."*

There was more to say about thought and how it relates to spirit during our meeting of 22nd April 2002. It was a lengthy session and much was difficult to follow. It may be appropriate to just quote the salient phrases that emerged:

~ *"You understand 'thought' and how powerful it can be. You use thought many, many times throughout your living but mostly you are unaware of the unconscious thoughts that are sent out at all times from each one of you. I have told you my dear friends that it is most important that you take full control of your thinking … You are bound to fall at times, only because you are humankind and humankind at this present time of evolution cannot be perfect. That is why we come to help you so many times, not only in these small gatherings but as you know, we try to influence all leaders in your world, not only in your world but in other worlds. I do not apologise for once more saying to you that it (thought) is the most powerful thing that you possess. As spirit continues, so does thought; it goes hand-in-hand, as you would say on this Earth. You cannot have one without the other; in fact they coexist as one energy … Thought has always existed as energy … You have a human brain and the human brain perceives thought to be separate from the spirit, but all energy that exists is but one energy but on different and various levels … True (pure?) thought belongs to spirit, not to the human brain … Of course there is a form of thinking, that is why humankind has been given a brain, so that the thoughts of the spirit may be changed if you like, and transmitted through that thinking brain. That is not the thought of which I speak; call it (brain output) intellect if you like, call it thinking … Intuition comes to you from the thought 'pattern' … All thought and thinking has to come to you* **through** *the human brain."*

The overall picture presented seems to be a thought/spiritual energy that comes to us and is processed by our physical brains. In fact the impression given is that the brain is much more of a processor than a generator. And this perhaps helps to explain the power that thought can have. (If it is of soul/cosmic origin then its power need know no bounds.) I reminded Salumet that we had recently talked about the random number generator machine that seems to be able to detect collective-consciousness-thought energy. Looking for clarification, I asked if it would detect just spiritual energy or also brain output.

~ *"I would say to you my dear friend that anything which tries to capture energy cannot always be pure. Therefore I would say to you that not only spiritual energy but also negative energy would be picked up."*

George: "And the negative energy would connect with the human brain…"

~ *"Yes."*

The following month we were discussing the confrontation of problems in the world and that led to a further reinforcing statement from our teacher:

27th May 2002 ~ "All nations within your world today have problems of one kind or another but these problems will be worked through. Remember, and I say my dear friend you have used the word 'thought' and that, my friends, is the most powerful weapon that you have. It comes not only from our world but from within each one of you. Each individual has the power to change much, but again I say to you: it is within your hands to do so."

In concluding this topic it may be appropriate to refer to one awe-inspiring application of thought power. There are huge stone constructions that continue to exist from our ancient past. Stone blocks weighing hundreds and sometimes thousands of tons have been hewn, transported, raised to considerable heights and positioned with care. There are Inca and Mayan sites in South and Central America and there are the Egyptian pyramids as examples of what I mean. There have been many theories as to how such edifices could have been built using mechanical contrivance and slave gangs. Such strategy could conceivably explain some building work but certainly not all. The notion that all could have been achieved using mechanisms and muscle is really quite preposterous. It was during one of our early gatherings on 15th August 1994 that Leslie put it to Salumet that the answer had to be either levitation or de-materialisation followed by re-materialisation.

~ *"As I have spoken previously, there were races upon your Earth much more knowledgeable. And yes, the simple answer is 'levitation'. Materialisation/de-materialisation; this basically is what happens with healing today when you speak of your 'psychic surgery'. But that is a different matter. These 'ancient peoples', as you call them … I call them 'very young' … but let me say: their knowledge far, far outweighed anything that you have today. And yes, levitation was a way of constructing these huge, huge monuments … At that time there were people who (were) very much like today in your African societies where you have the doctors who heal … the 'wise men' if you wish to call them (that). There were people who had these powers, if you like. They were the architects of the time. They were the ones who would have … the blue print? They would have made the blueprint of the construction of the building … or the temple, or the pyramids, or whatever we are talking about. You would have a group of people as you have a group here tonight, to build the power. It is no different. They gathered together, they made the blueprint and they instructed the people on how they should go about their tasks. We are speaking of powers not known today. So to go into the details of how it worked would be rather confusing to your mind, but I will say this: one time I will bring someone who will explain in detail how this happened. But we are talking of times to come. But yes, levitation was the manner in which they were built. I don't say everything … every brick, every stone; but that in the majority of the building was how it was done. Again we come back to the power of thought. Of course … what is levitation?"*

Leslie: "Yes, just the power of thought."

~ *"I must stress to you all again ... the power of thought. It really ... it really is an incredible thing. I wish I could express to you in words just how powerful it is."*

In today's world we are aware of the legends and folklore from ancient times that describe flying and we hear of holy men who are able to levitate their bodies. We see pictures engraved in rock that illustrate such happenings. According to Salumet, past cultures have understood and developed the power of thought that springs from deep within the spirit self. Adepts could levitate both massive objects as well as themselves. This was a part of their knowledge/art that they put to use. It follows that those legends and folklore that reach our present awareness are accurate echoes from those ancient times. Modern mankind's intellectual development springs from physical mind output and this is something entirely different from developing the spirit self. Perhaps that is something that we should think on.

4. SOME FACTS ABOUT ANCIENT CIVILISATIONS

We are assured then, that thought-powered levitation was a principle used in the massive stonework constructions of times past.

The Egyptian pyramids: Use of levitation would explain well the many difficulties there would otherwise be in assembling such massive blocks. I have long felt that the original purpose of the pyramids must have been so very much more than just mere tombs or treasure houses. Considering the Great Pyramid: its incredibly precise placement and alignment to the cardinal points and its construction in ratio to a hemisphere of Earth is awesome. Then the precision of rock cutting and fitting massive blocks together in such an orderly way is something that is really beyond our modern technology. Four perfectly straight shafts are cut at different precise angles, two from what is known as the Queen's Chamber and two from what is known as the King's Chamber. They at one time accurately pointed into the heavens to:
- Sirius (Alpha Canis Major, also known as the Dog Star),
- Beta Ursa Minor, a star in the Little Bear constellation,
- Alpha Draconis or the Pole star of ancient times,
- Zeta Orionis, the brightest star in Orion's Belt.

Computer studies of Earth's precession tell us that the very precisely made shafts pointed to the four named stars in and around the year date 2500 BC [7]. Whatever the construction date of the Great Pyramid, it seems to have been designed *for* this particular time.

The many subtle details that have been carefully worked into the Great Pyramid belie any mundane usage. Salumet had something to say on that in response to a question concerning the pyramids and drawings of people flying that was put on 23rd January 1995:

~ *"Much is spoken of pyramids and pyramid power. Pyramids were sources of direction. There were indeed those who could travel at that time. Pyramids pointed to other galaxies ... other stars if you like. I will try to keep it simple. Each point of the pyramid pointed to a direction of the universe ... to the open skies. That is why ... you had a civilisation that could indeed fly, as you put it. This is a little known thing about the pyramids. They were not places of worship. They were used for a directional function."*

Leslie: "So the fact that they were used as tombs was secondary?"

~ *"They were not there as tombs. That was not what the function of them was. That was not the intention and I can say to you now: there was a much more complex reason for them."*

The reason must indeed be complex. It looks as if we need to re-think our ideas about the pyramids. There has been further commentary concerning space travel and we shall come to that later. Suffice to observe at this point that one cannot progress far into space travel without first mastering a de-materialisation/re-materialisation procedure. (In fact our science tells us that the atoms and molecules of ordinary matter can never travel beyond the speed of light. This is an axiom upheld by both theory and experiment. Hence, de-materialisation as a means to entering that experience beyond light velocity, presents the only way forward in any serious attempt at space travel. This is a useful product of scientific reason and intellect.) It follows that, in consideration of this basic principle together with certain details of pyramid construction and the directional factor, the pyramids may well have functioned as de-materialisation chambers as well as the means of fixing direction in the heavens. This would justify the elaborate details of alignment and of internal construction of which we are at last beginning to take more serious notice.

The Nazca plateau markings: Several months earlier, in response to a question about the Nazca Plateau markings in South America, the subject of space travel had also been mentioned:

10thOctober 1994 ~ "I have said before, there have been civilisations upon this Earth who have had superior knowledge ... far superior to that which you have now. The lines on the plateau that you speak of were in fact directional lines for those people who travelled in space. I think I have spoken before that there were travellers from this Earth, because of their extended knowledge. This also applies ...it did not happen in just one area of your Earth, but in many. Particularly we have spoken of the Egyptians. The South Americans ... all over, and I too can say, around your North

Pole area there was a civilisation with much, much knowledge. And still there is to be discovered the remains of that civilisation. It was a directional point if you like, for space travellers to home onto. Is that helpful?"

It was indeed helpful. I thanked our teacher for his statement and asked that he confirm the space travellers were of this planet and not visitors *to* it. He repeated that they were indeed of this Earth.

More on the pyramids and space travel: Moving on to our meeting of 10th July 2000, the subject of materialisation had just been discussed. This led to an opportunity to place a question concerning the opposite process of de-materialisation and how it might apply to space travel:

~ *"Yes, I understand your question. De-materialisation as you call it, is an attribute of spirit; it is something that you all are capable of. I do not pardon myself for repetition of my words but each one of you as spirit has the capability of much ... Yes, I agree with you that many space travellers have used what you call de-materialisation for their own good and their own benefit, but what is more important is that you know and understand that it is an attribute of spirit. To you human beings who have lost much of your natural capabilities, de-materialisation and materialisation seems to be an exception to the rule. It is not. It is just a matter of re-training yourselves, if I may put it so bluntly."*

It would appear then, that we material-bodied humans could travel in space with success if first we de-materialise. There is both scientific reasoning as well as the teaching in support of this notion. Such a conditioning would arise naturally from our spiritual development and would be classed as an attribute of spirit. If the Great Pyramid were in part a pre-conditioning chamber leading to space travel, then this would of course begin to explain its complexity. And clearly Salumet sees an ability to de-materialise as just a normal function for humankind that should in no way be seen as exceptional. It does then begin to look as if the 'users' of the complex construction that still remains there in the desert today, were able to travel in 'alternative energy' form. And this would have been, not so much a triumph of material technology, but more a development of the spirit within.

More was said on this topic during our meeting of 5th May 2003. On this occasion I put a further question on the pyramids with particular reference to their complexity and how that might relate to energy manipulation and dematerialisation function:

~ *"Yes, let us first take dematerialisation. To you it seems such a strange and unusual happening. To those of us who know more, it is a natural happening. That is first and foremost what you need to know."*

George: "Yes, and that goes with a much stronger spiritual development..."

~ *"Yes, of course. You have enough knowledge at this time to understand."* (I had been reading much and pondering the issue in the light of Salumet's previous words.)

~ *"I told you when first I came that all of these great happenings, as you call them, were quite natural occurrences and that people of your past times had much more spiritual knowledge than many do now. Yes, originally those of greater knowledge had those ... we will call them 'points of light' ... points of light because all structures are light and energy. This you understand.* (That is, as scientists would agree, the molecules of all physical matter that we see are comprised of light and energy; also the pyramids themselves would be seen in the way of spirit as light beacons.) *The pyramids were built as points of travel for **those who came from other worlds.** The drawings you speak of within the walls of these great rocks came later ... they came from man and man's assessment of what they should have been. We are speaking of two different things here. It is a topic that we can enter into another time if you so wish, but we must not mix the original construction or dematerialisation within, with what you find in the inner walls of these structures. I will clarify it for you and make it a little easier for you to understand. There has been much written, there has been much controversy, but I will tell you how and why and when so that your understanding will be greater."*

There was general enthusiasm and agreement at this prospect:

George: "There seems to have been a time of..."

~ *"There is a lapse of time."*

George: "There was a time of very early knowledge when the major pyramids would have been first built..."

~ *"And mankind has not been correct in his timing (dating)."*

George: "... And then there has been further usage of the pyramids since their original construction."

~ *"Yes, you must always bear this in mind, but we will go into more detail..."*

I thanked Salumet for his further words on the subject. It was the end of a session and time had run out. But the information given is clearly very important. The original construction and purpose would appear to relate to de-materialisation and to space travel of **those from elsewhere.** The internal wall inscriptions came later. This scenario makes sense of a number of things ... the inability of the early treasure-hunters to find any tomb treasure to begin with!

As our teacher says, there has been much written and there has been much controversy. I am bound to say that the information received is consistent with certain publications by Graham Hancock, Robert Bauval, Erich von Däniken, the Coptic scribe Abu'l Hassan Ma'sudi and the Greek historian Herodotus. Evidence for the construction date of the Sphinx, the Great Pyramid and the Giza pyramid general layout is well presented by Hancock [8] as being around 10,450 BC. This date is supported by the assertion of Abu'l Hassan Ma'sudi [9] that two pyramids, one of which is the Great Pyramid, were built before the flood. Then there is the testimony of Herodotus [10] that is both detailed as well as remarkable...

Herodotus had travelled to Egypt where he had discourse with the priests of Thebes. He was shown a statue of the last priest-king, Sethôs in the temple of Vulcan; also 341 statues representing all the Egyptian priest-kings from the very first one. Each he was told was the son of the former, so that the span of time amounted to 341 generations. If we base a calculation on an average generation gap of say 29-30 years, then we have a time span for the generations of almost exactly 10,000 years. Counting back from the time of Herodotus brings us very close to 10,450 BC. Herodotus was also told that no gods appeared in human form during this period; the entire series were Pirômis (gentlemen). Then he was told that prior to this period it was different and there were indeed gods in Egypt, living together with mankind. Always there was one who was supreme. I understand from my further reading that the last god-king was named Horus, known to the Greeks as Apollo. He was the son of Osiris, known to the Greeks as Dionysus. Horus had deposed Typhon to rule Egypt as its last god-king.

It is highly likely then, that the beings Salumet describes as *those who came from other worlds,* identify with those Herodotus describes as the god-kings of Egypt. Advanced beings from other worlds must have seemed as gods to the ordinary humans of that time. Their names also identify with the religion of the pharaohs and relate to the mythology of the Greeks. In fact, in his history, Herodotus also makes the clear statement that nearly all the names of the Greek gods came originally from Egypt.

Early mankind … Homo erectus: Let us now look back two million years. It is the custom to refer to ourselves as we were then as Homo erectus. In reply to a question on the spirit character of Homo erectus, Salumet reminded us that spirit has always been and of course continues to be a part of us, and indeed the major part. Spirit communication and influence existed then in its various forms as it does now. During another session it became clear that we might well see the human biological body as a material 'vehicle' that can receive input of spirit from a parent soul. But of course, in spirit, there are souls and souls. There are the souls that develop in the 'ordinary' sense in association with this planet. There are also more 'advanced' souls with developmental associations elsewhere in the universe. Clearly then, in the wider scheme of things, there is the possibility of implanting spirit from elsewhere in order to provide humans having advanced knowledge potential. Our teacher spoke on this:

10th October 1994 ~ "When man originated, he started off with very little knowledge. But always on your Earth plane there have been … I would like to say: Masters of knowledge. They are people who have come to this Earth plane, not as simple people, but as people with already extended knowledge, if you like. Originally, some of the people (who) settled here came from another time. We are beginning to go into difficult subjects, but I will try to say as plainly as possible how this occurred. In earlier times, there have been people on this Earth who have travelled through space. Let me say: your Earth is very young as far as the planets go … There are other places that hold … I don't want to say 'superior' beings, but beings with knowledge that far outshines your own. They were placed upon your Earth to guide, to impart the knowledge they had already obtained. So you see, although you had man who knew very little, you had 'masters of knowledge' too. These are the people that inhabited those places that you find difficult now to recognise. It was nothing for them to travel in space. The object of their lives here was to teach, was to encourage, was to help mankind gain the knowledge that they already had (but which remained un-accessed within the parent soul). That was the beginning, but what happened was that these settlements became greedy, became egotistical and

*wanted to outshine each other. So in the end, what had to happen was
that they actually destroyed themselves with their own superior knowledge
… in the same way that man now has gained sufficient knowledge that
he too can destroy himself. I speak of your nuclear energy. So, although
you think you have gained in knowledge, you have in fact done the very
same that those previous settlements of people had done. The knowledge
they had became too great for them. They misused it … and they lost all
that they had gained.*

*That is why we have gathered … to prevent the same thing happening.
You have been reaching a peak of knowledge. You have already started
to travel in space. You were beginning to reach the point of extended
knowledge … and I am sure if you spoke with your astronauts who have
travelled in space, they could tell you much, much more than they have
already divulged. So you see, it is almost like something that is repeating
itself, and we cannot allow it to happen."*

George: "So it's a question of having the spiritual maturity to
be able to control what we have invented or learned?"

~ *"Yes, the knowledge that is given to you must be used for the well-
being of all of the peoples of the Earth … not for segregated communities,
not for the people with the knowledge. Knowledge that is given to you
is meant to be used for the good of the Earth. Man has increased his
intellectual power, but that does not mean he has grown in his soul-
growth. In fact, very often it can mean the opposite. Life should have
progressed when these people of knowledge lived on your Earth. It should
have been the beginning … it should have been a 'paradise on Earth' as
you like to call it sometimes. But unfortunately that did not happen. And
I have to say once again that their own egos, power and greed, lost all of
their knowledge until they extinguished themselves."*

As often happens, we have digressed … on this occasion
from the nature of very early mankind to the nature of early
civilisations and this leads us on to one in particular…

The civilisation of Atlantis: An interesting point was made on
this subject on 25th June 2001. The subject of Atlantis had come
up before in our meetings, and I think I would be correct in
saying that there are two published major and important Earthly
sources of information from that time (and I am aware of one
other important source as yet unpublished). There is the account
by the Greek Philosopher Plato [11] who states that his information
came via Egypt, and there are the many 'life readings' received

in trance through Edgar Cayce [12]. Cayce had a noteworthy connection to Egypt of the 11th millennium BC. It seems that in past life, he was a Carpathian that came to live in Egypt as the priest Ra-Ta in a position of some influence. At that time, there were many refugees arriving from the foundering residual part of Atlantis. I also state that, on a previous occasion, Cayce's past life readings were mentioned and Salumet confirmed that he was indeed *a man of vision*. A topic of our evening this time had been reincarnation and questions followed:

George:"In talking about the many reincarnations, we are very often I believe, talking about tens of thousands of years, perhaps hundreds of thousands of years … so that there are many today that had past lives on Atlantis. Perhaps I could mention this … and misuse of power was one of the problems in the days of Atlantis, so we understand. Could one see our recent confrontation with the nuclear bomb, as a chance for those same souls of Atlantis, to re-work that old problem?"

~ *"Yes, those who existed at the time of which you speak would of course have to readjust to the conditions which they had caused. After all, everything is cause and effect, as you know."*

George:"Yes, and the learning that goes with that…"

~ *"Of course. Any opportunity that would arise within this world … for many of those souls to redress the balance of their existence … they would take the opportunity of some situation in this world to do so. And yes, that could be one of the opportunities open to them … because mankind has abused the power that he has been given, throughout the existence of this planet. Not only the people of Atlantis, but many of the civilisations on this planet have abused power. And I will give you one example … the people known to you as the Egyptians, who had much knowledge also and who also abused that knowledge. There are many situations within your world where these people could return in another form, to redress the balance of their abuse. I will not say 'all', because that would not be correct. There would have been many opportunities for them, but of course, when so many are involved, then very often they choose to return as a group, to redress that balance."*

It was an intriguing exchange that serves to illustrate just how much our remote past lives can be entangled with present day happenings. Such karmic matters are sometimes difficult to comprehend. The idea that numbers from spirit may reincarnate as a group for shared purpose is fascinating and may possibly relate to seemingly irrational political change on Earth. The deterioration of the wonderful culture of the pyramid period in Egypt clearly relates to abuse of the knowledge that they once had. And along with this decline, I would deduce that it became no longer possible for them to 'activate' the pyramid structures.

Conclusions: During the course of our meetings, there has been reference to several great civilisations of the distant past. They include: Atlantis, Lemuria, South America, Egypt and a 'North Pole' culture that may possibly relate to the mythical Hyperborea. My understanding is that there has sometimes been an input of more highly developed spirit from elsewhere in the cosmos, for the purpose of promoting advancement on this planet. Unfortunately, there has also been attendant abuse of power and knowledge leading at times to some degree of spiritual decline. This has resulted in the physical loss of entire civilisations (only physical loss of course). Though this may have happened thousands or even hundreds of thousands of years ago, advanced cultures cannot disappear without leaving remnants in some shape or form. The remnants that remain include: the sphinx, certain pyramids, various huge stone edifices, the Nazca plateau designs, written records, myths, past life readings and the knowledge that continues to be held in spirit. That knowledge can of course, be accessed and divulged by Masters such as Salumet.

Although this is fair conclusion for what has been presented so far, the picture still remains sketchy as an expression of the whole vista of our continued 'being'. More recently, and now with the advantage of receiving ten years of the teachings, I had the opportunity to seek further clarification. It was our final meeting of the year prior to Salumet's Christmas recess until his return in the New Year:

"… We think of them as past civilisations but that description really perhaps only relates to the physical Earth. I imagine there are groups in spirit who continue those past cultures and some reincarnate into later cultures for further learning, and all that knowledge is still there in spirit … it is not lost at all. Is that a fair picture of how things are?"

8 December 2003 ~ "Yes. Your words are admirable, but just let me simplify it for the others. Past, present, future are but one, this we have discussed briefly, but time as you know it is but energy and energy cannot be destroyed. *Therefore, when you speak as you do, of course it is never lost. You of course think of time within your own Earthly planet, but it is but a small, small part of all that is. Energy cannot be destroyed. Therefore, what has gone in your minds indeed has not."*

George: "So it is almost an erroneous thought form to think of them as past civilisations…"

~ *"Yes, but it is acceptable, because mankind's thinking is so limited. You understand? But my answer to your question would be: yes, in your thinking."*

Then followed Salumet's words of farewell as he left for short recess (that we know provides the opportunity for a kind of 'cosmic conference'), and I include these words because they help to illustrate again both the warmth that abounds and his multiplicity of being:

~ *"I will leave it with you this time. I feel when these moments come and I have to leave you for a little while, I feel somehow your Earthly emotion sometimes, and I wish to say to each one of you, that although I may not use this instrument to speak with you, I am indeed with each one of you at all times. And know always as you call my name in need, I will be with you. So my friends, until we meet next time, I wish you all much love and happiness in your daily lives, and no matter what troubles you, know that I stand by your side."*

5. EARTH AS A SPECK IN THE LIVING COSMOS

In the past, there has been the occasional visionary who has looked to the wider horizons of creation. More often however, spiritual matters have been considered in terms of just our one inhabited world ... or even in terms of one single faith that sub-divides our world. That has been the accepted, restricted view of recent past, and of course there must of necessity be at some point a beginning to life's spiritual journey. Now, in the 21ˢᵗ century, it is becoming more and more evident that we are not the only life form that exists. Others live material lives on other material worlds. Others live in spirit in association with this and other worlds. Others live in non-worldly pure energy forms that are beyond our wildest imagination. There is a need for us to see that the oneness of spiritual existence extends throughout the cosmos in its entirety.

Earth is a relatively young planet, so that there are many out there who outshine us in knowledge and many who are far beyond us in their spiritual growth. And some by virtue of their wonderfully developed attributes are able to visit us as 'space travellers'. It is perhaps the time for us to think less in closeted Earthly terms and more freely as the cosmic beings that we truly are. On a number of occasions we have been encouraged in this more expansive view and Salumet has dwelt at some length on the nature of the guidance that planets throughout the vaults of the heavens receive ... planets that are at all sorts of different stages of development. He has also talked much on the guidance that Earth receives within the greater scheme of things. It may help in piecing together a picture if excerpts from that voluminous commentary, as received, are presented here:

17ᵗʰ July 2000 ~ "... *There are many worlds within this great universe and many that have beings upon them ... beings with much greater knowledge than this very young planet Earth ... All planets answer to a greater Divinity. All is part of a greater plan.*"

1ˢᵗ August 1994 ~ "... *Let me say: you are indeed limited by what you know and understand. There are other galaxies. Let me say this to you:*

how do you suppose there were 'space travellers', or are 'space travellers', if they do not travel quicker than the speed of light as you know it? … The speed of light is only the Earth's conception of speed. There are many things that the Earth is not aware of … but you will become more and more knowledgeable in these matters as time progresses."

George: "And beings that are able to travel faster than the speed of light, would be concerned with a more 'rarefied' state of matter than atoms and molecules, with which we on Earth are more familiar?"

~ *"They indeed operate on a much higher vibration than you at present understand. Yes, that is true."*

17th April 1995 ~ *"… There are beings who always have been formless, if you like, who have not possessed human forms. It means not necessarily that they have risen greatly, but shall we say, their starting point is different. When I first came to you, I said many, many were gathering. This means not only within your Earth, but in many planets. Do not think that yours is the only planet which is in need of help, because I can tell you that it is not so."*

18th January 1999 ~ *"… What you perhaps do not know and understand is this: that each inhabited planet, is overseen by those of us who have been guided, to oversee the evolution of these planets. There is I believe amongst you, a vision of one guidance for all …I must emphasise at this point, that **there is only one creative force** from which we all come. But I do not think you understand that many planets are guided individually by many principles and forces … The over-ruling guidance comes from a number of beings; from great, shall we say, consciousness … higher consciousness than you would perhaps expect … When we have spoken in time past of visitations to this planet, I have told you that that indeed exists, and I believe you now fully accept that many forms of life exist throughout the cosmos. You must now accept that these 'space travellers', as you call them, are also governed by higher consciousness from their own worlds. You have to now accept that they too belong … and I will use the words of my dear friend (Leslie) … they too belong to a 'chain of command'. So what visitors you have on this planet, have already been guided here …There are many forces and many principles, many forms of consciousness which emanate, and are created into human form, into many forms of existence, into all forms of life … Does it not show you that this planet Earth is reaching a point in its own evolution, where knowledge is being given around your world, in order that you can evolve in the same way that many, many others have? You are very* *young in as much as knowledge goes. You know very little in the way of existence. But your time is coming, and that is why in your time, (now) comes the emergence of others ... to show themselves to the human beings of this planet, in order that you understand that much greater knowledge is known by others throughout your universe."*

27th July 1998 ~ "Those beings from other times, other energies, other planets, who sustain more knowledge than yourselves. They of course have the opportunity to travel this space area ... the intention of these beings is that more contact be made. As each of your years pass, more and more communication will take place. But because of mankind's natural inhibitions and fear, this must be done at a slow, slow rate. Beings from other times have shown themselves upon this planet, but in the main, as with most things not fully understood by humankind, it is being ridiculed. The time is coming when human beings must accept that they are not the sole forms of life within the cosmos ... they will lose all fear of foreign beings. Using the words 'alien' or 'foreign' is not useful to you ... better that you say 'brother'. (On another occasion, 'cosmic friends' was suggested.) Their form may be slightly different but the energy within is the same energy of which you exist, but (geared) to a much faster degree of evolution on their part ... They may have more advancement in their travel but you are an entirely new world to them. Would you go to another planet and expect them to understand, or would you understand their language automatically?"

Leslie suggested at this point that we might understand their thoughts if we had sufficient spiritual development.

~ *"Yes, now we have an inkling of what this is about. Contact is being made on a higher form of energy. Therefore they are expecting mankind to respond in the same way, although they know them to be lesser beings in their development. Humankind cannot respond because they do not have their knowledge. They have left many 'pictures' (crop circles/pictograms) ... in the forms of their writings in the fields. But it is mankind's downfall that they do not understand these forms. It will come. There is already amongst many of you, an understanding of what is being done. It is being used in many forms, as the ancient civilisations in your world used to use drawings in order for others to understand."*

Leslie then observed that they could have shown us pictures of themselves.

~ *"My friend, they **have** shown **themselves** to mankind. They have shown themselves as they truly are. Not only is it in the crop circles and other phenomena, but they have shown **themselves** to man ... to those* *people who they hope will understand and pass on the truth to the rest of mankind. Do you not know my dear friends, that many in governments in your world have witnessed for themselves what you call 'aliens'? ... And I do not like that word. I would prefer you to call them 'brothers'. They have witnessed for themselves many of these beings, but because of their fear for mankind, because of their lack of understanding, much has been kept quiet. Do not assume that corn circles are the only form of communication. In many areas of this planet there are more of these showings of crop circles because of the entry of the spacecraft. In the same way that your antiquated aircraft need pathways of flight, so too do the spacecraft. It is assumed that these craft can lift and fly and go in any direction they wish. But I can tell you they have to follow the airways of travel. That is why there is an abundance of these happenings in certain areas. The time and the place is most important and certain times of your days and nights, in order for them to enter this planet. They also have to abide by the cosmic energies that are available to them. But I assure you, my dear friends, communication has taken place. Much has been shown to all governments within your world, and much is being denied, but the time will come ... and I will not say that it will happen in 100 of your years or 200, but it is a gradual introduction of new beings. As your world has become a smaller place, in knowing each other, so too the time will come, when interchanging of beings from other planets can take place."*

Many books have now been written on the subjects of UFOs, crop circles and pictograms. A recent publication by Andy Thomas[13] presents a very well illustrated record of the crop circle phenomenon to date. It has been described as a definitive work and I would agree. My own earlier book[3] includes a summary of crop circle incidence to year 2000. It also includes a first introduction to the Salumet mission with his 1994 commentaries on UFOs, crop circles and the attempted 'cover up' that will not be repeated here. But as time and the teachings have progressed, it has become clear that there is more than one kind of space traveller. There has furthermore been one with whom (by wonderful arrangement with Salumet), we have been able to communicate. He conveyed to us amazing facts with a certain logical, forthright directness that made us take a hard look at ourselves:

13th March 1995 ~ "... Your past century of Earth life has seen many forms of communications with others from other dimensions whether you know it or not ... The object of my visit here with you, is to show that closer communication is possible without fear ... It (the information given) should not be kept, it should be made known ... I believe where you humankind are failing, is that you are developing your brain power instead of your mind power ... That (mind power development) is what we are trying to bring. It is the work Salumet and other Masters are endeavouring to do. I can tell you, as time progresses there will be much brought to you. He would not have made his appearance unless that was to be so ... I am instructed on languages of each (culture). But I have to tell you, not all are as base as you. Communication in other spheres is easier because of mind contact communications – not with words (with telepathy). Perhaps I can come another time when I have better command of words and use of energies..."

But in fact our visitor was able to stay a little longer and Leslie was able to put further questions, enquiring next of his natural home:

~ *"You will find this answer difficult to comprehend: I am a child of the light of the cosmos. I do not have home base as you say ... Your Earth within your galaxy (is) only a baby as far as your development goes..."*

Then he expounded on what lies ahead for mankind, well beyond the horizon of our ordinary thinking:

"You are tiny dot. You, my friend, have many 'realities' (planes of existence after physical death) to journey through ... there are many stages, each one becoming more of a reality than the previous one, until you reach such levels that the baser energies are left far behind you. The only reality becomes the one ahead of you ... As you pass through each stage of reality, you become more and more refined and that which you have known as a body, or even a mind, ceases to be ... You are reaching to the very top, the very refined. You leave behind all Earthly reality, and so too galactic reality, until you enter the Cosmic Flow. Then we begin to get somewhere."

Leslie had ventured that 'time' as we know it would by then have ceased to exist. On learning that we could not possibly understand any explanation of that that could be given, Leslie then said midst some general laughter that we were beginning to have a very low opinion of ourselves:

~ *"No, my friend ... don't. Salumet is appearing (to me) saying: Do not allow him to say such a thing!"*

It was a nice intervention that introduced a welcome note of levity and reminded us that Salumet was still with us, ever watchful. Leslie also touched upon our awful 'space-wars' sci-fi presentation of galactic violence on TV and how this is such a thoroughly bad and misleading advertisement for our cosmic brothers. It was explained that we are primitive people and so our brains over-awe our hearts and we have allowed our brains to become contaminated. I think some of us at least have now become aware of this, which is a step forward. There is of course no sense in kidding ourselves that that kind of belligerent behaviour extends beyond Earth! The final message from our Cosmic Flow communicator was:

~ *"I would say to you: develop your minds. That is my message to you."*

It left us with impressions of the utter vastness, both of the cosmic complexity as well as our way ahead that stretches well beyond the domains of earlier thinking. We had not thought of evolving beyond mind or beyond galactic realities!

Salumet has on occasions had much to say about 'light beings', many of which would have the ability, like our selves, to be born into a physical body and live a planetary life:

29ᵗʰ April 2002 ~ "... Mainly they are 'light beings', but you would need to have the awareness to recognise it ... There are many amongst you in your world ... call them teachers, call them people whose light shines out to many. They are the beings of light in your world ... they are the beings of light whose whole purpose is to help the people on this planet ... There are many in your world at this present time who lead what you would term an ordinary life but whose light shines so brightly that people are influenced by it. So do not assume that they are always people of great knowledge or that (they) are known to many people. There are of course many who exist in that state, but there are also many more who wish to come to this planet to be an ordinary person amongst you, but whose light is too strong not to be recognised."

There are so many different types of being that influence our lives. As to the light beings, some further clarification came in response to a question put a few months later, the central part of which was:

George: "... Are they beings that have gone through the usual incarnation process and have Earthly bodies? Would this be so? But the difference would be that they have a different-from-normal soul connection? And I think you said that the spiritual light beamed from them..."

~ *"Yes, you are correct in what you say. There are beings of light that live in your world, and the only way they can live in your world is to don the cloak of human flesh. They do have a different soul connection because (as) beings of light, their task is to look after this planet. When they incarnate to human form, their light can never be dismissed, diminished or extinguished. Their light shines forth like a beacon. Their light shines forth with such brightness that no one can doubt that they are beings of love and light and goodness. There are many in your world at the present day. Their task is to protect this planet Earth. Their task is to show humankind the way forward ... You will know them if you should meet ... Their spiritual energy and light would not be mistaken."*

A question had been put two years earlier about the proportion of children coming into the world that seem more spiritually aware:

15th May 2000 ~ "Yes ... many more souls, older souls from our world have entered this planet more recently in order that we can help the planet ... There are cases where the soul who enters the human form retains more memory, that is all."

These would not be light beings, but the reply illustrates that there can be and is at the present time, a degree of selection of soul input to suit general advancement on the physical planet.

A question put regarding more advanced physical beings that are living on other planets, received the following reply:

26th March 2001 ~ "Although they may be clothed in different garbs, may I say, they are still operating on individual free will, although it may be entirely different from your way of thinking. There are of course, much more spiritual beings on other planets but the process remains the same. All are going forward in the same direction. You must remember this. It matters not where your placement is within the cosmos. All are seeking that purity, that love, that higher being that we all belong to."

It was a general statement on physical planetary beings that reassuringly places us all on similar or parallel journeys forward. It would doubtless be this general category of being that would be able to visit by means of the so-called UFOs, many of which have been observed, reported and often ridiculed. A simple statement on UFOs was made in reply to a question about intermittent luminosity of some that were reported in Porto Rico:

*11th December 2000 ~ "The luminosity is nothing more than energy, and their control (of energies), as I have said, is far superior to humankind on this planet. **Their visitations do exist.** There are many ways of entry into the solar system..."*

It all adds up to a complicated picture of a cosmos populated by many different beings and there is much interaction between them. All are advancing. All look to the one Creative Principle. Earth as well as other planets is being helped along the way. While it has been customary to 'fear the unknown' in our darker past, this is clearly a primitive idea that we need to rise above. There is no place for such irrational fears in an enlightened future. In the past we could afford to ignore the rest of creation. Now, the rest of creation is involved in our progression and not only that, we now have awareness of that involvement. Therefore we are no longer in a position to ignore.

6. ANGELIC HOSTS AND HIERARCHY

There has already been passing reference to the higher beings that oversee our planet. They, as angels, are probably the most regularly acknowledged of the normally invisible beings associated with our Earth. They are in our everyday expressions: 'Do be an angel and…' and 'He's been a little angel today'. Even towns such as Los Angeles are named after them. They are respected and the knowledge of them is innate within us. We comfortably accept their existence and they probably deserve more of our attention than they receive. Our literature is well sprinkled with reference to them, sometimes with serious and accurate pronouncement, as in Saint John's Revelation[14], in which he attempts to describe his vision of an angelic hierarchy who watch over Earth's evolution.

I had first placed a question with Salumet concerning angels on 21st August 2000. It followed a discourse about communication and it being *the very essence of truth*:

"Mankind has, in the past, had communication with other beings, and I think in our literature we have given them names such as angels and archangels. Would that be an accurate statement?"

~ *"Yes … I am not fond of the names, but yes, I would say to you my dear friends, that those descriptions are apt enough for mankind to use. There are indeed what you term angels and archangels, but probably not in the same way as you would think. I can tell you that the true angels have not lived on any (physical) planet. They are supreme beings, and because of this, it gives an aura of lightness which creates in mankind's eyes, the look of an angel as you visualise … What would be your question upon this matter?"*

George: "I just think it is nice to look back on our literature and observe that there has been communication with non-physical beings, and mankind in the past has given names to these … perhaps unsatisfactory names…"

~ *"Yes, I can tell you my dear friend, that this part of what you call literature is indeed correct. This is a topic that we have not touched upon, but is a subject for a future time. But let me tell you, there are such beings in our world. They have never been 'mortalised', shall we say, on any planet, because they are supreme beings. But they do come to many planets in the form of help, and many people have become aware of them in your world. And, as you have stated, have given them names, to which I might add, they are pleased to respond to."*

Salumet then referred back to a previous matter concerning a difficult healing, suggesting that the one known to us as Gabriel might be called upon for help.

It had been a 'taster' before the subject of angels was more fully dealt with several months later. Our teacher then began by speaking of the greater angels or those of the higher realm. They *have always been* and *were here when the Earth was created.* A question on the subject sought a connection with Revelation:

George: "Could I mention St John's writing about his vision in which he describes angels and four intelligent beings and twenty-four elders that I took to be some of those who would be watching over the planet. Does that connect at all?"

5th February 2001 ~ "Yes ... you have to understand that these elders, as you describe them, belong to the group of angels of whom you speak. These angelic beings are responsible for much of what governs this planet. There are many, many types of angelic beings who all have different stations of work. Much of what has been written in what you term your Bible is in fact quite correct, but as you know, much is man-made. But when I speak of visions of angels, I can assure you my dear friends, we speak not of visions of the mind or self-seeking visions, but we are speaking of that form of Divine Light that was much stronger in the days when your so-called Bible was written. There are many, many variations along this (line of) evolution of angelic beings. You have angels of healing. They are one form of the great angelic beings ... we have angels of many types of work, but I would say to you at this present moment in time: it is important for you to realise that this greater angel and the evolution of these angels, has existed and they are closer to what we seek than any other form. Again I will say to you: they are purity of light. They come from the source of all life. They have the knowledge, the wisdom, the understanding and the love of all things."

Lilian's question then led on to 'guardian angels':

"As each child is born into this world, an angel will come with them?"

~ "Yes, you all have a guardian angel. These guardian angels come from this group of angels. They will never leave your side from the moment

of conception until your death or re-birth. Whether you become aware of them is dependent upon your own consciousness, upon your own spiritual growth and remember what I have said … they are not your guides. You must not confuse the two. These angels govern the soul consciousness … the whole consciousness of this planet Earth as well as many others. I will tell you now that many of these beings have come from a spiritual planet of light, to help with the evolution and lifting of consciousness of humankind. I believe this fact is not widely known."

Lilian: "Could I ask about healing … if they help with the healing? The energy that one can feel … would they be behind the energy?"

~ *"I would rather say that the 'healing guides' that superimpose themselves upon you would be the energy that you feel because the angels of the group I speak of come only for the protection of the soul. You have the interaction in healing of both the angel and the 'angelic' guide. Try to differentiate between the two if you can."*

Sarah: "… It may seem a silly question, but what would happen if we didn't have one of these angels?"

~ *"That is not possible. Each one of you has a guardian angel."*

George: "Would the guardian angel have the power to influence consciousness to prevent a physical accident that wasn't meant?"

~ *"No, you are speaking of the guides. They are the ones who would look after form in this human existence. They are the ones who will try to influence you in many ways. The greater angels are more responsible for the whole outcome of consciousness in the planet…"*

Sarah: "Could I go back to something you said … that George was talking about … in the Bible? Did you say the light was greater than it is now?"

~ *"… Only those who have come to that stage of quietness and self knowledge, if you like … only they and they alone will have a glimpse of these magnificent beings. And remember … they **are** magnificent beings. They have never touched or been in human form. They are purity of light. We are speaking of creation now, in its almost pure form. This is what I wish you to try to understand. These guardian angels … their task is to try to protect you throughout your life if they can … but that purpose is for the expansion of soul and consciousness and all that is spiritual. They are not concerned with everyday living as your guides are. They are the essence of being. They are the providers for this planet of love,* *wisdom, power and many other spiritual attributes ...Are you beginning to understand my dear friends? I feel an awe amongst you..."*

Lilian: "With each reincarnation, would we still have the same guardian angel?"

~ *"Yes. You will always have the same guardian angel no matter how many reincarnations there are."*

George: "During our disastrous periods, would they be saddened by what has happened or would they simply not have that reaction?"

~ *"They are beyond human reactions of that kind. This is the point that I try to put to you, that they are beyond all of these emotions, and in fact, until you can place emotions to one side, it is highly unlikely that you will have a glimpse of these beings."*

George: "Going back to St John's account again, he mentions one great angel with one foot on the land and another foot in the sea, which would suggest a huge size by our standards..."

~ *"Yes ... remember that form means nothing to these beings. They are not limited by conditions as we would know them, and of course, how they show themselves to those who can perceive them is something that seems amazing to humankind ... There are indeed in what you call Bible, many angels and also archangels. They are the highest of all these angels, not because they have more power ... that is not how the Divine plan works, but there has to be order. For this purpose alone you have that group of angels who are called archangels ... because of their magnitude, their great knowledge and wisdom."*

Jan had then put a question about guidance, the answer to which further clarified how angels are different from spirit guides (who may have once had Earth life):

~ *"They travel along a different evolution. The line of evolution for these beings is entirely different. What I speak to you tonight about is a Divine and purity of light which cannot be intermingled with the (human) evolution ... I want you to understand this time, how much wider, how much greater (is) the knowledge that these angelic beings have ... how much more expansive is their knowledge ... and the help that they can bring to this one little planet."*

It had been a difficult subject for us. We were slow to grasp some of the points and there was further exchange with some degree of repetition. But our teacher was as ever patient. It seems that on Earth, some of us use the term 'angelic guide' to denote 'spirit guides' who are helpers in respect of everyday needs. These are not angels and they are not referred to as such in spirit, so that 'angelic guide' is really an Earthly misnomer. This had caused some confusion. The reality is that angels, as pure energy beings, follow their own lines of evolution and watch over ours. They are numerous! We each have one guardian angel for a start, so that there are more angels in association with this planet than there are people upon it. That is a breathtaking thought!

There were other details discussed that I will mention only briefly here. There was much about angels of light and of darkness, how they are mirror images of each other, how they are so much like our own selves and how they are a necessary part of our progression. There was discussion of the 'lower order' angelic beings and how they, like us, can exercise free will to good or bad result. Misdirected free will has sometimes resulted in what we know as 'fallen angels' … they do indeed exist as is evident from historic record. Much has also been spoken about angel wings. It might be said that wings are a 'figment of our perception'. There is a spiritual light that emanates from the upper body and curves to encompass the body. It is this light that has led people who have seen, to think of them as having wings. (There is no mechanical function and they do not need wings to get about.) The 'Angels of the Sun' are of the greatest of beings and there is a spiritual light of the sun in addition to the physical, solar output.

The planetary guidance and 'chain of command' mentioned earlier is of course largely angelic. The order of angels guiding our evolution is overseen by the four great beings. These are the same four great beings witnessed by John in Revelation. Although I accept Salumet's teaching without any shadow of doubt, I still find it a joy to see agreeing detail from written record reaching across two thousand years. Truth is somehow 'self-evident'. Salumet has said on a number of occasions that knowledge is innate within … within soul that is, so that the better the soul-connection, the stronger will be the feeling about truth. But I think correlation with written record still has its appeal if you are part human as we all are. I would also observe that the teaching on angels is so very much in line with that teaching received by others, in different time and place, from White Eagle[15]. If in one of our quiet times we are fortunate enough to glimpse our guardian angel, then 'he' will present himself in the form he wishes and to suit the perception that we have. That is the way of pure energy beings

7. TRUTH IS INNATE WITHIN

It is clear from Plato's dialogue between Theaetetus, Theodorus and Socrates, that he was of the opinion that the human mind is equipped with certain knowledge from birth. Descartes later elaborated with the idea that the mind has a certain 'predisposition' to acquire knowledge as it enjoins with the world; the worldly contact acting in some way as a trigger to bring it forward. Kant talked of 'a priori' knowledge as distinct from the 'empirical' knowledge derived from experience. A priori knowledge would be independent of any experience, coming to us directly from heaven. As such, it would be superior to other knowledge gained from experiment and experience. Not only did Kant recognise this intrinsic a priori knowledge to be the essential nature of the best form of knowledge, but he also indicated that it relates to every possible universe and not just to this one. Sir James Jeans in his book Physics & Philosophy makes excellent presentation of these facts[16].

There have been in opposition to this way of thinking the 'empiricists' who maintained that knowledge comes from experience alone. You discover facts by experiment and by encounters with the world. This became the more down to Earth (and away from heaven) view of knowledge that suited the fast developing materialism. But then there was also Einstein and relativity to be considered. Before Einstein, time and space had been seen as separate items. Now, these had to be seen as a 'space-time' unity. This new departure had attracted the attention of an Australian philosopher, Samuel Alexander. He accordingly developed a view of space-time as the fount of all that is, leading to matter, leading to life, leading to consciousness and leading even to Deity. In philosophy, it represents a huge step that reverses an aspect of earlier thinking. Space and time had earlier been seen as creations of mind. Now, Alexander saw mind as a creation issuing from the space-time.

As a considered fount of creation, it is tempting to compare space-time with the spatial 'ether' that had been a part of the thinking of earlier decades. Both are thought of as filling the same inter-stellar and inter-everything void. Each may be seen as the fount of creation or primary flux for building the atoms and molecules of matter. Each has been thought of as arising to meet 'logical need'. The difference is that space-time is expressed in mathematical terms having been derived from mathematical process. The ether has no such root and is not expressed in this way. But that is not to say that it does not relate to the world of matter in a way that *could* be expressed mathematically if required. It is possible then that ether and space-time are in the final analysis, two names for the same thing, the latter being a more sophisticated presentation that yields to mathematical testing.

One might oversimplify this overall picture of existence that the above selected great thinking minds have produced through a 2400-year period as:

1. There are two kinds of knowledge ... a priori (innate) and empirical.

2. ' A priori' is superior and comes to our minds direct from heaven.

3. *Einstein demonstrated the unity of space-time.*

4. *Space-time is a primary flux or factor at the seat of creation.*

5. There is a sequence according to Alexander: space-time > matter > life > consciousness > Deity (Creative Principle or universal consciousness).

It is a small step to make a circle of the sequence given in 5, so that the Creative Principle also powers the space-time creation (whilst also being the creation that unfolds). This makes a self-contained and ongoing scheme in which the Creative Principle drives all, including itself. The creation emerges from space-time as matter, leading to life and to consciousness that ultimately aligns to the Creative Principle that continues to drive the creation forward. This portrays creation and evolution as an ever-ongoing cyclic process. And all-knowledge will be within the Creative Principle, and we as life and consciousness, have our connection to that all-knowledge. But the connection is subtle. If our soul linkage is strong, then so will be our intuition and awareness, and for Masters such as Jesus who walk the Earth, soul knowledge will have no bounds.

Having presented a selection of the work of philosophers prior to the last seventy years, let us now compare the various statements made by Salumet that relate to the nature of knowledge:

Firstly, it is clear from a number of his teachings that we have a general picture of a vast bank of knowledge in the realm of spirit that comes to the physical Earth in various ways. How and when, is linked to our spiritual and mental advancement. Knowledge will not be 'released' to the world if the world is not yet ready to receive. Masters that teach, withhold that which we do not yet have the wisdom to use or the mental development to understand. Our knowledge is therefore in a state of balance dependent upon our maturity. Artists, scientists and seekers may be helped from spirit at the 'individual' level and perhaps one could see this as reward for endeavours. The whole world is also helped through certain periods from time to time as required or as becomes necessary.

*20ᵗʰ March 1995 ~ "There is no **one** guidance around you. All of you have more than one helper. We have spoken … about your scientists, about your writers, about your musicians. All are inspired from our side of life … I am not saying **all** your thoughts are inspirational ones, but at certain times, when your awareness is heightened, then of course we come close to you."*

21ˢᵗ February 2000 ~ "The galaxy to which this planet Earth belongs is now in a state of its own spiritual growth. To that end there will be many changes. You will find that the men of this Earthly planet will come to recognise that within your space-time, much is happening. Not only are you in times of much development, you are in a time of great evolution not known to you before but which will take effect and will make itself known to you human beings upon this planet quite soon. You of course depend upon the knowledge given to you by those you call scientists and astronomers. You depend much upon their knowledge. I can tell you my dear friends that those in my world are already working with them in order that this knowledge can be brought to them. The time has come for expansion and growth … allow your selves my dear friends, to become part of the cosmic consciousness rather than the Earthly one. You can achieve this and the time is now ripe for this to take place…"

The next statement follows a question on the observed wonderful abilities of a number of Indian saints and yogis:

15ᵗʰ October 2001 ~ "… They have not achieved greater things. What they have done as a group or as a nation of people is that they have

retained *that which should be natural to all of you ... those spiritual gifts that all of you could have if you but spent the time and the dedication to the spirit rather than to the physical living. They have not **gained** but* **retained.** *(... I have told you, many, many people that have existed on this planet at many times ... they have gradually lost all those spiritual gifts which are natural to you.) These people have retained the knowledge and bettered themselves with the use of it ... It is the deep meditative state that achieves ... it is the inward knowledge of who and what they are. It has been passed from one to another ... it is not that they have anything special or created anything special. It is just that they continue to use that knowledge which has been lost to most of you on this planet."*

29ʰ October 2001 ~ "... There have been many times upon this planet when mankind has almost become self-destroying. That is why my dear friends, it is important at this time, for people of your understanding spiritually, to work closely together with those from our world, who at this time will succeed, although it will not be in the shorter time (term?) ... But we will succeed in bringing to this planet a form of love and peace, hitherto unknown to your world ... so my friends, I will say to you once more: go inwards, know yourselves. Therein lies all the answers to the problems of this world ... this planet. Therein lie the answers to all your life problems. Therein lies the source of love, and let me tell you, when that source of love is reached, nothing can destroy it."

2ⁿᵈ September 2002 ~ "... It is not as simple as it may seem but it is a step forward in your pathway that you must endeavour to understand, and if I may put it simply, it means going deeper within. All answers lie within as I have told you on many previous occasions. That is where all of your questions will be answered."

Then Salumet added a little more about what results from meditation ... from going deeply within oneself:

~ *"Mankind creates his own problems but what I wish for you my dear friends is that that spirit within comes forward ... in order for that pure light to shine. I am sure there have been many times in your existence when you have met someone, without even exchange of words, where you feel that they really are beacons of goodness. They do not need words. They do not need to do any deed, but ultimately you can see with your own human eyes the goodness that emanates from them. Is that not true my dear friends? There, in those individuals, you are seeing truth and genuine people..."*

The next statement follows Salumet's regular Christmas recess during which period he returns to that far domain in spirit that is 'home':

20ᵗʰ January 2003 ~ "… My heart is full that I am with you once more, that we may begin this Earthly year knowing that there is to come to you, this group, new knowledge … but again remember my past words: no knowledge is new … only to those who need to obtain it whilst in these physical garbs. Therefore, when I say 'new knowledge', I mean knowledge that you will regain but which you already know as spirit."

There was some considerable embellishment during two sessions that came two months later during which we had the opportunity to put several questions:

10ᵗʰ March 2003 ~ "… As all-knowing beings you would say to yourself: what do I need to learn? Would that be a human question?"

George: "I think you have said before that knowledge and wisdom are growth factors. We can grow in respect of knowledge…"

*~ "Yes. Let me take you a little further along this road of discussion. As all-knowing beings, the power of all-knowing is within you. You understand this? … Yes …So in human terms, there should be nothing to learn. But, in a sense you **are** learning and the problem here is using your Earthly word 'learn'. Yes, in a sense you are learning, but what I would say … you are **re-learning** that all-knowingness."*

I think the meaning, on reflection, is that we have full knowledge when we are soul-in-spirit, but when we are born onto the physical Earth, the link to that knowledge is lost apart from what 'filters' through as intuition. The knowledge can be re-learnt through our strengthening of soul connection (and gateway to God-connection).

24ᵗʰ March 2003 ~ "… with the all-knowing comes the pathway that is indeed 'heaven' as you call it, and that is your Earthly word for 'God-connection'. Yes, heaven already exists, but it is up to each one of you to become aware of it here and now … it is the all-knowing part of you that already exists. Do you see the difference? Each one of you on this Earth, except for the ones you call Masters, Masters of the seeking …strive for what you call 'spirituality' or searching for 'God-energy'."

And later, Salumet was saying:

~ "… But you should not strive to seek what you already know. You should not strive to find what you already have. You should not strive to

understand who and what you are, because all is already known to you. Can you see where I am leading you my dear friends?"

Paul: "So if we manage to attain this awareness, is it something that we can then continue with, as opposed to a state of mind that is a bit transitory? This inner-knowing is more permanent ... we can live it through our daily lives?"

~ *"This inner-knowing continues throughout all of your existence. It is this all-knowing that you need to find whilst on this Earth. We have spoken briefly that it is not so much that you need to seek yourselves and to return to what you already know. Last time I spoke about that awareness growing within you. We cannot go too quickly, because what I am telling you now, has taken many of your years to reach this point for your understanding. It is important that each one of you takes in and understands each step as we go forward. Each of you as you know, are at different steps of your own growth, therefore it is important that you understand my words as we go slowly. If you have questions or doubts, then remember when first I came to you, I told you if any of my words were to sit with you uncomfortably, then you must let them go until such time as the realisation comes that what I bring you is truth. Are there questions you would wish to ask?"*

George: "I will just observe that the way you have taught us is rather like a natural process ... like the opening of a flower. When the flower is fully opened, then there is all-knowing."

~ *"I like your description ... and think of the beautiful flower that is opening. Remember how many veins within one petal and then you may have some idea of how much there is to understand before you reach the middle of the beautiful flower. That is why we must go slowly..."*

Salumet went on to compare the 'seekers of truth' of today, with one from much earlier times known to all as Moses. He was indeed a seeker of the truth, and there is more about Moses that comes later.

Exactly how and to what extent innate, 'a priori' knowledge or 'the knowledge within' is accessed by us, is clearly an important aspect of Earthly life. And I would say that it comes as no surprise that philosophers should have addressed this issue. In going within and seeking the soul connection, we find the God-connection and we then find 'heaven'. When Immanuel Kant stated that the 'a priori' knowledge comes to us through the gates of heaven, he was perfectly correct. He was also more clearly thinking than most in regard to the general format of the creation ... a creation that is in one sense 'steady state' and in another sense, is creating itself. The Hindu Vedas that describe the universe as God's dream also fit the picture and of course, the dream is dreaming itself. And just as we are able to access our own personal dreams and recall their content ... equally we are able to access that 'greater dream' for the all-knowledge contained therein.

One further observation: within Christianity, much has been spoken of 'God the Father, God the Son and God the Holy Spirit'. Within the above picture, the Father is the Creative Principle. The Son is the visible created living being. The Holy Spirit is the immortal factor within the created and continues journeying throughout eternity as a part of the Creative Principle. The thought ... the dream ... is indeed creating itself.

8. HUMOUR LAUGHTER AND UPLIFTED SPIRIT

Some of the teachings have led us into matters of deep philosophy, on occasions, deep and difficult philosophy. But then there also has been the subject of 'humour'. Salumet has said on more than one occasion that he is beginning to feel the way of our humour. It must be one of our more difficult facets to understand and sometimes difficult enough to fathom for we ourselves who live on the physical planet. But he has been quick to point out how laughter can, like a number of other attributes, raise the spirit. It was during the meeting of 2nd November 1998 that the topic of our being only part human had again come up. Leslie had been speaking of how difficult it is to speak of the spirit to some people, declaring:

"… I'm not mentioning names of course and I *am* trying hard not to do that … and frequently I would love my physical reactions to take over. But I'm afraid your teaching always gets in the way and stops me doing it…"

~ *"Ah! We do indeed have some growth do we not? That my friend is an achievement, if you can at least recognise that there is a choice."*

The exchange continued as Leslie continued in buoyant style while the rest of us bubbled with gentle lightness of mood. Then Salumet was saying:~ *"But, my dear friend, may I say: continue to try hard."* Leslie: "I shall have to. You don't allow us any option you know…"

~ *"We will be close by next time and help you in your task."* Leslie: "Thank you very much!"

~ *"And I don't want to hear the words: I am only human!"*

Leslie: "I promise I won't say it. That's no longer an excuse after what you've taught us."

It was a wonderfully light-hearted exchange that came at the end of a session when it was a good time to lighten the atmosphere. In fact it is often the pattern that, following a more serious session and after our teacher has left, a chatty visitor comes through from spirit simply to lighten us up.

Laughter and upliftment certainly have their place in the scheme of things and it might be both interesting as well as amusing to list some of the between-worlds witticisms and jokes that have occurred, beginning at the beginning:

1st August 1994: Leslie was concerned regarding certain extraordinary religious beliefs and had put the question:

"There are beliefs as you well know, held by people who will not knowingly kill even an ant or other insect, lest they should have to return to this Earth in the guise of the insect. I can't believe for one minute that it would be necessary for anyone to return in what we call a lower form of life once they have begun here as a human…"

~ *"I am sorry if I smile … no, that does not happen."*

Leslie: "I couldn't imagine it…"

~ *"What would be the point of evolving … if you would (then) take a step backwards? No, no … that is not the case."*

Leslie: "I have always denied it emphatically, that it would be necessary or even possible…"

~ *"It is a belief of many, we know. But we are trying to put these things in their proper perspective. It is difficult to break the thoughts and ideas of many lifetimes."*

Leslie: "Quite. And again, it is wrong teaching by those responsible."

~ *"I would have to say that if that was the case, you would be over-run by insects!"*

That of course was the punch line.

12th September 1994: Brent was one of our more intellectual sitters, before he went to live in the United States. He had discussed our meetings with a colleague who was sceptical and asked that a question be put, the answer to which he could then check from scientific data. Accordingly, he passed on the question to Salumet.

Brent: *"What is the weight of the moon?"*

Salumet was quick in his reply:

~ *"I can tell you the weight of the moon … it is weightless!"*

Following a brief silence, there was on this occasion explosive laughter. It was an unintended joke. Brent ventured that he thought he must have meant the 'mass' of the moon. This would have been different. But, as to weight, gravitational pull exactly balances centrifugal force so that what we term 'weight' is indeed exactly zero ... and Salumet had very quickly delivered the correct answer. He followed up, not with any dissertation on 'mass versus weight', but with comments as to the best way to convince sceptics of spiritual existence. I think what I found so devastatingly funny at the time was the very idea of posing such a question to a Master of all-knowledge and infinite wisdom ... and then for it to go wrong and sound like something from a joke book!

9th January 1995: One of us had returned after an absence of several weeks. Leslie had doubted that he would indeed return.

~ *"I have no doubt. I have said he would return did I not?"*

Leslie: "You did indeed, and it's very nice to see him with us again."

~ *"I must say that I am most fortunate, that I do not have your Earthly doubts."*

Some gentle laughter followed ... then, with humorous tremor:

~ *"Forgive me ... I don't mean to put you down."*

Leslie: "Of course you don't ... I know that. We enjoy your humour."

~ *"Thank you. It helps do you not think? It is good that you all sometimes should laugh. Do you know, each time you laugh ... you smile ... it actually raises your vibrational energies? Did you know that?"*

Leslie: "Yes, I could imagine that."

~ *"Yes, so please all of you ... laugh, especially in your times of troubles. That is when it will be of more benefit to you."*

6th March 1995: Debbie had asked a question about the nature of superstitions ... about it being bad luck to walk under a ladder, to break a mirror and such:

~ *"Oh, who am I to say how your minds work?"*

It was a joke. We laughed. And of course, we should really seek to understand what goes on in our own heads!

~ *"Forgive me please. People are so varied in their thinking. I'm sorry if I seem amused, but so often we see these feelings. And you see, basically superstition stems from fear. It is a fear of something ... of the 'unknown' usually. But eventually these superstitions are dispelled. But I would say to you: FEAR NOT. FEAR NOTHING WHILST IN YOUR PHYSICAL BODIES. After all, what is there to fear? You know life is eternal. Let go of all your fears and you will find that your life plan falls into place ... I beg your pardon if I should seem so amused."*

There was some further discussion about the human brain conjuring up its own 'devils' and how our power-of-thought can produce either good or bad ideas. But the overall picture is that superstition stems from a fear of the unknown, and it is really down to us to organise our thinking away from this and into logical process.

20th March 1995: Half way through the evening, Salumet needed to work quietly with Eileen while another from spirit came through Sue. The visitor explained that his instrument (Sue) would be experiencing some odd feelings because she has human form whilst he was not of human form. A bizarre conversation followed. Leslie asked if he normally lived on another planet, to which he replied:

~ *"If that is an easy explanation…"*

Leslie: (seeking some clarification) "And have you ever lived on **this** planet?"

~ *"Not this time … no … not this time. But in what you would call your future, I will walk your lands. But that is not for some time yet."*

Leslie: "I see (hesitatingly) … you **will** walk upon this Earth at a distant time in the future…"

~ *"That is the future plan … yes. But it will depend upon whether your planet improves and becomes less hostile place."*

Leslie: "Yes, I understand. So am I right in saying that you are what is known on this primitive Earth as an 'alien being' from another planet?"

~ *"Yes, but that word brings to mind in your minds: LITTLE GREEN CREATURES. I am neither little, nor am I green!"*

This was seen as a punch line and brought much laughter and Leslie gallantly struggled as best he could to continue:

Leslie: "I do hope … I have not offended you, but in **our** minds, no such things exist."

~ *"No, that's right. It will take longer than I can afford here to explain my appearance, but as you are aware, after the physical appearance becomes thought only … yes, you understand me … therefore I can say that I have no real physical attributes. You understand me?"*

Leslie: "I do understand."

~ *"My words are being given to me by another. Therefore the words I use are not easily recognised by me, you understand?"*

Leslie:"Yes, I do indeed and I appreciate the effort that it must be causing you in order to communicate with us, primitive beings that we are."

~ *"That is* **your** *word. I would not be so unkind. I say, not 'primitive' but 'unworldly' ... yes, you understand me?"*

Leslie: Yes. But we do consider ourselves to be primitive in many respects. We have so much to learn."

~ *"Yes, but it all takes time. Not one lifetime, but a whole universe of lifetimes. Now instrument needs rest from my words and personality ... yes that is right ... personality. Needs to return to her self. Yes. I leave with many, many thoughts of love for future and trust and hope for this planet in time. Farewell ... farewell to you all..."*

Leslie expressed our extreme gratitude. The exchange is reported in full because, although it carries the humour of the 'little green creatures', it also is a wonderful dialogue with a REAL extraterrestrial being ... a being of feelings, of love and consideration for others such as ourselves who are steadily making their way in the universe. Visitors from other parts of the galaxy have come far and have developed well beyond any absurd 'star wars' mentality. We should clearly count ourselves lucky that they take interest in us and we should afford them the courtesy and appreciation that they deserve.

18th March 1996: Salumet had been saying that being confused is not a bad thing if it leads to another small step forward. Leslie replied:

"No, it's certainly one thing we do excel at ... being confused."

~ *"You are all doing very well. I will use one of your Earthly terms this time to say: I am 'proud' of you all. And I don't use that word to give you ... how would you say? ... BIGGER HEADS!"*

It is a fact that, when exchanging with a teacher having all-knowledge, there is no such danger. The size of head can only be diminished, but it was good for us to receive a little mortal-style banter from one such as Salumet.

21st October 2002: Salumet had been talking about our link with Divinity and our 'going within' and recognising our true selves:

~ *"Yes ... when you go inwards, that knowledge that you recognise ... that spark ... peace ... that is what you are ... that is what we all are."*

George: "When we go inwards and make contact with our soul-body ... then ... I couldn't help thinking while you were talking ... that when you come to us as you do, it's a little bit like getting an extra portion..." (There was spontaneous general laughter at the thought).

~ *"I am appalled that I am seen as an extra portion! I have never been called that! (More laughter) ... But I thank you my dear friend for that. It makes me feel ... fuller! (More laughs) ... I am glad to see that humour exists in your lives ... because laughter, my dear friends, is something that you should always encourage. Perhaps I shall be known as 'An Extra Portion'!"*

It was a nice period of levity that once again came at the close of a session. A few minutes later, our teacher was bidding farewell saying:

~ *"... I will leave you this time. Again, I hope that you will go inwards and find that true being ... the gentle loving beings that you all are. Make no mistake my dear friends ... you are beautiful beings, but you have many difficulties, each one of you with the past and what you call the future to overcome. But nevertheless, that should not hold you back in striving to find peace in your mind, in helping others in need. I leave you feeling lighter and surrounded in the love which I bring to you."*

Lilian: "Thank you ... our love goes with you."

4th March 2003: Again it was at the end of a session. A question had been asked about Earth Protectors or Ancient Site Guardians as they are sometimes called. (These are accounted later.) During Salumet's answer there was an increase in energy such that voice volume doubled and voice pitch changed:

~ *"... I hope my dear friends that you can feel the energy that is here with you. I hope that each of you has been aware that not only my presence but that of another has been quite significant in these past minutes."*

George: "Yes ... and a small detail, but the extra energy sometimes shows itself with a little whistle in my hearing aid ... so that it is physically manifest!"

After the chuckles had subsided, Salumet added the punch line:

~ *"I do not know whether to congratulate you or to apologise..."*

I assured that in any event it was entirely accidental. But it is perhaps an interesting fact that on a number of occasions, the energy in the room has built up and registered as a feedback in the sensitive aid. It has happened especially at the start of proceedings just prior to Salumet speaking.

The value of humour has been stated. It can raise the spirit and that can only be of benefit. It is also good to observe that humour is understood and appreciated by those in spirit and those from other worlds whom we may have erroneously thought of as 'little green creatures'! And those in spirit will also share a joke between themselves. There was one occasion when we were visited by a 'light being' whose work it is to escort those departing this life to the next world. She spoke at length about the interesting and loving nature of her work, reported fully elsewhere[3], then spoke of the need to return from time to time to her natural domain. There was some hesitation in giving the reason and she was being helped with appropriate words by those in spirit closer to Earth.

~ *"We all need to do ... I think you would term it: 'to recharge your batteries'? Someone just told me: 'Say that and it'll be fine.' ...* **Recharge your batteries!** *... Yes ... I am telling you: I am a being of light and I need to charge my batteries! It is quite amusing!"*

We were quite helpless with mirth on that occasion. Leslie was struggling and managed to say:

"Yes, it is an expression we can completely understand."

And our dear visitor added:

~ *"Yes. I'd rather forgotten how amusing you beings could be ... I had long forgotten. That is not to say we do not have* **our** *fun..."*

Humour is then, not just a quirk of Earthly living. It is a universal resource that can raise the spirit. In fact, there is more to humour than catches the eye, or should I say ... tickles the tonsils? There was one occasion when I had placed a searching question with Salumet ... a philosophical question about humour that sought its value from a spiritual perspective, and I was looking for its possible modification with spiritual advancement, observing that on Earth it includes both 'coarse' and 'nice' varieties. Salumet gave a really excellent account and Leslie joined in. I think they should have the final word:

30th October 1995 ~ "Let me say this to you my friend: there is indeed much of what you call humour on your Earth. It is part of your physical make-up. It helps to make life easier for you, from what I can see. But I think I can tell you that, even as matter refines, then of course, humour is retained, and I would have to say, any matter which is heavy and includes coarseness of any kind, will eventually be gotten rid of. As you become finer ... become more attuned to that part of your being which exists on a higher vibration, then all coarseness disappears. But how would you define humour?"

At this point, our teacher seemed to become reflective and took a most interesting departure:

~ *"I suppose you would say to some extent, that I have on occasion been humorous whilst with you..."*

There was general agreement to this.

~ *"But I have to say, it is a memory of humour that I bring with me. It is not something that is natural within me. Firstly, you have to understand that there is no need of humour, as the energies become more and more refined."*

George: "Ah yes, thank you. I wondered about that."

~ *"We have spoken about the time when all speech ceases to exist and only the power of your thought remains as communication. But I think you are asking me the question: is there a particular point in your development when humour disappears? I would think ... say to you: 'yes', but it would take much time for this to occur, because you see, it mainly belongs to those physical attributes that you possess ... I suppose, in a sense you could say: good humour was a form of love, and that my friend, is how I would look upon your term 'humour'. It is an interaction between two people."*

Leslie: "I would agree with that description absolutely. We have often been asked by those in the immediately succeeding plane of life, to make sure we bring our sense of humour with us when we go to them."

~ *"Of course, because we have spoken previously ... when you leave your physical being, you do not suddenly become someone so different. You are still you and all that you have been, remains with you for some considerable time. That includes what you term 'humour'."*

Leslie: "The laughter that has been brought back from the next life and which has been recorded, has been of extremely good value to those who have come investigating this work. They have been astonished at the laughter and to know that it still exists in the next world."

~ *"You see, all that is good exists for longer on those energy vibrations. All that is love, that is good, will continue for so much longer. Can you see this?"*

Leslie: "Yes, and I see what you mean about humour being love, because it does unite two people in the sharing of something beyond the immediate physical problems."

~ *"And those of you who have that bond can share what you call humour, without exchange of your words. You have a little of what humour would be in the very best sense."*

Leslie: "Yes, we enjoy our laughter together."

~ *"Yes."*

9. HEALING AND VARIOUS MEDICAL MATTERS

Healing is so often linked to raising the spirit. It follows that, such things as laughter, love, music and birdsong can sometimes heal and there are many accounts of 'miraculous' healing that can only be understood by reference to their spirit connection. But it is a vast subject with many connections and considerations. I will not attempt to organise Salumet's teachings into any particular pattern in this section, other than to simply present the statements in date order as they arrived. They arise mostly from our haphazard questions prompted by news media, particular interests, books read etc. What follows is a valuable catalogue of information that often takes our understanding beyond the ordinary domains of known medical science. Certain topics such as psychic surgery and transgender can ONLY be understood when considered in relation to their spiritual involvement. Although what follows is merely placed in date order, the reader may nevertheless feel that a pattern in regard to understanding the general nature of disease steadily falls into place.

Psychic surgery: Let me first briefly state for those unfamiliar with the term that certain mediums may form an alliance with a doctor or surgeon in spirit, enabling that spirit to work through them, to perform what seem to be amazing medical wonders.

*11th July 1994 ~ "... What is occurring ... there is work on the **spirit** body. When that is whole, then the effect passes to the physical. Then, and only then ... mind, spirit, body must be one. When you talk of psychic surgery, we are talking on a completely different level from your understanding of **physical** happenings. When a problem manifests itself on the physical body, the problem lies within. That is the part that has to be dealt with. Sometimes the problem is with the 'etheric body'. That is the part that is put right. Does that answer your question?"*

Brent: "Yes it does, but we all wonder how that can affect the physical in such a dramatic way..."

*~ "First let me say: you are **not** a physical being. You are spirit. Mind, spirit, body are one. If one level is not right, then everything is not right.*

The mind affects the body, the spirit is affected, and very often it is the etheric body that needs treatment. There are those of you on this Earth plane with the ability to be used by us in this way. To us, it is nothing extraordinary, but to explain it to you is difficult in your terms. It is the etheric body that is worked on, which (then) produces the result in the physical. I cannot explain to you this time about the methods used, for the simple reason you would not understand. It is a spiritual happening, and therefore a spiritual thing to explain … do you want an explanation of what is happening physically?"

Brent:"Yes … I can't understand how bleeding can be stopped and blood can disappear and scars can heal … because our doctors can't do that."

~ *"Your doctors are working only on the physical body. I'm sorry I cannot be more explicit than that."*

It is clearly stated. A doctor in spirit may work through a medium/instrument to perform healing on the etheric/energy body. The benefit then automatically transfers to the physical body. I will add only that this method of healing is very often 'permitted'. If however, it is a matter of karma … it is the soul's requirement or way forward to go through life with a particular suffering, then the healing will simply not be allowed. It follows that if the person cannot be healed, the reason is not really failure by the doctor, but refusal by the higher self to allow the treatment. The wonderful work of a number of spirit doctors has been well documented[17, 18] in recent years.

Self healing exercises: Salumet was asked about the value of the graceful T'ai-chi exercises that originate from China:

18ᵗʰ July 1994 ~ "Of course! Of course! We go back to energy once again. They (the Chinese) are a race of knowledge when it comes to these matters … what is your healing if it is not an energy being used? So why is it difficult to understand? Call it by any name you wish, it makes no difference. Yes, to use the energy for self-healing is of course quite possible, and to us is nothing unusual. It is no different if you sit still and meditate, or if you do a yoga exercise, or if you sleep and let your mind be free. Let me say: it matters not what you call it, it all comes down to the same thing … using the energies that are available to you. And you see, by these movements that they use, they are attuning themselves to the higher realms. It is something as simple as that."

As with psychic surgery then, it is again working with the energy body and not to be seen as a physical exercise.

Mercurial fillings in teeth: The question placed was about the possibility of counteracting the effect of mercury in the mouth:

22nd August 1994 ~ "... If there is a problem with a mercury filling ... I would say these things are not good to be used within the mouth ... and that knowledge is now becoming available to those who deal ... your dentists, your orthodontists as you call them. That knowledge is being made (known). We have many problems when you speak of such things. I would say to you: cleanse the mouth with something that is natural ... something like elderberry juices. That would be very good... rinse continually daily and that should counteract the problem from mercury."

AIDS and the general nature of disease: We asked if AIDS, which influences the immune system, has any special significance:

*22nd August 1994 ~ "There is no special significance. There always have been diseases while man has roamed the Earth. Firstly let me say: man is the creator of many diseases. They are not things to suddenly appear from the sky. We hear so often the pleas and the cries: 'Why does God allow this?' I say to you: why does **man** allow this? Disease is exactly the word that it says ... DIS-EASE. There is an imbalance when it comes to disease. It means that somewhere along the life of man, something has gone wrong. Again, we get to cause and effect, or karma as most of you wish to say. I know these things are difficult for you to understand. You say: why is this allowed to happen, why is that allowed to happen? We don't allow it to happen ... man does. We often hear in your prayers: why are there disasters? Man must look to himself for the answers to his problems. The responsibility lies with him. We don't say: there are too many people on the Earth, we must get rid of some! Would that not make our work all the harder when they come to spirit? We do not say that. Man and the Earth must take responsibility for its own problems. Man has interfered with nature. That is the basis of most epidemics. It is simple. It is clear. But to you ... you find it a problem. Man ... man has interfered too much with nature. There will be a cure for this disease (AIDS), not yet, but it will come as it has come for many diseases that have been around on your Earth. But until man allows that inner knowledge, wisdom and love, there will always be disease. Does that answer your question?"*

It did. It was a clear answer that placed the entire vista of disease into sharp focus. Diseases relate to the Earth and to our living and are very much our own responsibility. It was expressed to our teacher that, whilst it was not at all well understood, nevertheless, in the hearts of many of us, this was indeed what was felt.

On colour as seen by the blind: On this occasion, Leslie picked up on something that had been mentioned the previous week:

"… And you did mention 'having no sight', that being unnecessary to appreciate beauty. Of course we can understand that somebody who has had sight and lost it, still has thoughts to draw on … and memories. But, in the case of a person who is blind from birth, are they given any particular sense to enable them to appreciate that which they cannot see?"

*29ᵗʰ August 1994 ~ "Yes, let me speak on this. Of course, their other senses are more developed if they **are** without their sight. And, if you can imagine, closing your eyes … in your dream state, are not things as vivid as they are in your awakened state? Something similar occurs to those who have been without vision from birth. As the sight is denied them, so too is that sense within their mind, developed. So, in effect, they can see pictures if you like. They are almost 'inspired' … perhaps that is a better word … with vision, vision without sight. It is almost another thought process … something that you would find difficult to understand in your everyday terms. But they do see colours, they do see visions, they do see pictures. So the development of their touch, their smell and their hearing, is enhanced. And so too comes the inspiration for the pictures within their minds."*

Leslie: "Yes. Thank you. I thought it must be something like that because there would have to be some compensation for what they're losing in having no sight. And when you spoke of being blind but still appreciating beauty, that's the only way I could imagine that it would be done … by impressions from your world."

~ "It is what I was speaking of last week. When your senses are enhanced to the highest degree you are feeling the energies that are around you. Do you understand?"

Leslie: "Yes I do."

~ "So if the one who is without sight is to touch, let me say, a newspaper, that person is picking up those vibrations of energy within

that paper ... something that most of you have lost. But that is why those senses are developed to such a great degree. They develop ... it's a natural development. It should be a natural development for all of you, but of course it is lost..."

It is no doubt a subject that many of us have not really thought about, but it is good to have reassurance from one who knows and understands these matters, that colour may still be sensed without use of physical eyes. And it is an interesting thought that we could all emulate that small minority within our midst, and develop our sensitivity towards various 'energies' if we put our minds to it.

Hypnotherapy: There is no doubt that hypnotherapy can achieve good results where such problems as heavy smoking and over-weight are concerned, but not always. Dawn had asked if success rates could be improved:

12th September 1994 ~ "Yes, I know what you are speaking of. Let me speak of individuality again ... and I understand your hypnotherapy and the work that you do. But (in) everything you do, you may be successful or you may not. If the individual mind is not ready to accept ... let me say: their 'higher selves' ... that is a better way of putting it. If they are not ready to accept, whatever the problem is, be it smoking, be it weight, be it whatever it may ... you will not have success with that person. There is nothing more you can do if the higher selves do not accept the reasoning, the talking that you do with your hypnotherapy, then it cannot be successful. Do you feel there is something more that you should do?"

Dawn: "I think sometimes some people need extra help..."

~ "Yes of course, and that is how it would be. But let me speak of those persons. They are sometimes not even aware of what is held in their own subconscious minds. And sometimes with some individuals, you will never reach that point. I know that is difficult for you to accept. But ultimately, each individual holds the key to their own way of living, and if they are not ready to accept that, then whatever is done in the way of hypnotherapy/hypnosis, it will not be achieved. So too, we can speak of the healing energies and rays. If subconsciously that person is not ready to accept it, then there will be no healing. If the spirit is not touched, how can there be a healing? And that is what we are speaking of. What you are doing basically with your hypnotherapy is a form of healing."

Quite simply then, the spirit must be touched for healing to take place.

Illness in its broadest context: Brent had posed a question about healing and as a result, drastically changing a life. This seemed to go against life plan and prophecy. This led to Salumet speaking on the healing of illness within the broad scheme of things:

17th October 1994 ~ "... What is illness within the human form? It is a disease of spirit, which manifests itself through the physical body. How can the physical body be cured if the spirit is not touched? Your physical being is a covering for the spirit ... that is all. So when something goes wrong, you leave the 'straight and narrow' as you call it ... you take the meandering pathways. You in the human form create your own illnesses. It is not the pattern of your life usually (to be ill) ... I don't say in all cases, because sometimes that is the path that you (as spirit) choose. Some choose to have some form of disability. Some choose to have some illness. When that is the pathway of the spirit, then no spiritual healing can change that. But in the main, I would say, all illnesses are man-made. Therefore how can you say it is foreseen? It is caused by the free will of man in his human form. I am trying to keep it simple. As always, these matters are not straightforward. Man comes in many forms. Spiritual healing comes from us to help you along life's pathway. But (it) is mainly to touch that spirit ... to spark that side of you that needs to be expressed. Can you see that? Man is responsible for his own life, although it is known what the ultimate end will be. You cannot hold us responsible for the way you live your lives whilst on Earth. I know it is a difficult subject for you. But you are endowed with your free will to do with your life ... to make the best of it, and go forward. And unfortunately, we see so many who reject what they know (what they feel within?), and take the wrong pathways. Have I been helpful to you?"

Brent: "Yes, but I don't think that I'll ever understand how the ultimate end can be understood if free will is allowed to operate. I don't think it is possible for us to understand that, because we think that either things are determined or they are not."

~ "They are only determined within a structure. Your free will allows you to do much that is not within that structure. Let me try to simplify it. If you have a playing field ... we have a playing field with ten players. The ultimate goal is to reach the other end of the field. Three or four of those people will go directly to the other end of the field. They are the

people who are following their 'true destiny' if you like. Let us take another three who may meander all over the field, to the left, but ultimately, they too will reach the end of the field. They may have more obstacles to go over, but ultimately they too reach the end of the field. Let us take the other four. Perhaps they think they know a short cut. They leave the field entirely and for some reason they find it difficult to find their way back, but they do eventually. You see, all of those players within the field have their own free will, but at the end of the day there is a destination that they must reach. And within the structure of the field, it is up to them to decide which way they go towards their end. I know it is very difficult for you all to understand these things ... but somehow you seem to think you are all placed within this Earth, that the knowledge is known ... which of course it is ... but there have to be some guidelines. You must agree on that, otherwise there would be chaos, and there cannot be chaos within a perfect structure."

It was a fine effort to win through to us with such a difficult subject. The bare bones of the matter seem to be that illness mostly connects with our free will (but not always). And it is easy to see how such things as smoking-related diseases or the effects from alcohol and drug abuse and things of that general nature are connected. Stress lies at the seat of many physical illnesses and that also can be seen to have its free will connection. But in relation to the grand scheme of existence, these seem to be mere hiccups along the way. Elsewhere it is stated that the exercise of free will has only a fractional input within the grand scheme so that true prophecy by those who have the gift remains substantially correct across thousands of years.

Cancer: Two weeks later, Brent again pursued the subject of healing. The example of cancer was cited with the observation that spiritual healing can sometimes result in the most amazing remission:

31st October 1994 ~ "The change my friend, is really within the spirit body. What is cancer? Shall we speak a little on what that disease is all about? I have spoken before that each one of you is individual but part of a whole. What is a cell within your physical body? It is one part of a group within an organ. An organ is a part of other organs within a body. The body is an individual that is attached to other individuals (spiritual attachments). So let us go back to the one cell. What happens when a cell within the organ, within the body, begins to change? Let us make a comparison here. The cell is in fact saying: I want to do my own *thing. I am keeping this simple, because again we get into difficulties in trying to explain. When we begin to speak of structures as cells, it is difficult. But one cell decides it wants to do its own thing. Who can stop it? So it progresses onwards, onwards, onwards. When it reaches the stage that it invades other organs, then we have the disease called 'cancer'. And you all know that it is a disease that spreads throughout the body. When it has invaded (taken over?) the body, then the physical being dies. So in fact, your cancer disease has won. You have the power within your spirit body to change these things. That is why you have the cases ... especially through your spiritual healing ... when these things can be changed. It is not so much that the cells are de-materialised and made whole again. It is the fact that the spirit body accepts ... accepts that there is something wrong within. The individual cell is reacting in the same way that the person himself is reacting. Can you see the comparison there? It is almost like the cell is that individual person within the body structure. (Pause with intake of breath). **Cancer is a disease of humankind that should not exist.** It has been the scourge of mankind for many, many years now. I say to you: it is a disease that is unnecessary, like so many of the diseases have been. But unlike many, cancer is a disease of ... the mind ... the mind. The spirit body can alter the way it reacts, and the way that it feels. I can make comparison with many illnesses that exist now ... for example, let us take the person who suffers from back problems. What would you say the comparison would be for that? It shows that the person is 'rigid', is unbending in his way of thinking. I could continue with so many comparisons, but let us say this: cancer is a scourge of the times, which, only when mankind realises what he is truly about, will the disease be eliminated. I know that you will tell me that it has many physical ... physical beginnings (causes?). But I say to you: no it is not (the cause). For the cells to become 'rogue cells', then the problem begins within the spirit body. Try to compare the cell to you as an individual. I know these matters are probably new thoughts to you. But if you can think along these lines, you will see that it begins to make some sense. You beings only see yourselves as flesh and blood with feelings, emotions ... you are so much more! You have to see yourselves on a wider, deeper scale."*

Brent: "What you have been telling us would imply that those who spend a great part of their life in meditation, often in solitary conditions, ought not to suffer from any physical illness at all. Is that so?"

~ *"If the meditation is pure, it should result in a perfect physical body. Of course, there are 'outer influences'. But basically I say to you: those of you that raise yourselves to that greater consciousness should not suffer from physical illnesses. You were all meant to live your lives whereas the body becomes older and goes naturally ... when the time comes, your spirit should leave that physical body easily, without trauma and without disease."*

The statement endorses the idea that disease begins deeply within and is in no way a direct affliction of the physical body. Salumet asserts that cancer is a disease of the mind. Our doctors use the term 'stress' ... stress as being the prime underlying cause. Stress is an aberration of mind. Salumet later confirms that stress indeed equates to disease of the mind. It is easier to take in perhaps if we can look unemotionally at ourselves from afar as opposed to a view midst life's complex details. But the message is clear, that disease is really of our own fabrication and once we manage to raise ourselves to that greater consciousness and have strong soul-connection, then that is an end to disease. That is the salient teaching that comes to us from spirit. I should also point out that it has been made clear to us at other times that disease can be carried over as karma from a previous life. Life in the physical and in spirit can each be complicated it seems, and there may be interactions between the two.

Spontaneous combustion: It is a very rare occurrence, but it occasionally happens that the body of a living person is suddenly almost completely consumed leaving a small amount of ash. The phenomenon is known as 'spontaneous combustion'. In recent years there have been unconvincing attempts to explain it in physical terms and several theories have been suggested. These matters have been presented in forensic science journals. But, as with the general nature of disease, the root cause does not begin in the physical body. It was following a few words on poltergeist energy that Leslie had enquired if the energy involved would be the same:

16 January 1995 ~ "No, no, it is an inner energy. It is an energy that has ... to put it in simple terms, gone wrong."

Leslie: "I see, and would the person so consumed have been responsible...?"

~ "They are totally, yes. They may not be aware of that, but yes. Let me take the word 'consumed' ... that is exactly what has happened. The body has been consumed by the overpowering energies."

Leslie: "And the person so consumed would be responsible for it?"

~ *"Yes ... it may not be from one life. It has to be a build-up of abused energy. That within the physical becomes contorted and has to have an expression, if you like."*

Salumet went on to explain that these are energies not widely known to man. But of course, the phenomenon itself does serve to illustrate the very power of the energy that rests within us. Leslie probably at first had in mind the comparable degree of power that can be manifest in poltergeist activity (but we now understand that to be quite different). But we must observe that the energies in association with life can indeed be powerful! Sometime later I chanced to read a work by Swami Rama[19] that led me to pose a further question on the subject:

"... It has been documented in Sanskrit writings that certain holy ones who are sufficiently in tune with their spirit-selves, know their time of departure from this life, and will actually use 'spontaneous combustion', through a method of contemplating the solar plexus ... using it as a method of disposing of their body at time of death. I'm not sure if this is a particularly useful thing to do. Would you have any comment on that for us, and could you say if those writings are correct?"

~ *"Yes my friend, I will speak. I did tell you when we spoke upon this matter that this combustion, this name you have given to this burning ... is not understood by those of you on this Earth plane, as yet. I told you then and I will tell you now, that it is only a change of energies within the body that makes this happen. When you speak of these men ... who I must say have (indeed) gained such insight and knowledge about themselves ... then they would be capable of changing energy patterns within their own bodies. We have spoken briefly I believe, about how these people can leave their physical bodies behind, have we not?"*

Leslie: "We have indeed." (Leave the body, travel and return again, without further complication.)

~ *"We have spoken about many things. I have to say to you: I do not think that to leave the body in this manner ... in **this** manner ... is very good or wise. I do understand the reason why they do it. They think that they are sacrificing themselves ... they can leave the physical being more quickly and more neatly, by reducing it to ash ... because in ash, you see, they see purity. You understand?"*

Leslie: "Yes, the purification of the fire."

~ *"Yes, yes, but I do not totally agree with them ... but I do understand. Providing they do not hurt others with their ideas, then it cannot be wrong for* **them.** *Does that satisfy you?"*

George: "Yes, thank you very much."

Leslie: "That of course is always supposing that they are absolutely right in having picked that particular moment for their departure from this Earth."

~ *"If they have the knowledge, then the awareness would be great enough ... yes, most of them do know when their time has come."*

Leslie: "I see."

~ *"Yes ... they do have a great awareness."*

One might say that such people as the Himalayan adepts who have strong soul-connection would have very great awareness and Salumet confirms that they would have the ability to 'use' spontaneous combustion in the manner described. It is abundantly clear that we are not talking about an ordinary fire (fast oxidation), at all. The phenomenon is destruction-by-internal-energy that has become disarranged. (In terms of the body's sudden destruction, it might be compared to the hot air balloon basket that fouls power lines and in that instant becomes dust.) It would appear that spontaneous combustion has been known and better understood from early times and its controlled application recorded in Sanskrit.

Dr Bach flower remedies: Having heard interesting reports on Dr Bach's flower remedies, I asked if the doctor's described method of floating flowers in a bowl of water in sunlight would indeed collect the flower energy ... and then, would imbibing the prepared remedy help relieve people's fears and anxieties:

3rd July 1995 ~ "Yes, let me say this to you: you have been told of the energies that each and every one of you take from the sun, through your auras ...in a similar way the flower is attracting the rays from the sun ... the energies ... so you see it is energised, so too is the water. That is how it works. Everything ... you humans, flowers, animals, your Earth ... all are surrounded by these energies. I will say of this Dr Bach: he was a man of much awareness. He struggled in his lifetime to produce these remedies, and although many people scoffed at his ideas ... in actual fact he was unaware of the true energies he was involved with. But nevertheless they (his remedies) were successful for the very reasons I have stated. Is that acceptable to you?"

George: "Yes, that's most helpful. Thank you very much."

~ *"The flower ... whether it be in the ground or placed in water, is reaching out for the living energies surrounding it as you humans also are ... even those you are as yet unaware of ... yes?"*

Leslie: "So there would be many ways in which the flowers could be used directly without being floated on water, I would think?"

~ *"It is nature's way ... his method was his method, and of course there would be other ways. But his awareness instructed him in this direction."*

I must admit I did not realise the full import of Salumet's words to us at the time. The reader will note that in speaking of 'energies', Salumet's words are: ...*even those you are as yet unaware of ... yes?* Well, I have to say that it is in the nature of the teaching that it sometimes takes a while for the penny to drop, but fortunately this does not seem to matter. In fact, it was not until the meeting of 10th November 2003 that I found myself addressing our teacher and saying:

"Can I go back to the Dr Bach flower remedies? It was eight years ago that you spoke to us about that and at the time I think you intimated that Dr Bach was not fully aware of the particular energies that he was successfully using. Now it has taken me a long time ... and I think we are talking about the two energies that come to us from the sun: the 'physical energy' and the 'spiritual energy'. And I suspect that it is the absorption of the spiritual energy of the sun that is being so effective in Dr Bach's remedies. Would you be able to confirm that?"

~ *"Yes. I congratulate you on your willingness to dissect my words on that. Eight years may seem a long time to you but my friend it is not. That is why it is important that we go slowly with all of our information: that you collate the information, that you digest the information and that ultimately you can make sense of what I am telling you. That is part of your growth and awareness. That is what I am trying to cultivate within you, that your own awareness should grow to such a point that anything I tell you can be taken and dissected and understood. So, my friend, I think you should say to yourself: 'well done!'"*

George: "That also brings us to something else. This places flowers in a rather special category, and the gift of flowers from one to another?"

~ *"Not special my dear friend … natural. There is not one thing upon this Earth that is special: all things are meant to be. You understand what I say to you?"*

George: "My meaning was that the gift of flowers from one to another is a gift of spiritual energy…"

~ *"As too is your breath, as too is your sun, as too is your Earth … and water and all things …(all) are spiritual gifts to you. Mankind only feels things are special when he understands, but what mankind needs to understand is that all these (things) come from spirit for mankind to use to the very best of his abilities and in order that the spirit may grow in understanding, as did this gentleman (Dr Bach) who was influenced from spirit. Remember he was influenced to do what he had to do in order to help others. Always my friends look to the wider picture of life, look inwards for your answers and you will find that anything that you do not understand will become so much clearer to you."*

I have reported fully because a number of useful points emerge. First and foremost, the flower remedies indeed work. Dr Bach was a man of much awareness. He of course received influences from spirit in his work. It is the 'spiritual energy' of the sun's output that can be captured and recycled to good effect. Nor does it matter if we are a bit slow in the uptake … even if it takes eight years for the penny to drop! That is a blessing, and even then we might still get a 'Brownie point'.

Regression and regression therapy: Much has been written on the subject of regression therapy. Remarkable cures have been achieved for afflictions such as phobias and idiosynchrasies thought possibly to be psychosomatic. But the process does not always work, and is therefore seen by some as controversial. On this occasion Salumet introduced the subject and Leslie followed with questions:

7th December 1998 ~ *"… There are many disputes in your world about this subject, so I think this time we might answer some of your most pressing questions. Although, as you know, each one of you has the choice of returning to another lifetime, and many of you in this world have returned many, many times, you also know it is not always so. So let us speak a little on what you call 'regression'. Do not assume, my dear friends, that when you are under this 'regression time', that you are absolutely returning to 'past life times'. It is not the case. Indeed, there is not much difference than (regarding?) any communication between any instrument upon this planet. That is not to say of course that returning to a past lifetime is not possible. It is. But the dispute within your world is this: that you assume that any information from past times, must automatically be a past lifetime of each individual."*

Leslie: "Yes, you are quite right. That is the general assumption, but I have never been able to accept that myself."

~ *"Well, I would say to you my dear friends: hold onto what you feel, because you are partly right ... Regression is possible but there has to be a reason for it ... Well, let us now begin with your questions now that I have outlined for you the generality, shall I say, of the subject."*

Leslie: "Yes, I have never been able to accept the fact that **automatically**, the information being given by a person under regression would be that pertaining to a past life ... and also in my thinking, the power of thought of the person responsible for the patient ... shall we say ... that thought could also intervene..."

~ *"Of course, once more we return do we not, to the power of thought, and yes you are correct, that sometimes the person who is doing this regression has influence with **their** thoughts. I would say the majority of your regressions are indeed information being shown to the individual, but not necessarily their own past lives. What we hear then is: 'But it is so vivid!' But is not any communication between **any** medium upon your world when contact is made within ours? Then of course, that becomes reality at that moment in time. Always bear this in mind. But of course, then we come to those genuine cases where the individual **is** allowed to be shown, I would say **one** past life, not many ... for the purpose of freeing their soul (soul aspect) so that their lifetime can be helped. That is the only purpose of being shown any past life ... to, shall we say, unblock any emotional or spiritual blockages that may have been taken from that past life and is hindering that soul in its pathway in the present time. Does that make sense to you?"*

Leslie: "Yes it does, and I can accept that absolutely, but that presumably would only be permitted under certain circumstances if the information was in fact for the benefit of the progress of that soul?"

~ *"Yes of course. Any spiritual, any emotional blockage that the soul would sustain into the present lifetime ... then of course that information would be permitted to help the soul."*

Leslie: "So that would be parallel to what you have told us about being counselled before we return to any life of this time?

You did once say that we would receive counselling as to the best physical return we should have…"

~ *"Each soul knows and understands what its life's journey is about but sometimes the soul is unable to free itself from spiritual blockages/emotional blockages which have occurred and belong to the soul. The soul (soul aspect?) brings it (the blockage) with them and is unable to free itself in the present existence. That is the only permission that would be given to allow the soul to see a past lifetime whilst it inhabits this human form. Is that clear to you?"*

Following our general positive response Leslie continued:

"Which leads me on to the next question. If it is only permitted in certain conditions, would I be right in thinking that other information that is supposed to be coming from a past life, is in fact communication **from your world** to the person under regression?"

~ *"Information given of past life, is of course monitored from our world. Of course we have to protect the soul. That is another point you may take counsel with. Yes, you must remember the soul's progress is what is important. You could perhaps place a parallel with your healing. Only those … allowed-to-be-freed from illness would secure what you would term a cure. It is the same parallel …only those souls that are permitted-to-be-freed from illness (blockage) would be freed. The others would remain because that is the pathway they have chosen. Does this become any clearer to you?"*

Then, in response to Leslie seeking further clarification:

~ *"In the true regression where permission **is** given, I would have to say: the information is given from another aspect of the same soul. It is slightly different when you speak about healing and other matters. Although the information for the help comes from our world, it is not necessarily in those cases, from the same aspect of soul. Do you understand this, or am I confusing you?"*

Leslie: "No, it rather confirms what I have suspected. A person under regression is, to my way of thinking, equivalent to a person in the physical world allowing themselves to be taken over and pass on information given from your side … which need not necessarily have anything to do with their own past lives…"

~ *"That is the majority of cases of what you call regression."*

Leslie: "Thank you for confirming that. I have suspected that for a long time. That is why I have been opposed to regression-so-called being considered as such, because I have often maintained ... to me it is merely another aspect of mediumship as demonstrated at these meetings."

~ *"Yes of course, but you must not say: 'No ... regression to past life does not exist.' There* **are** *genuine cases, but the majority of cases, you are correct, they are receiving information but it does not belong to that soul."*

Leslie:"Now we come to a most difficult question which you may not be able to answer. How would one distinguish between the two factors of general information and honest information from a past life?"

~ *"Because the past life truths would free the soul as I have said from emotional and spiritual bondage (blockage) which could create in the physical being many problems, many phobias and many fears. The soul would then be free from them. That would be the indication that the regression was a true one."*

Leslie:"So it would have to rely on the physical reaction of the person after regression?"

~ *"Yes, because then the soul is freed from any blockage that it has brought."*

Leslie: "And that would be reflected in the physical differences..."

~ *"Yes."*

Leslie:"Thank you very much, because that does explain how the two could be separated."

~ *"That is the only way ... the soul would know. It is difficult when human beings are trying always to, and I use the word reservedly ... prove something. It is not always easy, but the soul (soul aspect) would be allowed to go forward on its pathway that has been chosen (for) this time."*

It was a laboured and lengthy exchange, but well worthwhile in view of the difficult and controversial nature of the subject. As I understand the position, regression therapy can work well and has a precise mechanism involving soul referral, and the cure of the affliction is the proof that a blockage has indeed cleared as the result of the soul's involvement. This validates certain literature references[20]. But, as is explained, what may seem like receipt of information from a past life of the patient is not always so. The teaching is also in agreement with that part of the Tibetan Book of the Dead that concerns rebirth into Earthly life, with 'samskaras' (emotional blockages) in place from past lives.

Laughter as a medicine: It was one of those evenings when, after a few preliminary words, Salumet worked quietly with Eileen whilst another came through Sue. On departure, she gave her full name and title as: Sister Superior Veronica Magdalene, but made it clear that she much prefers and is generally know as 'Sister Maggie':

11th January 1999 ~ "Good evening everyone! I trust everyone here is well. I understand that at this time of your year you do suffer in your human body from some aches and pains and different illnesses. I myself used to be afflicted with rheumatism, but of course you can overcome these things with the mind as well as the cough linctuses and tablets, can you not?"

The conversation moved on to the importance of having a sense of humour and how on occasions in her Earth life, it had got our visitor into trouble. Then Leslie was saying:

"And of course, you learn that a sense of humour is a very great asset in the work you do…"

~ "Goodness me! Come on, LAUGHTER … isn't it the best medicine in the world?"

On emotion and its control: Allowing emotion to well up and control our lives for a period is an error that all of us will have experienced at some time or another. Salumet spoke on this at some length. What follows is a slightly shortened account beginning with:

13th September 1999 ~ "… When you are encompassed by life's difficulties, what can you do? You should go to quietness and allow spirit to come forward. Then all physical problems should disappear quietly to where they belong."

Sally had then enquired about the mechanism that leads to such upsets and disasters:

~ "In being spirit we have only the finest attributes but when you are clothed with these physical garments, then physical thinking, feelings, emotions … are partly in control. What you must try to achieve my dear friends, although spirit and physical life must run hand-in-hand as you may say, you must let that spiritual knowledge guide your physical living … because without this guidance, always the physical emotions will overrun your thinking. You must have the balance in physical life…"

Sara had then queried the whys and the wherefores of feeling hurt and if this is an aspect of emotion that we produce for ourselves:

"… Let me say this to you: the only one who can hurt you is yourself. What happens is this, that when you feel hurt or injured by another person, you are allowing the emotional body to take control of your thinking. This is what I try to say to you: no one upon this Earthly plane can cause you harm unless you allow them to. Each one of you has the power to protect yourself whether it be physically or emotionally. When you understand these words you can truly be spirit upon this Earth. You can be free from all harm, free from all hurt, freed from all physical ailments. You in fact come as close to spirit as you can. Therefore my dear friends I say to you: ponder my words this time, come to know yourselves … after all, that is why you came to this Earthly plane, that you might come to know yourselves, that you might join with those you have chosen to be with, in order that you can create this harmonious way of life."

Then, following further exchange about being hurt and choosing our feelings:

George: "Would it be true to say that if the spirit within is sufficient influence upon the physical mind, one would not be hurt anyway?"

~ *"Yes, exactly my friend. That is what you have to cultivate. You do not have to try. All knowledge lies within you. All you have to do is allow it to come to the surface. If there is emotional hurt or distress, then I say again to you all: look within yourselves. This is not meant to be a judgement upon yourselves … do not think upon it in that way, but rather that it is a lesson that you all need to learn … to use that spiritual knowledge within…"*

Lilian: "And that would go for guilty feelings … if we listen to the spirit inside?"

~ *"This applies to all emotions … yes of course. When you have learned to allow spirit to come forward, then you will find that life brings you fewer distressing and upsetting emotions, but as I have said, the power lies within yourselves."*

Where health is concerned, coming to terms with emotion may at first seem vague and unimportant. It is not. If one follows the teaching, and the spirit self is not smothered then clearly, freedom from feelings of distress as well as freedom from physical ailments, should follow. On a separate occasion Salumet referred to illnesses resulting when the energy flowing within the body becomes blocked. I think the implication is that, with the spirit to the fore, the energy system of the body remains freely moving and in good order.

Longevity, care for the aged and time to depart this life: A question had been asked about care for the aged who no longer have quality of life and that life being so often prolonged the more by advancing medical technology:

15*th* May 2000 ~ *"... I have spoken about the human race and the fact that you should perform as well (as is possible) in the 'thinking' ... (you) can (then) live to a much longer age than you normally do. It all comes down to the 'thinking'. We have discussed illness and we have discussed responsibility and we have discussed the topics of doctors and medicine and the influence that comes from our world ... Doctors will be able as your evolution takes place ... to prolong life. Whether this is acceptable to you or not depends on the way of your 'thinking'. Each one of you my dear friends, could choose the time of your leaving if you so desired, if you could only reach that state of knowledge and awareness that tells you that it is time for you to come home, without any illness of the body or anyone looking after you..."*

George: "I believe there are many in the East who are more practiced than we are in the West..."

~ *"Yes, there are some in your world, but it is possible ... I know this seems a large statement to make ... it should be possible for each one of you, and the key to healthy longevity is your thinking. Your doctors that are inspired from our world have responsibility for all of those people who they have in their care. Each one of you has responsibility for yourselves as spirit and each one of you has responsibility for those you are in contact with. If you want me to express an opinion on this matter, I will say only that perhaps people who have grown old and weary and try to keep alive in whatever form by the medical profession ... could involve someone with spiritual knowledge who could advise on spiritual matters ... It would be much better to have someone with the spiritual knowledge and awareness to be looking after them. Then the spirit would have the knowledge to release itself. After all my dear friends, you well know and understand ... why do you need to hold onto these old overcoats if your time is ready to come to our world? And people do (hold on) because of your own free will. You can, because of the power of your thought ... and again I return to my favourite topic with you ... you can create many situations that would best be left behind. Do you understand? But again, because you are*

*human, you cling to human life for all you are worth. But mankind ...
and there are peoples in your world who live to a much older age, much
more healthily, and when the time is right, they release themselves."*

George: "This is perhaps the ideal..."

~ *"That is what each one should strive for. It can be achieved, but
with much work. Thank you my dear friends, thank you for listening to
me once again. As always, I hear your questions and cries for help, for
knowledge ... of understanding. They do not go unheeded, but again
I remind you that I cannot interfere. I can encourage and uplift and
influence, but I cannot interfere. But that is not to say I do not hear you.
I leave you this time with all of our love and until we meet next time,
know always that I am with you."*

The words came at the end of the session and it seemed fitting
to include Salumet's warm words of farewell. As he tells us, it is
the 'thinking' that is so important. Hopefully, if well nurtured,
this attribute should remain with us, but if it is lost and medical
science still keeps the body that remains alive, then this is clearly a
sad situation. Our responsibilities are also spelled out, but it is the
thinking ... its continued use, care of it as a precious attribute, its
preservation and finally, a recognition of the time to go ... to go
home to spirit. That is important. There is mention of the adepts
in the East who are familiar with this way of thinking. Books
by such authors as Swami Rama[19] and Paramahansa Yogananda[21]
bear testimony to this. The latter accounts the final moments of
Lahiri Mahasaya, 26th September 1895, describing his revolving
three times to finally face north in lotus position; this being part
of a Vedic rite used by Masters who know in advance their time
of departure.

Out of body experience: We had been discussing
dematerialisation and how it would be of practical use in space-
travel:

George: "It (dematerialisation) is documented in a number of
old scriptures..."

10th July 2000 ~ *"Yes, nothing is new my dear friend ... this I have
tried to teach you."*

Lilian: "I suppose it is what we call 'out of body experience',
is it?"

~ *"No, no ... you are speaking of something entirely different.
Dematerialisation is another form of spiritual life. 'Out of body*

experience' is just the freedom of spirit from the physical body … that is all that means."

Mark:"Is it an out of body experience when I have had dreams … when I've been flying and it has felt as if my physical body was flying? I wonder if that was an out of body experience?"

~ *"Yes, all of you have, what you would call out of body experiences because, after all, in your sleep state my dear friend, each of you leaves your physical body behind for a short time in order that the spirit be rejuvenated, if you like … but to most people, this is not remembered. But when you speak of the physical body flying, remember my dear friend, that when you come home to spirit, you retain all the knowledge of your physical being. Although you are spirit, you still feel like a physical being … that is why you would feel as if the physical was flying … it is not the physical body that is flying, it is the spirit…"*

It is good that we have a clear definition of OOB as temporary release of spirit from the physical body. I think I would be correct in saying that the sleep state example given is the most common form of OOB. Less common occurrences would be motivated by accidents, fevers and difficult operating theatre situations.

Physical death: It was just two weeks later when death was defined. It is good that this statement follows on from OOB because some might possibly see it as a special case of OOB.

Lilian: "I was talking to someone the other day about the spirit leaving the body at the time of death. As I understand it, it is immediate … as the body dies, so the spirit leaves. She had the idea that it takes three days…"

24th July 2000 ~ "The spirit leaves the physical body only when there is a severance of the cord. The spirit can leave the body, that in your world, can be said to be dead … but until the cord is broken the spirit remains close to the body. And on some occasions, this can take seconds. This may take minutes and even days. On most occasions, I can tell you that at the time of what you call death, the spirit is freed almost immediately. But again, you are both right … I am sure that each one of you here has heard many cases of someone who has been pronounced deceased and has returned to life. So the physical pronouncement of death is not always the actual moment of severance of the cord."

From the spiritual viewpoint then (and that is the more fundamental viewpoint), physical death occurs only when the connecting cord of spirit is severed. (In general OOB experience it remains intact.) I have an amazing story told me by an Indonesian friend that well illustrates this point. The family lives in Bali and the story concerns my friend's grandmother. The life seemed to have left her body. She was pronounced dead, a funeral service was held and she was buried. Fortunately it is the custom of the region to place sloping boards over the body, and the earth that is then heaped over is light and friable. Next day, following the ceremony, the old lady was discovered walking back to the village, clutching her burial wrap about her, having dug herself out. She babbled about the one she had met who told her that her time was not yet up! She lived on with family for a further two years.

Stigmatic holy ones: A question was asked about those who bleed from the palms, as did Jesus in crucifixion. The subject had been mentioned earlier in relation to power of thought and how it can be an influence. Since bleeding is usually seen as a medical matter, it seemed right to include the topic here:

31ˢᵗ July 2000 ~ "Yes, you would be fringing upon the help of many others when those whose power of thought is so strong. Remember that I have told you that the power of thought becomes reality ... but what also happens when the power of your thought is so strong, is that those who are close to you and influenced by that thought, can also connect ... to help the situation being created. There again, is no clear cut answer, but remember that the power of thought is all-powerful. Much can be created by thought alone."

George: "Yes, that is always the primary factor..."

~ "Yes ... there are many who are close to you (in spirit) and I have said that like is attracted to like. Therefore those powerful thoughts would be attracting those from our world who have the same vibrational thoughts. That therefore creates a vibration that becomes even more powerful. If you take the thought of one person within this room ... it would be strong, but the collective thought of all, would create a much stronger thought vibration. We have spoken about collective thoughts in the process of healing the world. If you think along those lines it will perhaps become a little clearer to you."

The bleeding of stigmatic holy ones is indeed a reality and Salumet very clearly points to the cause as the power of thinking. If the creation is powered by thought, then one can easily see that thought can create a body condition. (One renowned stigmatic nun was Sister Anna Catherina Enmerich who lived in Germany. She is the one that had visions of the location of the house near Ephesus, where Mary lived following the crucifixion. The visions were accurate and the expeditions that followed in 1881 and 1891 successfully located the house.)

Siamese twins: Difficult cases of Siamese twin separation attract media coverage and are generally reported in terms of the loss or survival of each one. The terms used and the heartache relating to loss, do not always apply to both. It was Lilian who sought clarification on a particular reported case:

"… One of the twins, she has no heart … she is virtually living off the sister who has all essential organs. Is that one spirit?"

9th October 2000 ~ "It is one spirit, but with physical complications. Remember that, when the spirit enters at conception, it is now in the hands of physical living. We know that these problems confuse and upset many of you on this Earthly plane, but that one child is probably here to be living as a human being, but the purpose of that malformation is necessary, although you may not understand why. But it is but one spirit."

Lilian: "So if they were separated and one continued to live, the other would be nothing?"

~ "Yes, there are many questions in your world (that) we know confuse you, but it all becomes clear when you return to our world. All I say to you my dear friends is: when you have such confusion within your thinking, then send out the thought to have it made clearer to you and you will have the answers."

Lilian: "That is something we forget. We must remember it more."

~ "Always I say to you, and again I do not apologise, but (I) say that your thought is the most powerful possession you have. Please use it in a wise way."

The exchange shows clearly that Siamese twins are sometimes a single being so that surgery to remove appendages does not in such cases involve a death. We should remember that firstly we are spirit and the physical counterpart comes second.

Medical advances in the 21st century: This is a general statement that Salumet launched straight into when he joined us on this occasion:

*23rd October 2000 ~ "Good evening. I have been this time more slowly (joining you) because the instrument has a small problem with her throat and I have been attending to it. Perhaps my dear friends, this is an opportune moment to tell you that from our world at this moment of time, there is coming to your world, many, many great advances within your medical world. Many of your so-called diseases of your Earth plane, you know full well to be activated by mankind himself, but also you know and understand that most of mankind is looking towards medical people for help. This is of course, offered to you by the people known to you as 'doctors'. But also you know that it (relief from illness) comes through those known to **us** as 'healers'. Many of your doctors have the (spiritual) healing gift, and through these people we are now working from our world with them, in order that mankind, not only has Earthly help but spiritual help also. Because, by now my dear friends, you would understand that until the spirit is touched, there can be no health problem solved. You know and understand my dear friends, that 'disease' is the 'dis-ease' of all bodies ... the Earthly, the etheric and the spiritual. But, as I have said, mankind in general relies on Earthly doctors for their so-called cures of disease. To this end, we are working in order that bodily needs be satisfied, but also (so) that the healers within your Earthly world can create for many people, the opportunity to grow and understand themselves as whole beings. What I would say this time, and it also applies to the instrument ... that it is good to give of oneself ... indeed it is admirable to give of oneself to others ... to give of the spirit to the spirit. But it is foolish to give of oneself and not to look after the spirit and body of that same being. Do you understand what I say to you my dear friends? It is admirable to give of course, and that is what love is all about, but you must look after your own spirit ... your own development, and only then can you give love and help to others. Not only are there many advances being made within the medical world ... it will come to light soon ... but great strides are also being made in communication with all of your electrical equipments. I have broached this subject before I believe, but now we are beginning to see the results of our labour with mankind. And there are many within your world that now have very good communication with others from our world."*

Salumet seems to be referring to a number of things, not always in quite the terms with which we are familiar. He refers to the combined consideration of physical/etheric/spirit bodies when he speaks of understanding oneself as a whole being. By our 'so-called cures of disease', I think he refers to the frequency with which we tackle symptoms and results without seeing the root cause that lies within … root cause being not of the physical body. Hence often the recurrence of conditions some time later. When he speaks of communication, he refers in part to that communication between our selves and those in spirit. And that of course can only improve mankind's capacity to heal. I have suggested in an earlier publication[3] that it would greatly enhance national health services, if mediums through whom spirit surgeons can work (backed by their teams in spirit), were to become an accepted part of the service. I must confess that it did not occur to me at that time that those in spirit would be taking the initiative! It appears, according to Salumet, that they are in fact beginning to influence doctors in their medical work, albeit not in quite the way that I at first had in mind.

The session continued:

Lilian: "So would this be all over our planet?"

~ *"Of course. There is no one place that has the attention more than any other. All races, all manner of people are finding that their equipment is being used in the best way that it can. It will become more widely known but remember that I have told you so. There also comes from our world at this time … and there is a great surge of love towards this mission … raising (of) consciousness among all people on the Earth planet. I can hear you say: 'But has this not already taken place?' Of course it has. It is an ongoing thing, but at this particular time in your consciousness … in your Earth consciousness, there is an upsurge of understanding, of great seeking of knowledge."*

Lilian: "I think perhaps especially in the younger people…"

~ *"Yes, in all areas of living, in all people, in all of mankind on this planet. They are working on many areas of living. We are trying to achieve … to be emissaries of that Great Divine Love … to bring to you understanding, reasoning, hope, all of these things which are necessary for the spirit to evolve on this planet."*

Lilian: "We are very privileged that you tell us these things before they come into fruition."

~ *"Yes. Many times we have attempted within your world to bring greater knowledge. Many times have we attempted to bring mankind closer together, but always there is strife, there is unrest, there is this power struggle … but I can now say that we are beginning to make great strides. I can hear you say: 'But it seems very slow' …in your time, yes I would probably agree with you my dear friends. But, as you know, time in our world means so little..."*

It seems then that if we attempt to take an overview of the situation, we are being helped from those in spirit to confront and deal with the array of health problems that have accumulated from our living. The problems can be dealt with through our better understanding, reasoning and aspirations. We are being helped in this and it is all a part of the wider scheme of raising consciousness. This should no doubt have been a steady process continuing all the time, but our power struggles have sadly interfered. But now as we move into the new millennium the pace of change for the better, increases.

Significance of a deformed gene: It was just three weeks later when Sarah put a question following a TV feature:

"You were talking about our medical advances and there was a programme on TV recently ... about the Icelandic people who can trace their ancestors right back to the Vikings. Many suffer from cancer and they can trace back generations showing the deformed gene they all have. You said to us that we create the disease that we have in past lives or in this life. If people come back with a defective gene, do we trigger off the problem with the disease whilst we are here by what we are doing now? And can these people avert getting cancer, even though they have a deformed gene, by the way they are living today?"

13th November 2000 ~ "I understand your question. Yes, let me say this to you: in the situations you have discussed, these are of course the karmic debts. You all understand that term I know, but of course you know the power of thought that is given to each one of you when you come into this incarnation is entirely your own responsibility. Therefore I would say this, that although this group of people have come to this lifetime with what you call a deformed gene, I would call (it) a spiritual debt. People have the ability to change their lives and rid themselves of spiritual debt. That would explain why not every single one of them would trigger off the disease. The way they live their life will dictate whether that disease will become ripe and vigorous or whether it can be changed. Let me say to you my dear friends that each one of you has the ability to change the very cells within your body. It is not easy I know, but each one of you has the ability to change it."

Sarah: "And would that mean that if we come with a spiritual debt, we can rid the soul of that debt in this lifetime?"

~ *"Of course! But again, it belongs to you and to you alone. But with the help of the many you call healers ... (they) are here to help and to advise you and to bring to you that touch of spiritual light that is needed for you to dispel that spiritual debt."*

Perhaps the important message here is that if one comes to Earth with a genetic disadvantage, it can be manipulated by means of thought and spirit, and I would imagine that some deep meditation would not come amiss. Our history is so chequered with such things as wars, crusades, slave trading and the like, that it is easy to see how whole groups of people could return with a common karmic debt to be worked off in some way.

Disfigurement and 'old souls': Our questions are sometimes triggered by something we read in the press.

George: "I read very recently about a lady who had a psychic reading, and it sounds as if it was a very informative psychic reading ... and at the end of the session a reference was made to her Down's syndrome child. The psychic said that this is not an ordinary child but an incarnated angel. I wondered if this would be possible or if there might be sufficient reason for this to happen. Could you comment on this?"

5th March 2001 ~ "Yes, I will ... I will try to clarify this for you. You know that all things are possible from our world. But I would say ... and the instance you speak about is of course a term used by the psychic and not in fact an angelic being that has reincarnated into the physical body. But in saying that, I do wish to say that on very rare occasions this is possible ... if indeed there is a special mission, but only then would this happen. And I have to tell you my dear friend, it happens only rarely. Of course, what I would wish you to understand ... and I know full well that you know that anyone who takes a body in whichever way disfigured or disabled is indeed usually an 'old soul'. So of course, they are special beings in that sense. So I would rather say to you: think upon those lines rather than that they are angels that have come into the physical being. It can happen, but very, very rarely, and there would have to be a special mission on this planet for it to happen."

Foot and mouth disease slaughter: At the time of our meeting, there had been an outbreak of the disease in the British

Isles and large numbers of cattle were being slaughtered. Margaret had tried to convince a concerned friend that the animal spirit continues, but she still wanted to know what Salumet would say about the matter, and so Margaret had put the question:

26th March 2001 ~ "... All those animals that you are so concerned about ... of course the spirit goes on, but it is not individualised. Only those animals that have experienced a bond of love, closeness with a human being, remain individualised within our world. The animals will go to a pool of spirit, where the spirit remains for some considerable time. But, as in humans, they do not suffer (in spirit)."

On other occasions also, Salumet has made it clear that all animals return to their respective spirit pool, unless they are those dogs or horses for example, that have formed a special attachment to a human during their lives.

Relating thought pattern to disease: There may be some who feel uncomfortable on reading through this section. If that is so then I apologise, but I would be failing in my task if information that I feel to be of much value were not presented. Salumet had been discussing the work of angels who heal the spirit that has left the physical Earth, when it has been depleted through lengthy illness. And it may be a wonderful reassurance to those who do not know, that this indeed takes place. Paul had asked:

"When you say it begins in spirit, does it begin with thoughts?"

14th May 2001 ~ "Yes, of course. Thought is the most powerful thing. It is thought, and mainly wrong thought that starts off many of your Earthly diseases."

Sarah: "Sometimes we have brought diseases with us from a previous life…"

~ "But still they have manifested from the original thought. Yes, of course you are correct, you can bring them with you, and that is why it is advisable ... and advisable only for that case ... to find out what is holding you back in this lifetime."

Lilian: "It's a pity there's not more awareness in everyone."

~ "Yes, but you see, whatever you think passes through the spiritual body and manifests into the physical. I feel it is something not fully understood, that as human beings, you have this feeling that the physical is the only body that creates disease. But of course, the mind belongs to the spirit, does it not? Therefore, think along those lines my dear friend and perhaps it may become a little clearer to you."

Paul: "Would you say the diseased person has to change their belief, and their thoughts will change?"

~ *"They do not change beliefs, but they have to change their way of thinking. It is the thought pattern that is at fault. Let us take an example. Let us for example, say we have a person who is highly critical ... not only of others but of themselves. And have I not told you that you must have love for yourself before you can extend it to others? So let us (now) take this emotion of being highly critical. People of that thought pattern usually have the type of disease in your world, of the body becoming gnarled ... I am trying to get the condition ... yes, you call it 'arthritis'. That is because the thinking becomes reality and that criticism begins to twist and become embittered and shows itself into the physical body. Therefore the way to dissolve that type of disease is to learn to love, not only your fellow man, but also your selves. Can you see the pattern? If you try to follow this line of thinking, I feel it will be a little easier for you. It is the power of thinking."*

Sarah: "So children who come over with arthritis, they have brought it from a previous life..."

~ *"Yes, yes! That is ... probably, I do not say all. That is probably why they have returned to this lifetime ... to undo that pattern of thought. It is a powerful thing I say to you. It is something that each one of you should consider most seriously, because you can change what you think. And have I not told you in the past, my dear friends, that if you constantly find fault with another, then look inwards to yourself ... therein lies the fault."*

Lilian: "So with the right kind of thinking, our physical bodies could stand us in good stead for as long as we are here..."

~ *"Yes, and you would have the ability to help others as do the angels of healing in our world, after all, that is what they are doing with the power of **their** thought."*

Lilian: "So, although the body gets frail, which I guess is natural..."

~ *"Of course, it is part of your physical evolution. You cannot live here forever. You have to return home, but your purpose here is to learn all of those things that are only for your own soul's growth, that you may return home and say that you have learned something. That is your purpose of living, if not only for yourself but for your interaction with all other people who come into contact with you. You have great responsibility my dear friends. Do you have any questions before I leave you this time?"*

George: "I think we are beginning to grasp the connections between physical ailments and spirit. And I was reading something recently about buildings in the latter days of Atlantis, that were described as: 'between a hospital and a temple', where spiritual connections with healing of physical matters were looked into. This came out of past-life-readings of one Edgar Cayce. I think he was probably a very genuine individual ... but the idea of something between hospital and temple rather stuck in my mind, and seems to connect with what you are telling us now..."

~ *"Yes, I can say to you: this man was a man of vision. But I have to say to you my dear friend, that these ancient people have or had a much closer unity with spirit. Their knowledge was much greater than it (ours) is today. Therefore their knowledge would have been such that they would have understood spiritual matters much more deeply."*

George: "Yes, I can see that..."

~ *"They were much more aware of the spiritual aspect of man, and of course healing and places of healing would have been influenced from our world. Yes, thank you..."*

The reality that our thought patterns are responsible for illness and disease, is itself a sobering thought. And disease always manifests first in the spirit/energy body before passing to the physical. It follows that treatment of the physical body is treating the final material result and not root cause. Whilst this may be useful, it is often in the long term not enough. Thought pattern also needs to change, and understanding the basic nature of what is involved can of course help facilitate this. Understanding can be a first step. This general scenario may help to explain 'miracle recoveries' that have followed a change-of-heart or the impact of deeply inspiring music. Such things can alter thought pattern and wipe the slate clean for a new beginning, one might say. As salumet has stated many times ... thought is powerful. It can 'disorganise' the energy within ... equally it can unscramble that disorganised thought form and make well again. As Salumet confirms, Edgar Cayce was a 'visionary'. The information that he was able to channel concerning life on Atlantis[12] makes it clear that they understood well the connection between disease and spirit; hence their temple-hospitals. I have more recently had the good fortune to meet another having past-life memory of Atlantean times and Salumet's words have received further confirmation from this additional, independent source.

Improved health as spirit moves forward: On this occasion our teacher said more on advances within our medical profession in this first decade of a new millennium:

30ᵗʰ July 2001 ~ "I have told you of happenings that will occur on your planet in time to come, but what I wish to tell you my dear friends is that within the next ten years of your Earthly time, many advances will be made within your medical professions. These can only be good for mankind. But what I also wish you to know is that until mankind recognises spirit within, there will always be unrest within the human frame. The time will come when mankind will find within himself the perfect body if he so desires. There will in time to come be many more healthy people because the spirit will come forward and knowledge will become greater. The information from our world to those within your medical professions will be greater. I am sure my dear friends, that you are not unaware of the change of attitude towards what you call I believe, complimentary therapies. This of course is not new. This planet has always been provided with the cures to many of mankind's unrests and disease. It is only that in your time, much of it has been forgotten. But, as in all things, a new awakening has begun to change many attitudes and ways of thinking. But, as I have said, mankind has to realise that physical living should no longer be the power struggle that it is within your planet at this present time. Until each individual finds that spirit within, until that recognition is greater, then mankind will always struggle with the many aspects of human existence."

The statement clearly endorses the importance for us of recognising the spirit within, and that can be seen as a first step in making our lives run so much more smoothly.

Transgender: This is a topic that in general is not well understood and cannot be understood, until the spiritual nature of life is considered. Then some small degree of understanding falls into place leading to an easier ability to empathise. There had been dialogue several years earlier that had seemed to suggest that it arises from spirit being eager to return to Earth life. We referred again to this:

4ᵗʰ November 2002 ~ "Yes, it is always the problem, and you must remember that there are those in our world … and let me remind you firstly that when those who come to our world are anxious to return and will not be guided or will not be patient enough, they will use their free will that they still have. They will take any opportunity…"

Salumet went on to speak of internal conflict, the pathways forward and how one simply cannot and should not judge. I paraphrase the salient points made:

~ *"Yes, I would say: if you look spiritually to these people, that is why their lives sometimes seem to have this conflict. Not all I would say, but many …Let us not forget that gender belongs to the physical world …The spirit is eager to return and creates many problems … Mankind can do much to alter the physical makeup … There is nothing to stop mankind from using medical advancements … the spirit within does not change. It is a complex issue that cannot be spoken of lightly because there are too many issues at hand here …Yes, the spirit within is the one who is striving to come forward …Remember that spirit beings have free will … as you have those children in your world who are guided but will still always go their own way because of their free will. But that is something not to be decried because it is a learning process …"*

I had read something by the Dalai Lama[22] indicating that, at time of conception, the spirit enters the egg by one route for female and a different route for male but Salumet would not be drawn on that. He reiterated:

~ *"It is a complicated subject and not one that everyone can accept eagerly…"*

I thanked our teacher for his words on a difficult subject, adding:

"… because as you will appreciate, there are all kinds of different views that people have."

~ *"Yes, and this is always the problem … there I would say, lies the fault of humankind in trying to decide what is right and what is wrong. It is confusing, and this is something that all of us who come to you have to try to dispel, because there has been many, many of your years when information given to you has been misinterpreted, or mankind has decided that he is best at knowing the right answer. That is our purpose in coming to teach you and to help you to understand, and to open your minds more fully to what is happening. As always my dear friends, look at all of these issues … from a spiritual standpoint and you will have a much better view, you will receive a much better answer to your question."*

Sara: "Certainly, when we appreciate the complexity of things, we appreciate that we cannot judge…"

~ *"Yes, always it returns does it not, to my simple teachings: never to make judgement upon another … because how can you know the circumstances of that spirit? All too often Earth people are quick to judge, are harsh in their judgement, whereas the spirit eyes should see the wider picture … and, even if the understanding is not there, at least give the heart a chance to feel and accept another's life. It is not always easy I know but that is the way forward."*

It is a complicated issue and we are advised that we simply cannot expect to understand completely. The causal factor clearly relates to the journey of the re-incarnating spirit. But the detail of this is something we cannot and should not attempt to judge … how can we when the wider picture cannot be seen? And in any case, the whole sequence that then follows is a learning process for that soul aspect, just as all our lives are learning processes. It is made clear that none of us has any right to harsh criticism of another. Different individuals will doubtless have varying degrees of the conflict within (that is referred to), so that a percentage will be driven hard to find a solution that feels more comfortable. And of course, one must always respect that right of another to seek a best way forward. But the causal revelation, as I understand it, is that diverse problems can arise out of eagerness to return to Earth life.

It is my understanding that those having male physical body and the internal conflict have certain brain details (hypothalamus region) that are more aligned to female than to male. If the brain can be seen as a processor of information from mind/spirit, then perhaps some may see this detail as evidence that spirit input does not suit body biology. The research really needs to be continued further however, before speculations can be entertained or conclusions drawn.

Healing and karma: The subject of the evening had been 'healing' and how best to place our thoughts before the Great Creative Principle:

Lilian: "I just wondered if the thoughts of the healer would…"

27th January 2003 ~ "There should be no thoughts of the healer. The healer should be but an instrument … a channel that comes from that Great Creative Force. All that a healer offers is either their words or their hands. The healer should have no participation and does not have any participation in the healing; that is between the person and God if you like, or as I prefer, the Creative Force."

George: "And only the Creative Force can take into account karmic considerations? Do the karmic connections to illness

… I imagine they would come to an end at some point when certain things have happened. I sometimes wonder if the karmic consideration would be for a whole lifetime, or would it be lifted at some stage during a lifetime?"

~ *"I do not like the word 'lifted', as if the person can be exonerated. That is not how karma works. It will be released when the soul recognises what the karmic debt is. Then, and only then, in any one lifetime or another will the soul come to the realisation that the karmic debt must be paid and released. Remember free will. You must always remember that we have been bestowed with free will, not only in this human form, but the soul (soul aspect?) retains free will. Do you understand?"*

Following our assurance that we did, Salumet continued:

~ *"Of course, the spirit can be helped to release karmic debt. There can be inspiration, there can be a change of thinking, but the spirit must release their own karmic debts."*

Sarah: "When people are healed … when they go to Lourdes and become well after being ill for so long … is that maybe when the spirit has recognised what it has done wrong?"

~ *"A healing that you speak of can only take place when the spirit is touched. But having the connection with the life force, inspires the spirit to work for good … but no healing can take place until the spirit is touched."*

Sarah: "So this is why you said to us that sometimes people are healed and sometimes they are not?"

~ *"Yes, the desire alone to be healed is not enough, especially as we are speaking about karmic debt … that is something to be worked through by the spirit alone. Always there will be help and upliftment, but a healing will not take place whilst there remains karmic debt. Is that clear for you?"*

It was … at least it was as clear as we were able to comprehend. It is a difficult area. But one can always view things in their simplest form, and for myself that means that healing can take place only when the spirit is touched and when any karmic debt has been released. Both conditions must be satisfied. And of course, at such places as Lourdes, many 'miracles' of healing have occurred whilst many who have visited, have not been healed. That is precisely the result that one would expect from the teaching.

The healing power of music: During the evening of 14th April 2003, Salumet worked with Eileen whilst another came through Sue and talked to us about music and how it can raise the spirit:

~ *"... I ask you if you can feel music ... feel the vibrations? It can help you in so many ways. There is a healing colour to music. Does that make any sense to you? Music has colour. All music, whether you consider it to be the lowliest or just a cacophony of noise, it has a healing colour."*

George: "Does that relate to the colours of auras of people listening to music and how music changes the colour of the aura?"

~ *"Were you able to see auras, you would see a change in the spectrum of colour ... yes, you would ... and more so with those who are in need of some spiritual help. I say to you, the sound of music can be far more beneficial than your potions and powders. In your world, unfortunately, they are used far more than they are necessary, but we can do little about that. Certain of your powders can be like poison and we are hoping ...in time, that these will be replaced. (We are moving on now to deeper things that it is not my purpose to speak of)."*

George: "I have read of one who cured herself of cancer by listening to music, so that is very much in line with what you are saying..."

~ *"The power of the healing colour of music ... music is a powerful healer. I leave that information with you, and hopefully it will be of benefit to you in times to come. All music, I repeat ...whether it be birdsong, which is of the spirit, or whether it be the native drums of your jungle area ... all has the power to heal."*

Paul: "It is all vibration..."

~ *"A very good word my friend ... vibrations which show themselves in sound. When you all come to our realms, the music you will hear will be nothing like you have ever experienced in this world. We have healing areas where music is a constant source of healing power. We send lost souls into this music and it envelops them like a soft down, and the spirit that is troubled, absorbs the vibrations of music. That is something I hope one day someone more learned than myself will be able to talk to you about in greater depth."*

George: "Tibetan Buddhist ceremonies have some very strange sounds that one would hardly describe as music, but I suspect those vibrations are very subtle and may well be healing and reaching the spirit...?"

~ *"What you consider to be a strange sound, to another may be as the song of the mistle thrush."*

Sarah: "It is the same with language. Each language sounds different to each person so that must be true of language. The voice is vibration isn't it?"

~ *"Were you to be spoken to in a language known only to, shall we say the Inca tribes, it would be a cacophony of sound would it not? But to the Incas it would be melodious and understandable. You are right. It is the same with music, which is why… I speak lightly now … but some music to young people in these times is most unacceptable to the elderly people. That has gone on generation after generation, but to each one, they can hear wonderful music. Yes, each one accepts their own music and lets it do its will to their spirit. We must all learn tolerance in these things must we not?"*

Sarah: "But you also, when you hear things enough times, you get used to them … and then you begin to like them, just because you have heard them so many times…"

~ *"Think of that not as physical but spiritual. The spirit is rejoicing in that sound because it is bringing joy to the spirit."*

Lilian: "I was just thinking of lots of sounds that we take for granted … like the buzzing of a bee or the purring of a cat, which are all very pleasant…"

~ *"Those sounds, like the birdsong, are musical … therefore come from spirit. I leave you to think on that. May you hear your music through all the days of your life. Thank you for allowing me into your room. It has been a privilege."*

It was a useful instruction and so nicely put. We ourselves felt that *we* were the privileged ones. There is also physical evidence as to the beneficial effects of music and related vibrations … not just anecdotal and not just in relation to humans. Sufficient experiments have been carried out on plants for example, for us to know that they too respond in their growth rate and health[23] when music is played to them.

Sleep is an essential part of our living: Graham had watched a TV programme about sleep. A small number of people find great difficulty in staying awake. Investigation of their difficulty had led to the discovery of a drug released at the brain centre that relates to the condition, and speculation had followed as regards the possibility of a future (drugged) society being able to live without sleep. Being aware of our link with spirit world during sleep state, Graham had queried that speculation with Salumet:

30th June 2003 ~ "Let me say this to you, that as I have told you many times, your scientists are impressed from our world for all and many things in this world. Information gained for the good of mankind ... we have to say scientists in this age ... are not accepting with full love and understanding. I have just said that we cannot interfere in your lives, and this still stands. We can influence, we can uplift, but we cannot interfere. Therefore, if information given to these scientists is abused, then again it brings to you responsibility. But to go further and answer your question, I must say this: that to interfere with the sleep state of an individual cannot be good for that spirit, because as you have rightly said, in the sleep state the spirit frees itself from the human form. I believe you will find that this state of affairs will not happen. The spirit will always find time to leave the body ... to be rejuvenated in our world while sleep state exists."

Graham: "Yes. If that rejuvenation did not happen, then I would imagine that the consequences would be awful..."

~ *"Yes. I will not go into that just at this present time, but it does not leave much to your imagination to consider what the consequences might be..."*

As with so many of the above topics, I think it shows that one cannot formulate new ideas or grasp full understanding unless both the spiritual and the physical sides of the issue are considered together. This way of thinking will surely as time moves on, come to the fore and will be seen more and more as the rational way forward.

Depression as a side effect of prescribed drugs: We had been discussing the effects of spreading good energy in the world. This led to the idea of energy never being static but it would be less active when people are depressed:

21st July 2003 ~ "... But yes, those people who are in the depths of despair and who need the love energy to lift them ... yes, their energy is restricted for that time they are in that darkness..."

George: "There are so many people on prescribed drugs and medication which does have the effect of making them depressed. (This is a physical happening, but it seems to make many people depressed in spirit)..."

~ *"And after all, you cannot separate the spirit and physical while you are in this world. Each has an effect upon the other."*

George: "This artificial way of accidentally making people depressed seems very sad … and something of our times…"

~ *"Yes, but your world finds it all too easy to deal with people in this way. They are not looking within. They are not seeing the whole picture and it is too simple to say that you must take these chemicals, which are not natural to the human being, but sometimes necessary."*

George: "It is our fault that we tend to treat symptoms with chemicals instead of getting down to root cause…"

~ *"Yes, and always there is a reason why the soul is in the state that it is in. I have told you on many, many occasions that each one of you is responsible for this housing of the spirit … this framework that covers the spirit … and always people find this most difficult to accept. But as you well know my dear friends, the power of your thought can change mountains, but this knowledge is not widespread amongst your physicians. It is available to them but they choose for the most part to ignore it. There are those leaders in your medical profession, who are showing that mankind is more than a physical body. It takes time, but slowly we are seeing changes, and so it must be. But you my friends who have knowledge, who have all truth if you wish to seek for it, those of you who feel the love and support of spirit as you enter this meeting place, you have the knowledge to be completely well and whole, as a spiritual being. It is a great responsibility I know, but it is your choice."*

I felt our teacher had chosen his words carefully (as ever). Our imperfections in regard to medication have of course to be accepted. But I think it follows from what has been said, that the more we can sidestep the taking of pills loaded with chemicals for the purpose of alleviating symptoms, the happier we are likely to be. And if only we can 'go within' and employ our power of thinking within spirit, this may get to root cause and could help us quite a lot more.

It is possible to simplify and sum up the overall picture that emerges where health is concerned in the following way:

1. We in various ways create our own diseases … through stress, through ingestion of harmful agents in food, air and water and through our disturbance of nature's balance.

2. Although illness manifests all too clearly in the physical body, this is secondary to what is happening within the spirit/energy bodies that underpin the physical.

3. Where illness is concerned, surgery and chemotherapy are so often treating the physical end product and not the underlying cause.

4. Thought is all-powerful. Erroneous thinking may create disease. On the other hand, adjusted or well-directed thinking may heal.

5. Healing may be achieved through another in various ways, and in this context, heartfelt prayers do indeed get answered.

6. Healing follows when the spirit has been touched.

7. The only complication in this general picture is karma. A lifetime sometimes actually requires the experience of an illness or disability to satisfy the soul's need, and so, that karma may be passed on from a past life situation.

It would probably be true to say that, in a world that has perfect living, there would be no disease … apart from karmic debt disease from what has gone before (before lives on Earth became perfect). And in such a Utopia, lives should ultimately all become free from all karmic debt. I see this as a hypothetical state because, after all, we inhabit a young planet of much learning. This present Earth must therefore be seen as a valuable but imperfect stepping-stone leading onwards within the Grand Design.

10. DIET AND FOOD RESOURCES

Appropriate diet is of course the other important factor where health is concerned. We have questioned our teacher on the subject of diet; also on world food resources. The two topics are of course well connected. Firstly comes a word on resources. The media had been saying much on world population growth and future need to produce more food:

Population growth and world resources: Our discussion had centred on the possibility of a 'population explosion' and Salumet's words on that were most positive:

29th August 1994 ~ "... There will be no explosion of population. I also say to you that resources on your Earth are not limited. They are 'unbound' but not limited..."

Leslie: "That's extremely interesting, but is there not a limitation on the availability of water?"

~ "My friend, as I have said, much in your world has yet to be discovered. There will be ways and means for all of these things to come to you when the time is right ... resources are not limited. The only things that are limited at the moment are your minds ... as to what is available. That is the only limitation placed upon you."

We accepted those words with a muted chuckle or two, whereupon Salumet explained very nicely that he did not wish to 'put us down'. Then he moved on to point out that much of our planet is still uninhabited and that there is a potential for the future in cultivating desert areas. It would be well if we were more forward-looking and less pessimistic in our thinking.

Sense of taste: It was two months later that several further statements on the subjects of food and diet were made, beginning with taste and how it may be such a powerful guiding influence:

31st October 1994 ~ "Let me talk about your sense of taste. This is a sense that all of you have very poor knowledge of. If only, when you are young children, you could be allowed to develop your taste buds naturally ... it would be much more helpful in how you develop your life's pattern.

So often children instinctively know what is good for them when it comes to nourishing the physical body. But so often they are forced to eat what the parent has decided is good for them. You must all be aware of the child who spits forth the food that is offered..."

Leslie: "Yes, we are indeed."

~ *"Not only are they using their sense of taste, but of smell too. All of you instinctively know what is good for you. And unfortunately, it is abused to such a degree that you sometimes become gluttonous in your appetites. That is why the more primitive forms of people on your Earth, and they still exist, have much better ideas of what is good for them. It is how it was developed ... the sense of plant life that became your medicines ... (by) the people who were highly developed in their sense of taste and smell. In primitive times, there was one person within the group who actually tasted new foodstuffs. He, and I say 'he' reservedly, because mostly it was a male. His job was to find out whether new plant life was suitable, either for food or for use as medicine within the group of people. It became necessary for this one to taste on a very gradual basis, each new food. Otherwise how could they have known what was poisonous and what was not? What I am trying to say to you is this: These senses have gradually become lost down the ages. But that does not mean they cannot be found again. It is a matter of discipline in trying to develop those taste buds, which also includes the sense of smell ... they are so closely connected. If only the parents of your children would look and see, and see for themselves what the child is trying to say to them, things would be so much better. The child has an instinctive knowledge that he brings with him in these matters ... Do not be concerned about the child who will not eat. He will eat when he needs to. And he will eat what is necessary for him ... Treat the child as the individual soul that he is. He brings with him the knowledge from within. And although he may not be able to speak in words, to say what he feels, he can tell you from his gestures and his actions... As age progresses onwards, it becomes more difficult for you, because of the habits that you have acquired over a lifetime. But that is not to say you cannot change. And in fact it is good for all of you that you do not allow your minds full reign over what you do... You must always follow that inner voice. It will see you much better off than all of your diets, as you call them. If you are taking in what is instinctively right for you, then you are going a long way towards keeping good health..."*

These simple statements could then, revolutionise the way we eat; also the way we care for young children!

Raw food in diet: There are those who advocate eating raw food and something I had read rather strongly endorsed that view.

George: "I believe Jesus taught something about diet. He advocated the importance of raw food ... this teaching was recovered from the Dead Sea Scrolls. Would you care to comment on that ... the importance of raw food?"

31ˢᵗ October 1994 ~ "Yes, I will comment for you. Let us go back to Jesus the Christ and his teaching. We know he was a Master who walked your Earth... You must remember, at the time when he trod this Earth, much of the food that was eaten, was consumed raw in any case. They did not have your utensils and your ovens, and whatever else you use nowadays. So food was consumed raw very often. But I will say to you this: the reasoning behind that is that when food is eaten raw, it contains its natural elements ... its natural energies... Although you think, when things die, they lose a certain amount ... for a little time they retain that essential energy ... that essential vibration. That is why it is always good to eat food while it is fresh and while it is raw. Once this is cooked, it loses all of those elements, and that is why it is written. Your fruits, your pulses, your nuts... all of those things, they are natural foods and of course need no cooking. But essentially, that is why it has been written thus ... (so) that it retains that vibrational energy that is good for the physical being."

George: "Yes, thank you ... I thought it might relate to the energy..."

~ "Remember always that you are spirit and that you are speaking of spiritual matters ... also, all things have their own energy, as I have said before ... also your foodstuffs always remember. So of course, it is better for you if your foodstuffs remain uncooked. But as we have spoken a little while ago, your palates have become used to food that has been 'tampered with', that has been, how shall I say ... 'molested' in a way. And so your palates have become used to food that is essentially dead. It is also a reason why you sustain so much disease within your physical bodies."

This statement is clearly richly informative. It is known that all living things have energy fields within and about them. (These may be revealed by what is known as Kirlian photography[23], or may be rendered directly visible by hyping our consciousness using a variety of methods). The energy fields exist. There is ample documented scientific proof. The energy fields of fresh salads and vegetables are a part of the foodstuff and a most beneficial part. This fact is not generally realised. It is important that we acknowledge the energy as part of diet. The energy dies away over a few days following harvest, or extremely rapidly on cooking. This is one particular reason why our raw food should be fresh. And it also follows that 'vegetable gardens' should be seen as important in lifestyle, since only they can yield to us *really* fresh produce that is known without any doubt to be fresh. We in fact must acknowledge that cooking removes from food: vitamins, enzymes and the energy field, all of which should be making valuable contribution to health. And perhaps we had not thought of cookery books as guides for the 'molesting' of foodstuffs or indeed that 100% commitment to cooked food leads to an inability to resist disease!

Over-weight problem: It is a well-known fact that some of us have a weight problem. To some it can be a most difficult problem and not at all easy to understand, and there are many diets some of which work while others do not. Our question reflected these facts and the dilemma that results:

31st October 1994 ~ "I would say to those people, if it is not a physical problem … by that I mean, if there is not a complaint of the physical body that prevents them from losing that weight … then I say: look within. Look within to find what the true problem is … what disease there is within that being (spirit) that is causing the quite unnatural forces of making fat within the body."

It was suggested that some people burn food at a faster rate than others:

~ "Of course, people's metabolisms differ. That is a physical fact. I am speaking more on a spiritual level. And of course, that applies to all of you. Here we come back again to thought. Your physical being is just a covering. It should be in fact, a perfect specimen. You have been provided with all that is necessary for physical well-being. You need to look to nature … she provides all that you need. Of course, each of you is different in your make-up, but that is a physical thing. Some of you do have physical problems … for example, if the thyroid gland is not working efficiently, then of course there is a problem. Eliminate the physical problems first. If that does not work for you, then I say: Look within, and use that 'mind-force'. Remember the power of your thoughts. What you see (mentally) is what you express through your physical beings."

The teaching seems to align to: once any physical problem is sorted, it really comes down to a question of mind-over-matter. But firstly the physical being should be in good order.

Vegetarian regime: We had put the direct question: 'Do you believe that people should be vegetarians?' The topic had already been touched upon earlier in relation to compassion:

31ˢᵗ October 1994 ~ "I think we have spoken on this subject … and yes, if you want my very simple answer, then I would say: yes … I do not wish to intrude upon what is your innate sense of what is right. But the question has been asked of me and I have to say: yes, it would be much better for all of you if you could refrain from your meat eating for the reasons that I have given you before (compassion and love for those beings with whom we share this planet). But I know, like everything else, your life patterns are all different, your viewpoints are all different, and you must follow your hearts. But I would say, your physical bodies would be much healthier if you would follow what I have said."

Leslie then made reference to a press report of a manual worker who had lived all his life largely on milk and honey.

~ "Yes, of course, you will say … some people are allergic to these things. Always I must say to you: you are individuals. Follow those instincts that are innate in all of you. You will not do wrong if you do this, because your own inner voice will only tell you of those foodstuffs that will help, and that will nourish and keep healthy, that physical being that all of you carry."

Leslie: "And to achieve that awareness we come back to your previous suggestion, that we all make the effort to devote a little time each day to meditation…"

~ "I don't think I need even put that into words. It should be part of your lives. How else can you reach that which is divine if you are not prepared to give the time to it? It will not come to you (simply). Nothing is easy. You must work and strive for that which is so good. I do not say the pathway for anyone is easy. You can only strive and achieve what is good ultimately, by hardship and by dedication."

On a later occasion, in response to a query from Lilian, the question of vegetarianism was further elaborated:

8ᵗʰ November 1999 ~ "… It would be best to refrain from giving animals for food, but it depends on the purpose or why you would wish to eat their flesh. In itself it is not wrong, but for your spirituality … I will explain this once more. To have true compassion you must have compassion for all things upon this planet. Again we come to free will and your purpose for eating the flesh of an animal. If that purpose is to sustain life, if you (mentally) thank that animal for the flesh it supplies, then you have in part helped yourself to that state of being which helps you to gain more knowledge of the animal kingdom. Do you understand?"

Lilian: "Unfortunately I don't think we remember that enough…"

~ *"I would say to you: in this world of yours today, there is too much suffering when it comes to the farming of animals for food."*

Lilian: "People are beginning to realise that I hope…"

~ *"As the awareness grows, so too does the knowledge that the animals have as much right … if not as much or more … as the human beings who tread this planet. That would apply not only to the larger animals, whether they be domesticated or in the open spaces, but to all forms of life. Without respect for all things, you cannot grow (advance spiritually), and remember too, that when you come back home to this side of life, you will see all that you have thought, all deeds that you have done, and you … and you alone will be responsible for those deeds. So my ultimate answer to you is that it would be best to refrain from the eating of flesh … but again, it depends on the reason why you do this. Again, there is no clear-cut answer. There is in your world much dispute about this subject, but be careful not to judge, because in judging unwisely, you create another problem…"*

It does seem clear at least, that vegetarianism is an expression of love and compassion for *all* animal life forms. Recognition of love and compassion has to be addressed from time to time in our living as part of the soul's progress, and these attributes find expression in a number of ways. If we simply choose to buy free-range eggs that can be seen as a compassionate choice that ensures more hens are kept in good conditions. The expression of love and compassion through vegetarian observance means improved health, and it is not by accident that there are groups of people on the planet that are healthier than others. In Europe, Bulgarians eat little meat compared to many countries and have more centenarians than any other country (1,600 per million population).

Vegetarian regime connects in no small way with our evaluation of world resources, and this physical connection also deserves a mention. In chicken farming, the conversion factor of cereals to edible meat is 4.4:1. Adjusting for water contents of cereal (12%) and of meat (80%), the overall conversion factor to solids in meat lies close to 19:1. In real terms it takes 19 kilos of cereal to produce 1 kilo of meat [24] and clearly many more people can be fed by the 19 kilos of cereal. It follows that even a modest swing away from heavy meat diet will add on handsomely to world food resources and all will be healthier as a result. A further factor is of course that cereals can be shipped around the world and stored without the technical difficulties imposed by refrigeration and the risk of undiscovered spoilage that occurs so much more readily in meat.

Genetically modified crops/foods: A contemporary matter that connects with crops, diet and resources; also ethics, is genetic modification. A question had been put earlier when GM crops first hit the headlines, and our teacher on that occasion had described it as *'an unnecessary step for mankind'*. Now we have progressed some way down that road. Disadvantages have become apparent, supermarkets boycott GM foods, people are taking sides in the issue and I had expressed the view that we are in danger of altering the course of planetary evolution. It now seemed appropriate to ask if Salumet had any further comments. He had. We were firstly reminded of individual free will and the attendant requirement not to judge another. Salumet then continued:

13th October 2003 ~ "… So firstly I would say this to you my dear friends: refrain from judgement, because what you feel to be right or wrong creates within you a tension of conflict … conflict within your own heart. What you must do is to stand to one side and allow these issues, whether you consider them to be grave or not, you must allow each human being their own trail of conscience."

Lilian: "Yes, that is quite a point."

~ *"Since the Earth has existed, mankind has made many errors … shall we call them … but also in that scope of error, ultimately has come some good. You understand? Therefore you must be wary of judging … because when there is conflict, ultimately there will come resolution … so I would suggest that if ever something goes against your grain of thinking, that you go inwards and seek the resolution from within."*

George: "I imagine it is satisfactory to express our thoughts without getting upset…"

~ *"Yes, you must always be true to yourself: that is your pathway, that is your true pathway, but what you must never do is to pass judgement on another because you do not see their thinking, you do not see their emotion, and what you consider to be wrong, in their eyes it may be right. I know it is difficult and with your knowledge you can see that mankind has made many mistakes along the way, but that is not for you to judge. Again, you need to see the wider scheme of life."*

George: "In some places, people are destroying crops that are being grown experimentally by others…"

I think Salumet then deliberately used a sentence of multiple meaning:

~ *"But what you sow you must reap. Remember, whether they feel right or wrong, the time will come when they face their own decisions … when they must face themselves as to whether their judgement was right or wrong. Remember, I have taught you there are two sides … white/ black … love/fear. Always there is the two-sided face to all existence. That is why you must not judge."*

George: "I think destroying crops has to stem from the feeling of fear."

~ *"It is fear. Remember, it is simple … all of existence stems from fear or love. That is why people on Earth are disturbed and create disharmony … it is from an inner fear. Therefore, what you must do is to send them love. Surround them with love and in so doing, their thinking will change, and then you will have created that harmony upon this Earth that will ultimately bring a little more of happiness."*

George: "Yes, you have brought us back to that very important motivation-by-fear-or-love statement again. Do I see a third motivation here … one of greed?" (I had in mind the financial profits to be had from the GM venture):

~ *"You could call it greed. I prefer to say it is but an offspring of fear. All of what I know you would term 'negative emotions' stems from fear."*

George: "Greed would be fear of poverty…"

~ *"Yes, you understand? If you can keep those two thoughts within you … fear and love … you will see the purpose of all of mankind's actions upon this Earth. Does it not become more simple for you to look at it in this way?"*

George: "It has brought us back to that very important balance (love/fear). Thank you!"

Sarah: "Also … going back to the GM crops … you told us Salumet that all new things are influenced from spirit. So, more than likely, the genetic modification … we haven't got it quite right. Somewhere along the line it will be used for something ... but we are not quite using it in the right way..."

~ *"Yes, as in all things that mankind has abused, it has been because of the power of his thought, that has prevented good within the world ... but that is his right because he has been endowed with free will and these things happen. We try to influence and we are mostly successful as your time of evolution goes along ... but as in all things, mankind is still learning. After all, that is why you have agreed to come to this planet ... that you may experience these two opposites of fear and love. That is basically what is happening."*

Lilian: "... I was listening to a discussion the other day on TV, and this farmer was into growing or planting crops or reaping them at a certain time ... maybe when the moon was in a certain position and it was bright in the moonlight. Would that help our crops ... to sow them at a certain time and would it also help the nature spirits?"

~ *"For this my dear friend, thank you for your question. This knowledge has been known in ancient times and almost forgotten."*

Lilian: "And it's now coming back..."

~ *"Always mankind in earlier times revered what they call 'gods of nature', which in effect, is exactly what you have said ... that they planted at particular times and they reaped at particular times, in accordance with what they believed."*

Lilian: "They also spoke of the energy..."

~ *"And of course your earth energy in ancient times was much purer. There was not ... how shall we say ... spoilt earth that mankind has reaped upon your planet. In those ancient times the earth was more pure because mankind had not abused it. Do you understand?"*

George: "I rather fancy that the stone temples, like the Avebury Temple that I think have been in place for perhaps 5,000 years..."

~ *"Longer."*

George: "Longer ... ah yes, I stand corrected. I think that places like that were deliberately built into the countryside because they had that powerful link with the Earth, with nature, with the Earth spirits probably..."

~ *"There are and always have been areas of Earth energy that are stronger than in other places; this is part of the Earth's creation. And, yes you are correct when you say that mankind at those times were much more aware of the Earth energy ... they were much more aware of their own energy than they are today. It is a combination of factors. There is nothing that mankind can do today that has not already been known to him. It is not new knowledge. It is knowledge that is being renewed..."*

The commentary on the GM issue at first seemed a far cry from the earlier stated 'unnecessary step'. But necessary or not, having taken that step, we are of course now well past that initial confrontation. The whole thing must now be resolved from where we stand well past the cross-roads, and resolved in the general terms of our Earthly incarnation if you like. The goalposts are in place and the ball game has begun. The terms/rules are really quite simple:

- Individual free will to be observed.
- We can express views but not sit in judgement of another.
- We can recognise the input of positive and negative emotion.
- Positive input springs from love and the negative from fear.

The matter will resolve, and we should not overlook the principle that love conquers all. And whatever mess we appear to be making of it as we muddle through, it looks like some good application will eventually emerge. I would observe also that the step that we have taken seems a far cry from the Avebury Temple days when nature was respected unconditionally, her elementals acknowledged and planting was in accord with moon phase.

Drinking and smoking: Concerning diet, it may be appropriate to include Salumet's replies here to questions asked about drinking and smoking, beginning with alcohol. I had felt that a question should be asked about this in view of the enormous scale worldwide of the brewing, wines and spirits industries. Drinking features so strongly as part of modern living, and there is also of course the fact that certain religions and organisations have chosen at times to require abstinence.

George: "… A little drinking of alcohol is a very common habit, and especially at the end of the week, people go down to a pub and have a drink and they relax … and for a lot of people I am wondering if that is a good thing and almost a first step towards 'going within' … to relax from the weekly problems. I am not looking at over-indulgence. I am looking at a small amount of alcohol at times to help people relax. I would be glad of any commentary you may have on that…"

30th June 2003 ~ "I feel my dear friend that a little justification may be looked for this time! But what I wish to say to you is that all of mankind has the responsibility for the protection of that housing that you call 'bodies'. Whether or nor we from our world approve or disapprove, does not matter, because as you know, you come to this lifetime with all of those attributes ... to see you forward in this life. You have free will, and mankind uses it wisely or unwisely as you may see it. I would say to you only this: that all of living in this world ... which at times for many is not easy ... whatever can help you go forward with understanding, with peacefulness in your heart, cannot be totally bad. Therefore I say to you, after all, the fruit upon your trees creates what you call 'alcohol' does it not? And who would we be to say that what is produced upon your Earth is wrong? It would not be right to say those words. Therefore, my words to you my dear friend (are) that, those people who need the crutch of alcohol, let it be so ... but I hasten to add that all of these substances are indeed crutches. Why do you need support to go inwards? All you need is but to close your eyes and focus your thinking. That is all that you need."

George: "Yes indeed ... those are nice words. I asked the question because it is such a common indulgence that I am sure it will be of interest to many, many people. Thank you for your words."

~ "Always each one has to take responsibility, and remember that these physical bodies are after all ... that temple for the spirit. Therefore I would say only this to you, that you can only do what you feel is best for each one of you, because each individual has the responsibility when they come to our world, to see more clearly how they have treated that temple called the physical body. Then and only then will the whole picture emerge, and the understanding that comes with it. I hope that is useful to you."

George: "Yes, and thank you for the word 'crutch' because that seems to be a particularly apt word to use."

~ "All of these substances are unnecessary, but as I have said, we cannot interfere in your daily lives and if someone finds benefit from it without harm to others, then so it must be. As long as they never harm another human being, then to them, it seems acceptable, then that is how it must be..."

Clearly then ... to each his own, but the point is carefully made that harm should not come to another as the result of taking a drink. And the body is a temple. It follows I think that respect should be shown for that temple and therefore we should take care not to overdo it. Finally, Salumet twice makes reference to 'other substances' that might equally be seen as crutches. I assume he means drugs that may also be similarly taken for relaxation, and possibly tobacco.

It was six weeks later that the opportunity came to place a question on smoking:

George: "You gave us your thoughts on alcohol recently. A problem area health-wise is smoking and it would be very good to have your thoughts on this. Now I have noticed that many who smoke tobacco heavily ... the smoking is linked to cancer ... but many who smoke heavily do not get cancer, many who smoke heavily do get lung cancer. I suspect that some people are smoking for pleasure, while others are smoking to relieve stress ... and it maybe not so much the smoking itself that causes cancer (which you have said is a disease of the mind) ... so I am wondering if it is more that stress leads to the disease? If you have any words that might clarify this area they would be much appreciated."

18th August 2003 ~ "I am always happy to give a few words ... It is well known that within the physical body ... it houses the spirit. It is for each one of you important that that vessel which you call the body be maintained in good order. I have told you that illness is (the) responsibility of yourselves and, yes, as I said of alcohol I say of cigarettes, that mankind does not need these crutches. But to answer your question simply, I say the difference between two people ... one who will have disease of the body, and what is disease but dis-ease of the mind? That is the all-important factor ... how each individual thinks. That is the key. You may have someone who smokes what you call cigarettes for the lifetime, and may pass from this life what you might call 'healthily' ... it is because that person's mind has retained some degree of positivity. So whether you call it stress that causes the disease ... then yes, you are right because the stress is fear. Again we return to either love or fear."

George: "So what we call in medical terms 'stress' is another word for 'disease of the mind'?"

~ "Yes. I cannot place it before you any more clearly than that. All of your existence depends upon the state of the mind, which as you know, is part of the spirit. That is why it is possible for healing to take place only when the spirit is touched. It does not matter my dear friends what you do to the physical body if the mind is strong, if the mind is pure and if the mind is full of love."

George: "I was just thinking of the American Indians who smoked the pipe of peace ... that would have been a good mindful thing to have done; although it was smoking, there was good purpose behind it..."

~ *"And they always gave thanks to the Great Creator of all life, so their minds were filled with love. That is the difference always. So many times you will see abuse of the physical body but you cannot see the light which shines from within ... you cannot see what is in the mind of another human being unless you are sensitive enough to understand that human being. It is part of your soul's growth that all of life's problems placed before you be dealt with love. It is such a powerful emotion my dear friends that I wish that you would say the word daily and feel the vibration that comes from that word. Remember when I said that words have vibrations, words have colour. Perhaps this time that is something for you to do, that when you go within you use the word love and see what you find from it. Does that make sense to you? Are you happy with that answer my dear friend?"*

George: "Yes, that is most helpful. I am sure that will be of great interest to a lot of people."

In putting the above two questions, I of course had in mind the vastness of industries committed to drinking and smoking and how we indulge giving scarcely a thought. But clearly we should think and take care to keep these 'crutches' within some kind of perspective. Our bodies are vehicles that deserve respect. The real self travels life within the body just as our body travels the road within a car, and we have sufficient respect not to give our car too much of a wrong fuel! Respect for body, respect for diet, respect for crop-growing-conditions, respect for nature ... all are important, all are connected, and our eyes had already been very much opened by our teacher where the workings of nature and the 'elementals' of nature are concerned.

Agriculture and elementals: Salumet has accounted in some detail the growing of crops in relation to Earth's elementals and how their work supports nature, so much so that humanity could not exist without them. Yet many simply dismiss the existence of elementals and their work as delusion. Paul, during one session was saying:

"I think it (belief in elementals) connects to the work that goes on in places like Findhorn, where I think people work with these entities and there is more of a loving relationship, so that vegetables grow bigger..."

28th August 2000 ~ "I would say yes ...that is one aspect of what we will discuss, and to take that example ... (it) is yes indeed a fine one. After all, that race known to you as Indians ... Red Indians ... they communicated with these beings, who enabled their harvests to be rich and plentiful. Yes ... my dear gentleman, you have touched upon one source of what we will discuss. But there are many, many beings who will come together to work together with you, provided ... and again I will say it ... provided they can feel your unconditional love, they will work with you, and for the betterment of your living."

Lilian: "Does it sadden them sometimes, the different things that are done to nature ... the trees (razing), pesticides and so on?"

~ "Of course, and without going into too much detail, which isn't my intention this time, I will tell you that, yes, they have feelings ... perhaps if I could use that word, and they will react to anger and violence and all those negative feelings that humankind is so prone to..."

The work of elementals in relation to what we manage to grow on the planet is not widely accepted at the present time. It is probably true that more of those in past times (and they include the Amerindians and the many originators of traditional fairy tales) have been aware of them and what they do. There is considerable evidence for the existence of elementals, as we shall see shortly. And the words of Salumet will describe how they form a vital part of nature's system, necessary to our planetary survival. It follows that we must develop awareness of them if we are to see ourselves as understanding our own nature-based environment and food production schemes.

11. EARTH'S ELEMENTALS

This subject concerns the very basis, the very structure of nature and our environment. Our teacher has clearly felt how deeply significant it is for us in relation to understanding the planet on which we rely and how we relate to it, and has accordingly devoted several sessions. Perhaps I might begin by putting a question or two to the reader. Looking at our more traditional children's literature, why do you suppose there are so many fairy stories and so many different names for the fairies and little folk? And why do you suppose that the stories about them go back many hundreds, or more correctly thousands of years, all over the world and in so many different languages? Just think on that for one moment.

The German *elfe*, the Danish *ellefolk*, the *alfr* of the Old Norse tales and the *elf* of English folklore are all different names for the same kind of fairy ... and yes, there are indeed different kinds. The elf-names all relate back to a word in Latin meaning 'bright, kindly spirit', and that I believe, is fair description. The word 'fairy' relates to an old French word ... *faerie*. But the roots go back much further than that. The people of Norway and Sweden have long called those fairies that are of the air *white elves* and those living below ground *black elves*. Other names for the ground-dwellers are: *gnomes, leprechauns, pixies, piskies, banshees, brownies, kobolds, dwarves, trolls, trows, goblins, hobgoblins, orcs, imps, sprites* and there is the Norwegian *nisse*. Then there are the *nymphs* of ancient Greece and the *naiads, dryads* and *hamadryads*. Some other fairy names are: *fay, sylph, sylphid, elemental, air spirit* and *peri* ... an Old Persian name. The Soviet countries have *domovays* and *leshys*. Islands in the Pacific Ocean have *meneheunes*. There are many more but the list gives some idea of the assortment of names and how they occur on a global scale.

The German brothers, Jacob and Wilhelm Grimm did a remarkable job in collecting together many of the old tales. And a number of fine books have of course been written. It was in the year 1828 that T Crofton Croker wrote 'Fairy Legends and

Traditions of the South of Ireland'. He describes the little folk as: *'a few inches high, airy, and almost transparent in body; so delicate in their form that a dew-drop, when they chance to dance on it, trembles indeed but never breaks.'* He describes them as having extraordinary beauty and … *'They are invisible to man, particularly in the daytime…'* That description seems to me to be just about right and I suspect that he was one of those quite rare but extant individuals among us who could sense their presence, and especially at dusk. There is just one further comment that I would make before presenting Salumet's teaching on this subject: as energy-beings, their fabric would be akin to that energy envelope that surrounds flowers (that may be observed by us in certain conditions). Their fabric is also similar to our own surrounding aura that, now in the modern world, can be detected and measured using scientific equipment and that can be seen unaided if we are aware and sufficiently attuned. In approximate terms, that is the kind of fabric-of-being that we are talking about. This being so, they are so easily missed and remain unaccounted by most of us. But that could change.

Several were away on holiday and our numbers were down for the meeting of 28th August 2000 and so, our teacher's words were introductory and designed to start us thinking about the fresh topic:

~ *"We have spoken of nature spirits, I know, but how many of you know and understand how many other beings inhabit this planet … in different form from the human being? All comes from spirit. How many people in your world have dismissed the creatures of the earth … the water … the air … the fire? … Are you of the opinion that all these beings are only figments of imagination? Or do you so believe that there is more than what you can visibly see? We are not speaking of spiritual beings, but different elements of beings (or beings of the four different elements). This is something we will discuss fully when the other members are present, because I feel the time is right now, for your understanding to grow, about your own planet. Who here would dismiss the fairies in the woodland? Who here would dismiss all those beings that help your nature? Who here would dismiss the fire elementals? So many beings inhabit this world with you. Would anyone now like to comment please?"*

Paul, who is very much a lover of trees and woodlands, replied:

"I was just thinking, when you're in a place that's quite wild … you feel there's a freshness and an energy around you, more than perhaps when you're in a city … as if the nature spirits are present."

~ "*Yes, so you do not dismiss these creatures?*"

Paul: "No. I think there is never any gap with nothing. Everything is full … full of beings and spirits…"

~ "*Yes. It gladdens my heart to hear you say such words my dear friend. This subject has been much maligned in your world…*"

George: "I think … this is something that people of our past on this planet, have been more aware of … in times when life was less material and less complicated. I think those of our past have had a greater awareness of these spirits of nature…"

~ "*Yes, but it is not only materialism that has closed mankind's eyes, but his fear and his own thinking … that have closed down his visions of these beings, who after all, are part of the whole existence of your planet. They are of importance to all of your existence, because without their help, life for humankind could not continue … I know I am speaking of a subject, as I have said, that has been scorned … that most people will dismiss as delusion. But let me tell you that those people are the deluded ones. So my dear friends, take these thoughts with you this time and think, not only of nature spirits that we have discussed in part, but see what else you can come up with. Think carefully, but more than think … FEEL.*"

Perhaps it is good sometimes, to just stop and think how the idea 'feels' before moving on. The following week, Salumet launched straight into the unequivocal reality of elemental beings:

4th September 2000 ~ "*… There is much within your world that has been discredited … it is time to put right many of these wrongs in your world. Most of you will be aware of what you term, I believe, 'fairy tales'. Every country within your world has its own tales to tell. These have existed for many, many thousands of Earthly years, but always it has been dismissed by most peoples as fanciful imagination. Let me tell you here and now my dear friends, that these tales are based on truth. Thus far it (the truth) has only been available to those who have clear vision (clairvoyance), and even those who believe in an after-life in whatever form, have dismissed these tales as imagination. Let me tell you, that these non-human beings are as much part of this Earthly evolution as you humankind are. Without them you would not evolve in the way that you do. What are these nature spirits, because that is what they are? They do not originate in mankind's thoughts; they are as you yourselves are,* *the creation of the Divine Creator, the great architect of all things. What do you say when you look at the trees and the plants and the flowers? You say do you not: it's God's masterpiece? Of course it is, but these great things, need workers to empower that masterpiece. I know that each one of you is aware of the four elements in your world: the earth, the air, the fire (and) the water. Within these four elements there are many, many others. Now we come to the beings of these elements. They are created within their own elements ... the earth element ... they are created in the earth-ether. That is why they are not visible to the human physical eye. That is why you need clear vision to be aware of them ... when you see those plants, those trees, those flowers, you are not aware of the workings behind them. You say: it is nature. Yes, you are partly correct, but behind what you term nature are those small beings that empower ... and I will address the earth-beings by the common name that you would know them by ... 'gnomes'. Without these small creatures that work tirelessly within your Earth, there would be no life-substance as you know it now. Yes, these little gnomes, as we will call them, have the appearance of tiny, small men. They have been seen and they respond to harmonious conditions and to love. These earth-beings work within the earth on all layers, from the mineral, they work on the jewels of the earth. They work on many aspects of the earth. But perhaps you will not fully understand that, unlike the human form that you possess, these beings are not immortal. They can exist for as long as one thousand of your Earthly years or until such time as their task is completed, and then they will return to a group soul. But they do not have the 'advancement' of the human being ... that is their only (spiritual) difference. Do you wish to say anything at this point?"*

Mary, an American colleague with us at that time, put the question:

"How does this tie in with the American Indians? Did they have a real grasp of spirituality?"

~ *"They most certainly did! They called upon their nature spirits, not only the earth spirits ... they truly believed in the fire spirit, as you may well know. These spirits we will call by the name known to man ... as 'salamander'. These Indians were well versed in spiritual matters. Because of their beliefs and their knowledge they had much success, not only with their animals but (with) their crops. Yes indeed, those ... and even to this day, those who remain true to that kind of living have great success with nature spirits because ... they respond to love and harmonious conditions. You will find them in many, many numbers in open spaces, in hills and woodlands and forests, where mankind has not caused too many harsh conditions for them."*

Lilian: "And would these places feel peaceful because of them?"

~ *"Yes, yes! If you send loving thoughts, create harmonious conditions, it should be possible for anyone who is spiritually aware, to see these creatures or beings or gnomes or salamanders. The beings of the air you would know as 'sylphs', and of course, water beings you would know as 'undines'. I am sure each one of you is aware of these things, but all I wish you to know my dear friends, is that they exist … I know that, especially with the earth spirits, that your geologists would give another explanation for many of the things that occur, but let me tell you my dear friends, they do not have the full picture…"*

Lilian: "They are obviously very much aware of us as humans…"

~ *"No, they are spirits largely unaware of human form. They are more aware of conditions … but they will respond to love and harmonious conditions…"*

Lilian: "So if we admire the flowers, they must be pleased. Will they pick up our thoughts?"

~ *"If it is loving thoughts … yes. What you may not know … and I will speak mostly this time about the earth beings … they almost live in their own way like human beings. They live as groups, deep within the earth. They exist on a type of air, which is different of course from the air that you would breathe, because it is partly physical air and air in the ether, that is of course much finer."*

Graham: "Do they have children in the same way as we do?"

~ *"They are capable of having families but not of course … not in the physiological way that human beings would. You must remember that all nature spirits are controlled by those … we would term angels. But within their own element, yes, they exist as families and groups such as your selves. You are not alone. The evolution of mankind and this planet are not reliant on humankind alone. That is my purpose in speaking to you about non-human beings."*

Lilian: "Could we in any way harm them by different things we do to the Earth?"

~ *"Of course. It would not harm them in the manner that you mean. But in corrupting your planet, then you make their task doubly difficult. By the power of their thought they also can change the way they look. They can become taller or smaller to suit the situation within which they work ... but they cannot enter another element ... they are restricted to the element to which they belong..."*

Mary: "Am I right in thinking that they give out an energy that enhances our own energy?"

~ *"Of course, because by looking after and appreciating the work that they are achieving, then you give back to them. Everything is penetrated ... nothing is isolated. All form is interpenetrated."*

George: "What concerns me sometimes is modern farming and farming methods. This must be seen as a distortion of nature and I imagine this might well cause some problems due to lack of respect and deviations from the natural process..."

~ *"... Of course, anything that causes disharmony within the earth is distressing to earth beings, and such as they are, like human beings, they can be mischievous ... if you come to the earth spirits while distressed, then you will see deterioration within that ground, you will see the dying of the tree, you will see the plant that is diseased..."*

George: "Yes, I think we have seen problems, and this is to be expected and would stem from lack of respect?"

~ *"If only mankind would acknowledge the work that goes on within the earth ... if only mankind could offer thanks to those beings who work so tirelessly and hard for your benefit, then things would be more acceptable to all. Can you see? But because mankind in his ignorance believes that he has total control of the Earth and what he calls nature, he is in fact destroying much of the good work that these beings have created. When next you touch the soil, the plant, the tree, the flower, why not give thanks for all they have done? Think about it my dear friends, that is all I ask of you."*

George: "I have a very special place in my heart for the bee populations. They are so industrious and they are so intricately part of the nature system. They visit so many plants and flowers and pollinate them that the natural order would be totally different without them. I have always thought that there is some sort of guidance behind the work of the bee..."

~ *"Yes, there is guidance. There is guidance in all things. You are correct in that assumption, but of course the bee belongs to the physical ... it is only another aspect of what can be achieved in this world. But the underlying power belongs with the beings of the earth and I would say, even more so, the bee population is guided by the air beings ... the ones we would call sylphs ... and whom people have seen close by to plants and water, and who do appear in smaller human form and with what would appear to the physical eyes as the formation of tiny wings. There are many beings ... but we will speak of the air beings another time. I feel your bafflement my dear friends!"*

Lilian: "We are deep in thought. I am sure when we are in our gardens we shall be thinking of them ... and hopefully see one or two..."

~ *"It is possible when you are spiritually aware. Speak to those people in your world who have evolved spiritually and I am sure they would be only too glad to tell you of all that they are capable of seeing. But again, because of much ridicule and disbelief in your world, they are loath to speak of these things. They are afraid of being called foolish, they are afraid that their fellow man will think of them as not being quite the thing ... I think you would say ... therefore they are hesitant of speaking of their visions."*

Lilian: "... you say, all over the world there are the little people ... in Ireland ... in Cornwall it's the pixies ... and with different names for different places..."

~ *"Yes, all over your world ... every country has its own fairy tales."*

Lilian: "So how did they start?"

~ *"That is what I say to you my dear friends ... they are based on truth. But as in many things, it becomes distorted ... it becomes to mankind in general a figure of fun to be dismissed as fanciful imagination. I am here to tell you my dear friends that there* **are** *such things in existence ... they are part of the great creation that enables this planet and your selves to evolve. You are not alone and never will be alone because there is too much that belongs to the great scheme of life. Humankind has been at fault too long in thinking that he is a superior being ... within the scheme of the great plan of life ... humankind is but one small part of what exists, not only on this planet but on all others. You cannot isolate yourselves from all the other energies and beings that exist on this planet. Let me just finish this time ... when you look into water, do you not see the power (in) that liquid? Can you not feel it? Can you not see it? Can you not understand that beneath that power there lie beings that are constantly at work to create a living force of that water? Water is a very good element for trying to capture the power within..."*

There are many points in the above teaching that might exact particular notice. It is confirmed that elementals have indeed been seen by some of us. Although 'Snow White' is a work of fiction, it is in the light of what Salumet says, based on the **fact** of gnome families living below ground and responding to our love thought. Bees receive guidance in their work, from the fairies. This I find not at all surprising, and I would mention here that the bee's visits to flowers are intricate in the extreme. Christian Sprengel published on insect/flower relationships as early in our history as 1793. A number of works have of course since followed. These include an excellent book with many flower diagrams and explanations by Lord Avebury [25] in the old Macmillan Nature Series of a century past. And more recently there has been Dorothy Hodges' wonderfully illustrated book accounting the variety of pollens carried by the honeybee [26]. Within the intricate and spectacular pattern of connections between bees and plants, I find it not at all difficult to accept that there is a guiding influence.

The following week, our teacher continued with the water elementals:

11th September 2000 ~ "... This time ... shall we discuss the water spirits? ... Sometimes in your history they have been called 'mermaids' ... in the larger expanse of your seas. Why should some see these things, I hear you ask, and not others? Well, because they belong to the ether and (are) not seen with the physical eyes ... unless with those physical eyes, you have momentary clear vision (clairvoyance), and only with clear vision will you see these creatures. The water spirit or undine can be seen on the waves of your seas, can be seen close to water of many kinds. Their task is to work with plants in water and (with) the very motion of water. They are created from the ether of water. They can be seen as shimmering creatures in the smaller places where water abounds, and upon the larger areas of your seas ... there you have the larger undines that are seen by many as the mermaid. Remember I told you ... these spirits have the ability to increase or diminish in size ... sometimes shimmer as mist or fog ... as (with) the earth spirit they are completely captured by loving thoughts ... by spiritual development. Now at this point my dear friends, I would wish you to understand that the water spirits are drawn to the human spirit by the very water element within man. And what is that, I hear you ask? It is the seat of your emotions. Therefore can you see, they would respond to good emotion? Let me try to say this to you: when the waters rage, these water spirits are working to full capacity. They can be stilled ... by the extension of love and the offer to work with them. Those human beings who have clear vision, who have love in their hearts, who have the best intentions for all fellow creatures ... not only their own kind ... they will in their evolvement, have the ability to have clear vision and to view these beautiful creatures ... the water spirits will be found anywhere there is water, even on your marshy grounds.

Now let us speak of another elemental ... the air spirit. Again, it is fashioned from that element to which it belongs. The air spirit is known as sylph. They too can increase or diminish in size, but what is important once more, is their involvement with human spirit ... with mankind. What would you suppose my dear friends, attracts them to humankind? We speak of the air element..."

Lilian: "It's the love again."

~ *"All are attracted to love, but what is it within humankind that would attract the air spirits to you? ...It is the mind ...the mind, the intellect ... they are attracted to many artistic people. But the air spirits or sylphs are indeed shown to you as beautiful creatures. They show themselves to you as tiny people or large people, depending on the setting. They are the ones that you would call 'fairies' ... who would have shimmering wings because they are fashioned from the air (air ether?). These creatures are indeed beautiful and ... attracted to love and beauty.*

And last but not least we have the salamander or the fire spirit ... of all the elementals, the fire spirit can indeed be mischievous ... as indeed the human spirits can be mischievous. Why should there be distinction? But all spirits no matter what element they come from, respond to love and will always work with mankind, providing you give those loving thoughts. I would like to make clear to you my dear friends, that oftentimes mischievous happenings have been accredited to human spirit when it is in fact sometimes the salamander at work ... especially when there is anger or trouble in households and such places. They thrive upon psychic disturbance. They oft times are amused when they hear of human spirit taking the blame for their own mischievous ways. Think on these words. I wish you to know my dear friends that you live in a world that is inhabited by many, not only the human spirit, but those I have mentioned and many, many others, some who have the ability to evolve and some who will never evolve in the way that mankind will.

But what I want you ... to understand: you upon this planet coexist with many others of various shapes and sizes, but all belong to spirit ... each interpenetrates the other ... no one group is isolated. Although mankind in his wisdom ... a word I am not fond of ... considers that he is sole beneficiary of this planet, now is the time in your evolution my dear friends, (and I know that I have approached a subject not easily accepted) but I do feel that you have reached a stage when you can begin to think at least and open up your heart and minds to other beings. Before

*you begin to reach for the planets and the stars, look inwards to your own
planet and those who are here to work for you in your own evolvement
of spirit. Therefore ... open your minds and hearts, give love and thanks
to all those who are around you, and you will find that your lives will
become enriched by the knowledge of these small creatures. Their beauty
is something to behold. And again I hear (from your thoughts?) that the
earth spirits or gnomes ... do not present such a pretty picture. Who are
you to judge? Do you suppose my dear friends, that you seem attractive to
them? So once again my friends, I say to you: do not judge, but accept and
keep an open heart ... if you have any questions my dear friends, now is
the time to ask them..."*

Lilian: "Would they be more aware of us than we are of
them?"

~ *"Only if you extend your love to them, (otherwise) they would be
most unaware of you. Disharmony would bring you to their notice ...
violent feelings. I must say that the air spirits are greatly disturbed by
what goes on in your atmosphere ... the noise within your skies ... but
as (with) all creatures, they adapt well. But of course they thrive more in
conditions of harmony and love."*

Lilian: "So that's where we'd go perhaps ... to visit a beautiful
garden, or woodland, or stream...?"

~ *"If your love and your expectancy is for good, it is possible for your
vision to be clear enough to see them if they so desire. But they, as all
spirit, know only too well those who seek them for the wrong reasons.
Harmony, love and the right reasons will bring you into touch with them,
but it is entirely an individual goal for you to achieve, but it can happen
if you so desire. Again I say to you my dear friends, the power of your
thought is crucial."*

Mark: "Are very young children aware of them?"

~ *"Their awareness would be greater ... because, you see, young
children still retain some memory of spirit. We have touched upon children
in other matters, and their psychic ability. Yes, they would be much more
aware."*

Mark: "And I guess the elementals would be more attracted to
the children because they are more loving and purer..."

*"Yes, their purity of spirit, their light and their love would be the
attraction. That is why their awareness would be so much greater. Yes, you
are correct. Again I say to you my dear friends, if only you could behave as
small children, then your awareness would be greater also."*

Sarah next expressed concern about the mischievous side to the salamanders and Salumet gave some further clarification about that:

~ *"... I have said that they can be mischievous but the majority of their working time is for good ... fire is as necessary as water, air and earth. After all, when there has been fire, what happens? There is new beginning, new life ... so do not dismiss fire as some kind of hazard. It has its place in the plan of life ... you understand?"*

Sarah: "When you said, if we gave out thoughts to them ... if there was a raging fire and we gave our thoughts to the salamanders ... could we help to reduce the flames ... or would that be interfering?"

~ *"Good thoughts are always helpful but the salamanders are governed by angelic beings ... they have the control over the salamanders. Therefore I would suggest that if you were disturbed by any destruction ... give thoughts to those angelic beings who would take control."*

There was some further discussion on the more fugitive nature of the fire elementals. Then Salumet moved on to say:

~ *"What I wish for you my dear friends, is that you find the connection between yourselves and all of these spirits... that they do not stand alone and neither does the human spirit ... that is why it should be imperative for you to open your eyes to these other beings ... to give them your love and understanding and help whenever you can. Give thanks for the work that they tirelessly do for your evolution. I know that mankind has developed an intellect that enables him to praise himself ... to think that he stands alone. That is not true, my dear friends ... that is not true."*

George: "Modern mankind has tended to think of fire, not as an element, but more as a process of oxidation and perhaps we could think of the salamanders as 'masters of oxidation'?"

~ *"Yes, I did say last time that your scientists and your, shall we say, more developed mentally clever, would always give you explanations for all that I have said, but I did (also) tell you, they do not know or understand, or accept the full picture."*

George: "I think the truly clever people are clever enough to realise just how much they don't know."

~ *"Yes, to keep an open heart and mind, that is the intelligent person."*

Sarah then asked for some further clarification in regard to elementals returning to group spirit:

~ *"… You know that spirit has always been and always will be. There can be no altering that statement. But there are some degrees of spirit (such) that it is not necessary for them to evolve. Those whom I have mentioned will work perhaps for a thousand years, having (then) completed their task. Humankind has much to evolve for. It is a much longer process, but the day will come as I have told you, when the human (physical) form will disintegrate and you will become but thought form. It is only that these elemental beings have a much smaller task to complete … and they will (then) join their group spirit to be blended with that greater mind … those who have succeeded in their task will return to spirit in the form that they know best … so they immerse themselves in a group spirit. This is a topic much maligned … and we see all too often so many people who think of those with clear vision as … crazy … crazy? But that is not true … what is important is that the task that is undertaken on this planet is done and dealt with and spirit can return."*

George: "I think you inferred that the elementals of this planet are just a tiny part of the general cosmic pattern…"

~ *"Yes of course, as you also are. Mankind needs to begin to view himself as part of the planet, not as the keeper of the planet. This is what you must try to understand. I am afraid that mankind's intellect has interfered in his spiritual nature for far too long … if you are to understand all that goes on within this planet, then you need to be simplistic in your outlook."*

Paul: "I remember once we had a lot of moles in the garden and we put out the thought to them suggesting there was another place they could go to … a field nearby. We tried to do it with love … a loving thought … and it seemed to work. Would that have involved any of the elementals?"

~ *"… The earth spirit would have been helping because of the love thought … yes, of course."*

Paul: "So the gnomes would have helped out…"

~ *"If the thought was given in love and for the benefit of the small creature, then of course you are being helped by the earth spirits. It is not only the power of your own thought in these instances … you are never alone…"*

The teaching on elementals left us much to think about. It was six weeks later that I was able to put a further question concerning our chemical usage in gardening:

George: "… Probably the most widespread fault we have is using chemicals to get rid of slugs. These seem to present a great problem. It may be that there is a problem because we have upset the balance of nature. It seems very hard on the slug to treat it with chemicals. Is this a problem to the elemental folk? Are we right to see this as a spiritual problem?"

~ *"… Yes, mankind has interfered in all areas of what you term 'nature'. But mankind is beginning to realise that it is far better to return to more natural ways. Yes, the elementals, as you have said, would find the use of chemicals abhorrent. You will find beauty in nature, in areas where there are not chemicals used … where mankind has had little to do with it. Therefore … mountains, woodlands (and) streams are much more beautiful places and where you are much more likely to encounter the elementals. So I would say to you my dear friend, that until mankind realises … because after all, this planet has been provided with … how can I put it to you? … Any problems that arise also have a cure, not only with mankind but (also) with nature. It takes but a little thought on the part of the human being, it takes much prayer and thought for those who govern your countries, to understand the seriousness of all that they allow to happen. That is why it is imperative my dear friends, that each one of you in your quest for knowledge and truth, seeks thoughts for all of this planet, in order that only good emerges."*

George: "And as you say, the growing awareness is so very important…"

~ *"Spiritual awareness is indeed what is necessary for all to be turned completely around … for man to understand his place in the scheme of life in order that harmony returns, not only to mankind, but to all natural things."*

I feel that the final observation … that spiritual awareness is needed in order that our concept of nature is turned completely around … sums up the various statements quite well. Many thoughts and details will occur on reflection. When Jesus stilled the tempestuous waters, he no doubt extended love to do that. The practical consideration of a further shift in the direction of organic farming (that a few fortunate countries still have), and towards organic gardening would seem logical. As to the worldwide fairy tales … well, they really did require some kind of explanation! So often as the picture unfolds we find that myth and legend have their origins in a distant reality. And if we think of elementals as 'working away like there is no tomorrow', that would not be quite right. They work so there will indeed be a tomorrow! Their place in the system is vital. Darwinism and

Mendelism describe processes in nature and do not account cause or the force that propels nature. We have to recognise that our sciences, although useful and meaningful, are merely descriptive of what is, without offering any explanation as to why or by what impulse. Recognition that our sciences are built around a 'non-causal' framework should perhaps be a part of rising awareness.

Given the general description of elementals, it is not surprising that the majority of humans today will not have seen them. They will however, have been seen by some people, and perhaps I should answer the question that may be on your mind. Yes, I can say that some members of the Kingsclere group have on occasions seen the little folk clairvoyantly.

Perhaps we might also observe that prior to the advent of space-time, our science had its dalliance with 'ether theory'. And in any event, it is clear to modern scientific reason that the space of the cosmos cannot now be dismissed as nothing as it was a few decades ago. It is something that exists and is necessary for calculations in quantum mechanics and to explain observed properties of black holes. So the ether-scientists of yesteryear might well have been onto something. The enigmatic ether was thought by them to occupy all space and to penetrate all substance. Now I see that as an interesting proposition, because Salumet considers that there are four ethers, each permeating one of the four natural Earthly elements: earth, air, fire and water. Since the atoms and molecules have different status within each of these four elements, it may well be that what we might call 'the ether' also has a difference within each of the elements. And that brings us to the four domains of the ether-beings. One might argue therefore that the idea of four different Earthly ethers is by no means outrageous when viewed as a purely scientific hypothesis.

As regards ancient times when deeper feelings were felt by many, it is not surprising that such wonderful places as the 'Avebury Temple' in Wiltshire, were actually built into the landscape. Its close association with nature and with the ley line energy of the landscape becomes obvious on inspection, and the energy of that place can be felt.

12. ANCIENT SITE GUARDIANS
...EARTH PROTECTORS

There are just so many different beings that participate in and who form a vital part of, life on Earth. There are the angels, the earth elementals, the air elementals, the fire elementals and the water elementals. There is also another class of being that we might mention at this point, known to a few as 'ancient site guardians' and to some as 'Earth protectors'. I had twice come across mention of these beings from reading of the work of Paul Bura [27] and he and I have since had interesting correspondence. It was during the evening of 4th March 2003 that I mentioned Paul and his work to Salumet:

"… I would describe him as an author and a powerful psychic, and he is able to channel the ancient site guardians … and some of these guardians have had Earth life, some have had life elsewhere. I don't think we have mentioned ancient site guardians. I am talking of ancient sites that are spiritual places such as the stone circles. I was wondering if you could say anything about the guardians. There is one in particular named Joeb whom he channels … are you able to confirm that this is possible?"

~ *"There are many forms of communication. There are many who communicate through many channels. Let me say this to you my friend: there are still within your Earth many who protect; this has always been and always will be while the planet travels through its evolution."*

George: "… I think they look after the ley line energies as part of their work?"

~ *"Yes, I can confirm that for you. This does happen. This is not something that I have approached with you, because we have spoken only briefly about angels, elementals and I would say that these 'protectors' are people of different* …(At this point Salumet paused and breathing became much deeper. It was unexpected. On resuming, the voice was much stronger and deeper. It was a very substantial energy change.) **They have not come under my teaching because their purposes are clear … for channelling through others. But I say to you my dear friends: the protection and power they bring** *to those who channel is indeed very strong.* (There was a further pause, then Salumet's voice returned to normal.) *I can tell you my dear friend that there will come to this gentleman another of the Earth protectors, not as yet known to him. You can inform him but he will soon become aware."*

George:"One thing I picked up is that ... the ley line energies are in the process at this present time of being upgraded and one of the protectors' duties is to watch over the upgrading ... and I think that is one of the energies used in crop circle formation, that we talked about..."

~ *"It is also the energy used for travel for other planet(ary) forms. Remember, energy comes from one source but in many shapes and forms. Earth's protectors are a group who are dedicated to the survival and evolution of these energy lines. Always there have been areas on this planet where energy is much (more) strongly felt by others. It is the unseen work that continues. It has continued from the time when this Earth was created, and it will continue until the end of this Earth's time, which of course ... you understand ... there is a time and an end for many things. But the Earth protectors are not widely known about and it is not something that teachers speak openly about, because too many people ridicule these things. It (the knowledge), is only given to those people who are ready to accept ... but I am happy to confirm for you that, of course, there are protectors."*

George: "That's very good to have that confirmed. Thank you very much. I am sure that Paul will be happy to know that another will contact him."

~ *"His work is not yet finished. I feel that this time I have spoken enough. I hope my dear friends that you can feel the energy that is here with you. I hope that each of you has been aware that, not only my presence, but that of another has been quite significant in these past minutes."*

We were all most certainly aware of the extra energy that had been with us this time ... and this was one of those occasions when it had caused my hearing aid to whistle! Needless to say, as soon as we had the transcript, a copy was sent to Paul, who said he indeed had a feeling there was more for him to do.

It had been a wonderful episode to conclude what had already been an interesting evening, and of course it confirmed the information I already had on the guardians. I understand from Paul that Joeb is of this planet, his most recent Earth life having been as a Burmese Buddhist priest. In an earlier incarnation, he had worked within the priesthood linked to a stone circle near Sudbury in Suffolk. Joeb retains knowledge of the ritual of the henge and reverence to the Earth Mother. I note that Joeb thinks of humans as 'Earth Addicts', which may be fair comment! (I would think he refers with some degree of humour to our apparent addiction to just the material part of our existence … that which we can see and feel). Paul has also channelled information from another known as Jeuz who is not originally of this planet, but from Sirius, the Dog Star.

13. SOME SIGNIFICANT EARTHLY EVENTS

The events of our living of course have spiritual as well as physical connection. We might, as Joeb considers, become 'addicted' to the one or the other, but it is as well that we continue to strive to take account of both. The questions on Earthly events take us firstly to the end of the cretaceous period some 65 million years ago:

Dinosaur extinction: I think, as Leslie placed the question, he was a little puzzled that people should still be talking about it:

"… Many people here are still discussing the reason for the disappearance, apparently in a short space of time, of the dinosaurs. Are you able to give any explanation as to what calamity caused that?"

29ᵗʰ August 1994 ~ "Yes, I think I can … at the time the dinosaurs roamed your Earth … (then as if reflecting with much depth of feeling) … they were magnificent creatures, powerful, strong, with everything there to sustain them. Their food, the Earth all around them made them strong. At that time there was … how shall I say … an explosion from space that hit your Earth at the time, destroying mostly the food that these animals survived on. It in fact changed the structure of the whole of the Earth, which meant … they could not survive without their foodstuff … and they lived in lush, lush green lands. With the explosion … so too came climatic changes. From hot, it became much, much colder. So gradually these great animals could not (continue to) exist. It was a natural happening that was meant to be. And so too, down the ages, each species has reigned supreme. I may say too, at the moment it is mankind, but he too is on a destructive course…"

Leslie: "Yes…"

~ "But the reason behind the destruction of all the animals was a geological one … an atmospheric one … a loss of food and other animals that helped to sustain these great, great dinosaurs. They roamed the Earth for a great, great time."

Leslie: "Yes they did. Well, thank you very much for that answer. It's most interesting because our scientists had developed a theory that it was a climatic change … an ice age … that destroyed them. But you've given further information. Thank you."

~ *"It was climatic but also a little more than that."*

A question that seemed to connect came up six years on:

Paul: "I have a question about animals that become extinct. Is it possible for any to be recreated?"

20th November 2000 ~ "No. You cannot change the scheme of life. If animals have become extinct upon this planet, there has been a good reason for it. We might (sometimes) say it has been the interference of mankind, but there is a plan for all of living and if these animals have become extinct, then there is not reason for them to return. This is a difficult subject for you to understand I believe, because we know that mankind has interfered so much within your world. But what you must try to understand is that these things would not occur if the plan wasn't perfect … in a way it is allowing it to happen. Can you understand this my dear friend? It is difficult I know, but what would be the purpose of allowing an animal to return to this world once all signs of life of it have been extinguished?"

Paul: "I think I understand … it is having faith in the perfect plan…"

~ *"Perfect plan … and after all, it is part of this world's evolution. Remember too that this planet has evolution and the life structure of it cannot be altered. Man can interfere, man can change, but it cannot change the overall plan of evolution…"*

I think it follows that whilst the film 'Jurassic Park' offers splendid entertainment and is a fine presentation of those wonderful dinosaurs, they have to be seen as a species that can never actually be recreated. Such an idea is fictional fantasy.

Noah's Ark: Having just read David Fasold's book[28] on what may be seen as one of the greatest archaeological finds of the 20th century, I questioned Salumet on the matter and was pleased to receive confirmation of the ark's authenticity:

10th October 1994 ~ "At the time you are speaking of, there was indeed a … how shall I say … 'vessel' made. But if you are speaking of the story as a whole, then no … it is rather a figment of someone's imagination. The story comes from an older … how shall I say … story if you like, although there is an element of truth. There was indeed a vessel at that time that was for all intent and purposes called 'Noah's Ark'. There has been found this vessel … I believe the one you are speaking of, which has been dated back to those times. When Jesus the Christ was alive, many stories circulated. When these things were rewritten many centuries afterwards ... how will I say ... they were elaborated. Much was added and much was left out. So if you want to believe the story as a whole, then I say to you that vessel is the one that is intended to be. But the whole story of Noah's Ark, gathering the animals two-by-two, is rather a 'fairy tale'. But yes, there was a vessel around at the time, but it comes from an older version of another story."

George: "Yes, I think there was another account of that story, written in the Epic of Gilgamesh..."

~ *"Yes, it goes back much. Let me say to you: your Christian Bible holds many things that have been put together, sections from here, there and everywhere. It made very good reading, I think. But as far as truth goes, you cannot accept it all. But indeed, the vessel you speak of is a genuine one."*

Jesus the Christ: Perhaps it is the start of the Christian era that is best seen as the 'event'. But first and foremost, we think of he who initiated that beginning. It was in response to questioning by Leslie that our teacher spoke on the true nature of Jesus. His view is of course, as seen from spirit (and not as conjectured from our reading and physical thinking):

*18th July 1994 ~ "... When Jesus walked your Earth, he was only one more incarnation of many who taught before. He was indeed not **the** Son of God. He was **a** Son of God. Let me say: I have difficulty with the word 'God'. 'Creative Force' / 'Universal Consciousness' ... are much better words. But Jesus **did** walk the Earth. He was a Master who came to teach the Earth people at that time. His gifts were great and these he tried to display. But he was not **the** Son of God. Never did he use those words. I'm afraid the words came from the people who wrote the words ... Much has been done that is wrong in (regard to) the teaching of those days ... He was denied what he came to do, to a certain extent. But no, he was a humble Master and still is ... much of what he taught has been denied. Throughout the ages we have had many Masters tread this Earth plane to teach exactly the same lessons ... that Jesus the Christ came to teach."*

Leslie: "Yes, thank you ... one point if I may: the resurrection was not a physical resurrection. I believe it was a materialisation of the etheric body, to become visible to mankind..."

~ *"Yes, why is there so much doubt here?"*

Leslie: "I don't know. It's pitiful."

~ "It was a natural happening. He did that. He told his followers that he would do it. It still happens today, and still it is denied … we find it difficult, that after all these many years, we are still trying to teach the same things."

It is a simple concise statement that endorses the fact that Jesus walked the Earth as the great Master and teacher that he was … and is. And following the crucifixion he materialised to be seen as the gospels describe.

Late in the following year, Leslie asked about Jesus walking on the water. That question followed one about the parting of the Red Sea waters during the flight out of Egypt. The answers to both questions follow:

27th November 1995 ~ "I will speak upon this matter. Of course, the waters did not part physically. No, it was written symbolically by those people who put pen to paper … it meant only that good always will come to the fore … that is the true meaning of the story. It is symbolic only, it has nothing to do with the power of the thought…"

There was some further exchange and Salumet reiterated that it was a symbolic story only.

Leslie: "Yes, and will I be right in presuming that the power of thought **was** operative when Jesus walked upon the waters?"

~ "Now we are speaking on a different matter. We now are speaking about a Master who was capable of doing such a thing."

Leslie: "Yes I thought perhaps that was so."

~ "Yes, now we are onto different matters and I can tell you that this did indeed happen."

Leslie: "Yes. I've always been able to accept that."

~ "You must remember that this man, although he walked upon the Earth, he was indeed a Master, come to help in those troubled times. Do not doubt that he did exist. Do not doubt what you call 'miracles' of those times … that most of it did take place … but not as it was written. A lot of it is symbolic. You have to interpret that book as such. You have to look at it from the viewpoint of spirit happenings and not Earthly ones."

It is sometimes difficult for us to see spiritually as opposed to physically, but this small section confirms without any doubt that Jesus was on the Earth at that time, there were miracles, he materialised after physical death and he indeed walked on the water. What a great privilege it is to actually receive from spirit the confirmation of these facts!

The Visions of Mary at Fatima ... 1917: This was a spectacular series of visions that occurred in our more recent past. The final event of the series also included manifestations seen by many who had gathered. The crowd was estimated to be 50,000. The purpose of the manifestations was to help people believe, and there were also predictions given concerning the ending of World War I and the beginning of World War II. Fatima and other visions are reported more fully elsewhere [3, 29]. The subject of our evening with Salumet had been 'the touching of the spirit', and I had made the link to Fatima, suggesting that this was a time when the spirit of many had been touched:

30ᵗʰ April 2001 ~ "Yes, that was the reason for the visitation ... that it was needed at that time to make people understand what was happening."

George: "It seems to have been a wonderful demonstration and it is a pity that mankind didn't heed the message that was delivered then, more strongly. But on reading about it, the spirit certainly seems to have been touched ... the spirit of many."

~ "The spirit of many was touched indeed my dear friend, but not enough. It was indeed a time of great darkness upon your planet, but I believe you would agree that, since then, that much has happened ... that mankind has opened up spiritually and emotionally and mankind in this time, is beginning to realise what his plan upon this planet is."

George: "And even then, at that time, Mary indicates that Russia move away from atheist communism ... which has since happened. It seems to have been a very important message for the last century..."

~ "There is upliftment, there is knowledge given to many in this world ... but it is a slow process. You must remember that time, as you know it, means little to us in our world. As we see it, much progress is being made. Mankind will not destroy himself, because at last truth is becoming known."

With a world war still in progress and the reasons for another already being set in place, it was indeed a time of great darkness for this planet. But how cheering it is to be reassured that we have emerged from that shadow and are making good progress! And of course, Mary's appearances in vision and the manifestations of that time, that today we can only read about, are all acknowledged for us as undeniable fact.

Saint Stephen Returns: Saint Stephen the Christian martyr was murdered by stoning as accounted in the scriptures [30] probably in the year AD 34 and, as he himself confirms, shortly before what would have been his 22nd birthday. During the 1970s he communicated with a spiritual group in New Zealand who were privileged to have question-and-answer sessions with him and who received wonderful teachings, in much the same way that the Kingsclere Group now receive. Stephen taught in the manner of an advanced soul. All is presented in extraordinary detail complete with quoted dialogue in a book by Michael Cocks [31]. I drew Salumet's attention to this and sought his comments. His reply came in a slightly roundabout way and I feel he has taken the opportunity to include a teaching for us within his answer.

George: "... I have been aware recently of links with other people, several others. One in fact, in New Zealand, is a priest ... who was part of a group in the 70s, such as our selves, and the one who came through to that group was St Stephen, the first Christian martyr of the 1st century. And you have told us that like attracts like, and it seems to me that St Stephen coming through to that very much Anglican church-orientated group is very appropriate. Would you wish to comment on that or say anything about that group in New Zealand? I would add that the person I have been in touch with has written a book about the channelling that happened within that group."

20th January 2003 ~ "Yes. I thank you for your question. I have told you my dear friends, in the past, that when the soul/spirit reincarnates into any lifetime ... they reincarnate in the knowledge of who and where they will be. But you know that spirit has always been ... the soul has always existed. Do you remember my words when I explained ... and I believe you my dear friend were the questioner about: did Jesus still walk the Earth, did the Holy Mother (still) come to this Earth? My reply to you then was that the soul has many aspects. This to you all must be the source of all your knowledge ... that there are many aspects to the soul that reincarnates into physical form ... therefore the connection with St Stephen and the friend that you have mentioned is not new. All who reincarnate, reincarnate for a purpose and of course they will return to the physical form to those places, to those people, where their purpose of life is most needed for the purpose of the soul ... not because of any name, not because of any denomination, but for the growth of the soul. So, if you keep this in mind, it will perhaps be a little clearer for you to understand.

*Remember there are many, many aspects to the soul and remember ...
it is not who or where that individual life goes ... but the reason behind
the coming to this physical life. May I say something to you my dear
friends whilst we are speaking ... if you are to achieve all that you have
to in physical garb, then the understanding of the being has to be the
understanding of who this individual is at this point in time. You have to
accept that any one being is not alone, but is but a part of a whole ... a
whole being whilst on this Earth. Do you understand? No man stands
alone. As each one of you within this group is connected, we call you a
group of light ... a spiritual group, because there has in past times been
many connections with you, but each individual here is connected to the
rest of this Earthly planet. You need to see the fuller picture."*

George: "All humanity is connected, and I imagine some
connections are stronger or more to the fore than others..."

~ *"Therefore in answer to your question my dear friend, if your friend
in the far-off country has connection with one from our world called St
Stephen, so too have many others that capability because of this one
connection. But I understand your question. Of course like is attracted to
like ... this is a fundamental issue when first you begin to recognise that
you are more than the physical being. Yes, like will be attracted to like, but
so too are the opposites attracted to you. Have you thought along those
lines? Why should this be? Because all things, all life is connected. We are
moving into deeper matters, but I would like you to think about it just
a little."*

George: "Can I mention ... Michael in New Zealand ... he
found that he has the ability to type a question on a piece of
paper and a book reference will then come into his mind, and he
will go along to the library, look up the book reference, and he
will find that it is the answer to the question that he typed. They
got into the way of thinking of this as 'the library angel'! Would
you care to comment on that?"

~ *"Yes ... that is good and humorous I feel. But let me say this to you
my dear friend: that is not something that is unique. You could be capable
of this also ... already I feel your doubts..."*

George: "It is a matter of listening within ... is that correct?"

~ *"Yes, this is the lesson that I try to teach all of you ... that you
are to go within if you are to find the self, and only by going within
can you allow those others to come to you to influence and to help you.
It is because he is an open channel ... a very good open channel ...
but it is not something that only he is capable of. It takes time, it takes*

dedication and it takes listening to those who come to you, to give you that inspiration which you seek. You will find my dear friend that there will be many more connections around the world for you to make. You will find as time continues that the evidence each is given will eventually be collated together, and each little bit will come forth as truth ... will come forth as knowledge that has always existed ... will come forth as evidential knowledge to each one in connection. All of these happenings will take place because your world, this Earth planet, no longer will be static ... it must grow in spiritual knowledge. There are many avenues through which this knowledge will come. When first I came to you, did I not say that much would come from far places? This, my dear friend is what you are now embarking upon."

We both agreed that there would be much spiritual joy in the journey indicated. The teaching is valuable in the way several points are reiterated ... how the soul's progress is all-important ... the connectedness that extends throughout ... how the mission to Earth progresses ... a gentle reminder of how important it is to go within and find the inner being ... the continuation of the work of that soul of which St Stephen remains an aspect ... and once again, the recognition of a fragment of humour. We are encouraged, as we have been from time to time, to look to the fuller picture of existence. And of course it is our pleasure to know of the group in New Zealand who have received from spirit, as we ourselves are receiving.

I can further report that a seminar was held in New Zealand on 15th May 2004 concerning 'The Stephen Experience' with the participation of Rev Michael Cocks; reported in the summer issue of *Network*[32] by Leo Hobbis. Included in the points made and reported are: Cherished beliefs are challenged ... Many beliefs can't be explained by science – they lie in a different domain ... The apparent intervention of Jesus during conversations with Stephen, for example concerning incorrect doctrine, was awe-inspiring for Michael ... The Stephen experience was valid for that group. Others must make their own journey. And the report ends: 'There are more things in heaven and earth...'

The Death of Spencer Perceval: I dare say there are not many today who will know that Spencer Perceval was a British Prime Minister or that he was assassinated in the lobby of the House of Commons. It is on record that the night before, he had a dream that he recounted to family and friends. In the dream, a man wearing a dark green coat with brass buttons confronted him pointing a pistol and all suddenly went black. Next day, 11th May 1812 he was shot through the heart exactly as dreamt ... by a man with dark green coat and brass buttons. I had queried with our teacher if the dream might have been in the nature of a warning from the higher self of an approaching possible accident:

24th June 1996 ~ "There are no accidents dear friend. I do not like the term 'accident'. If your time has come, then nothing will alter that. Can you see?"

George: "Yes, I see. Would there be a reason for dreaming the end before it happens?"

*~ "We have spoken briefly I believe. If all has always been and always will be, then past/present/future coexist. I know this is a difficult topic also, but how can you see what is to happen unless it is (already) written there? You see you cannot foresee what has not happened. We go into deep matters here when we go into past/present/future. All coexist ... he foresaw the event because it was **bound to happen,** if I could put it that way. You understand. So therefore you cannot term it 'accident'."*

The point is well made that our departure times from this life are fixed. We may at times foresee in dream-state, as did Perceval, as also did Abraham Lincoln, as also have many others. But it seems to be a preview and not an attempt to divert. The point about the 'overall' fixed nature of life path, in relation to past/present/future that are coincident in spirit realm, has been made elsewhere in the teachings. It is a universal truth.

The execution of Mary Queen of Scots: As has been explained earlier, the soul in spirit has within itself past lives of those who were once upon this Earth. Those lives form part of soul, and yet they can still be reached, and a Master such as Salumet has the ability to bring forth any one past life to a group such as the Kingsclere group, to speak through a medium. There would be purpose, of course ... a sufficient reason for doing so. On the evening of 20th November 1995, Salumet brought Mary Stewart to us and she spoke through Eileen. Needless to say, it was a wonderful, wonderful occasion. She came to us with the memory and carried with her much of the emotion of that traumatic last day. (Although such emotion will have long since departed from the spirit, it seems that its revival is natural on returning to Earth in this way.) The excerpts that follow are from the transcript of that evening:

~ *"I want to say to you, that my last day upon this Earth is still very vivid in my memory, as I return to you. It was a beautiful bright February day. The sun shone, and to all intent and purpose, you could feel that spring was around the corner ... I awoke that morning after a very sleepless night; because you see, there was much noise throughout the previous night. I was ready to meet ... how you would have termed then ... my Maker. I truly believed myself, that I was completely composed. I promised not to shed a tear ... that I had to be strong for those who had cared for me in those long dark days ... dear Jane and Elizabeth ... to them I owed so much in those last dark days. I will have to ask you to be patient, because memory torments me, even now..."*

Leslie said quietly: "Yes, we do understand."

There was some emotion concerning her jailor Sir Amyas Paulet whom I understand was a harsh man. Then Mary continued:

~ *"...I am sorry to display these emotions. I did not feel I would ... but you have to realise that on returning ... how painful these memories become."*

Leslie: "I can quite understand. They must be a burden to you."

~ *"What I want to say is this: much has been written about the words I uttered on my last breath. It is said that dear Jane and Elizabeth thought I uttered the words: 'Sweet Jesus'. I tell you now, that I had been praying, as my head lowered to the cushion ... I prayed earnestly to be taken quickly ... As it struck my neck ... I was saying the words: 'Je suis! Je suis!' ... 'I am! I am!' ... And so, I left behind the Earth plane torment, which had me jailed for so long. No one knows ... no one knows ... that my dear sweet little dog was gathered amongst my underskirts. How could they know? How could they know?"*

Leslie: "Of course not."

~ *"And this is something else I want you to know ... that only those close to me would have known ... that my dear animal was known to me as 'Piers' ... dear sweet animal. I know it has been written, that when I was disrobed ... that those who watched ... and can you ... can you ... imagine the humiliation, to be disrobed in front of so many? I was dressed intentionally ... intentionally I must say ... in red undergarment ... not ... not to hide the blood as it has been written ... but, being a devout Catholic, I wore the colour of the blood of Christ."*

Leslie: "Yes, I understand."

~ *"So I was preparing myself to meet our Saviour ... but on going there, I was shocked at my own stifled deep dislike and hatred of some of those who treated me so badly. I have to tell you also that whatever has been written about (Queen) Elizabeth ... she really did not move to sign my life away ... this has to be made clear to you. She also was unaware of the treachery of Paulet, who was indeed an evil man."*

Mary went on to say more and a fuller account together with historic reference has been reported elsewhere[3]. She affirmed the Earthly year as 1587 and told us that she has since lived a further Earth life. Before departing, Mary added:

~ *"... I have to be honest and say that truly, my heart belonged in France."*

Leslie: "In France?"

~ *"Yes. But it matters not. These facts are well dispatched. I hope that all of you in this time find your world religions much more humble ... that people no longer suffer for their religious beliefs. Because, truly, that is why I was put to death."*

Mary, born of a French mother, Mary of Guise, spent her happiest years, from age six to nineteen in France with the French court exceedingly well disposed towards her. It is plain to see why her heart belonged to France. Equally, it is appropriate that her departing words should be in French. During the difficult years of captivity 'dear Jane and Elizabeth' were Jane Kennedy and Elizabeth Curle who were closest to her and shared her bedchamber. Mary had had to plead for their presence in the hall of execution and had vouched for their good conduct. The noises that disturbed that last night's sleep would have been from the tramping of the guard and from the hammering in the great hall where the execution platform was being constructed. It is clear that the red undergarment was not lightly chosen, the choice springing from devout religious thought. I would also comment that Mary's words to us were delivered with such emotion ... tremor ... passion ... as I have never before heard issue from Eileen.

The visit was a clear demonstration of how things are in spirit and supported the teaching already received. It left me also with the feeling that a corner of history had just been re-written, by Mary herself. Historians do their best but cannot possibly always get the details completely right. And when there is some measure of error in the historic record, it is understandable that it may vex those who have passed on.

On the following Monday, Leslie was saying to Salumet:

"We do hope that the lady has a much greater peace of mind after having been here…"

27th November 1995 ~ "I hope that you have all realised by now, the purpose of her coming to you. It was important that some within the room realise how insignificant 'time' is, and also the purpose of showing to you … that part of that soul had now gone forward into a later time. I do hope you understand what it was about."

Leslie: "Yes, I think we did and we found it extremely interesting …"

Leslie made particular reference to her further life (also the further life of her son James who had also been mentioned).

~ "This is what I wish you to try to understand. Please try to forget about yourselves as an individual item. You are so much more. I want you all to realise that each one of you here, is just a spark of your whole soul."

Leslie: "Yes, I think we are slowly beginning to realise that. It's difficult for us of course, but gradually I think the realisation is taking shape in our minds. But we do have to recognise ourselves as a multiple personality."

~ "That is what I am endeavouring to teach you as well, as you well know … how powerful your minds are. This too I have stressed on a number of occasions, but it is an important teaching and I hope that you can gather it to yourselves to try and understand."

It is made very clear then, that Mary's visit to us was in fact an important teaching on the nature of our own souls and soul aspects. As soul aspects, we are each of us a representative of a timeless soul that has existed through all eternity. There is much more to this Earthly life than to simply be 'here now'. To see ourselves in this way would be a sadly blinkered view.

Saint Columba's journey to Iona: I had been reading of the time when Saint Columba established the monastery on the island and that had prompted a question.

George: "I've been reading what I understand to be some channelled writings about the setting up of a monastery. It is at the time when Saint Columba sailed to the Island of Iona. I've sometimes wondered if that was a chance landfall, but my reading has led me to believe that he would have been guided there, and that was a place of old energies. And the suggestion is that he re-awakened old energies there. Is there anything you can say about that?"

23rd October 1995 ~ "I can my friend ... the man you speak of, was indeed as you term ... a 'saint' in your world ... because indeed he was a man of spirit, who was guided by those beings who came to this Earthly life with him. From a small child, this being was touched from our world. Therefore it makes sense does it not, that all he did while he trod upon your Earthly world, should be guided? Indeed he was. I cannot say that of all who are termed 'saints'... but in this instance, it is correct to say ... I almost said: a Master of his time ... but he would not have been seen as such, but his gifts became well known as you have probably read ... and as we have spoken upon briefly before, there are many areas within your world that have energies which are special, if you like to term it that way. And yes, he was guided there, mainly to seek that guidance which followed him. That is why his footsteps trod that pathway ... for the guidance he needed for the rest of his Earthly existence."

George: "... That's very helpful. Thank you."

How very nice it is to receive such confirmation of the guidance and the saintliness of one from those early times. Following the founding of the important monastery on Iona in the year AD 563, Saint Columba strove to deliver Christianity to the Picts in the north of Scotland. Salumet went on to suggest that, if he is willing, perhaps he could bring him along one evening. How wonderful that would be! And as has been so clearly illustrated above, a Master such as Salumet is able to arrange such wonders. But that particular meeting is not as yet of our experience.

The Tunguska Event: It was in 1908 that the blue fireball appeared over Siberia. The explosion was massive and it literally shook the world. A huge shock wave travelled from it and a train driver on the Trans-Siberian railway felt obliged to stop. Hundreds of square miles of forest were affected by the blast, a central expanse being actually flattened. Readers of The Times newspaper wrote letters about the unusual brightness of the night skies that followed. It is remembered as the 'Tunguska Event'. Later, there were expeditions, a spate of scientific theories, not least the one involving a passing comet, and then the reply to our question put to Salumet:

10th October 1994 ~ *"... It was an atmospheric explosion. It was not a comet. It was merely nature taking her natural course."*

George: "Hmm ... thank you. It's surprising..."

~ *"Is that enough for you?"*

George: "I'm always interested, because this particular explosion ... has been a puzzle to those who like to think about problems of this kind."

~ *"They need to look to the Earth to find the answer ... not the skies. It was a combination of atmosphere and Earth together which created that particular disaster."*

George: "I would imagine a build-up of energy of some kind?"

~ *"Yes, a 'clash' I think you would call it ... in that particular area. You have to look down underneath the earth (surface), and you have to look to the atmospherics in the sky ... in the air. Together they can create ... how would you say ... a bang ... a bang? But they would have to investigate more, deep under the earth to find the answer. It was not from the skies."*

I think I would be correct in saying that the approach of a comet has been the favoured theory of explanation across the years, but interestingly, Salumet knocks that idea firmly on the head. There remains much we do not know of the energies within the Earth and in the regions that surround our atmosphere. And there has never been found, the expected surface debris evidence to support a comet theory. The blueness of the fireball from eyewitness statements, the heat-flash felt miles away and the absence of comet evidence are certainly consistent with an energy release of some kind.

The Bermuda Triangle Disappearances: There has been a history of disappearance in strange circumstances, of ships, aircraft and people in and around the area known as the Bermuda Triangle. A recent press report prompted our question.

Mark: "I read in a newspaper about an experienced pilot who was flying in the area known as the Bermuda Triangle, and apparently he looked out of his window and he was not where he was meant to be ... he looked at his computer readings and they showed that he was flying at something like 2,200 feet and somehow he had got over a mountain range at least 3,000 feet high. I think the suggestion was that he had entered this special

zone ... where the normal laws of physics that govern this planet
... had apparently disappeared. I wonder if you could shed light
on that?"

*4ᵗʰ December 2000 ~ "There are in this Earthly planet many areas
where mankind would say: it goes against the grain of understanding.
This applies not only to this planet but (also) to many, many others.
We enter into the realm of 'time' my dear friend, the subject that I have
thus far discussed little with you because I have always felt that your
understanding is not great enough as of yet. I would say to you that yes,
there **is** a time warp I believe you would say ... in many areas of this
planet. I am aware, as are many others, that these experiences are baffling
to many."*

Mark: "If you were looking at that plane as it entered that
zone, would the plane, to your eyes, just disappear?"

*~ "To your eyes it would disappear as it has entered, because it has
entered another dimension of time. To our (spirit) eyes it is a natural
occurrence ... it happens ... it is the ignorance of mankind about the time
zones and the dimension of time."*

Mark: "And in an instant, that plane suddenly is somewhere
else..."

*~ "Yes, it is another dimension of time. It is not unusual from our
side of life. The understanding ... is not always understood by many
here ... but it is a time dimension not fully understood by people on the
planet."*

Mark: "And I would guess that these zones ... the people that
know them and the energies, know how to use them ... can
do their space travel and can get to all kinds of places just like
that..."

*~ "Yes, the understanding of time dimension is a difficult one for you,
but yes, as I have said, there are many areas in your world that hold these
dimensions of time ... it is not unusual. After all, how do you suppose
the future is seen if it is not (by) the entering of another time dimension?
It is a little the same (similar) I would say to you, but used slightly
differently, by those who have the awareness and consciousness of seeing
what is ahead. After all, it has happened if you can see the future. Do you
agree? It is just travelling to another dimension whether it be with the
spiritual mind or ... physically travelling into the time dimension that is
encompassed within your planet. There are many ... but as of yet, little
is known about them."*

Mark: "I understand that quite a lot of people have got lost in them, so I would guess that they are not on their life path ... that they were not meant to be there, and I wonder what happens to them?"

~ *"You should not make assumptions my dear friend. Who are you to say that it was not their life path ... you cannot say that it was something that was not meant to happen. Perhaps for them it was their (designed) exit from this way of life. It does not mean my dear friends that you go into another time dimension and disappear forever. There are many in this world that would be able to tell you that they have entered into another time zone and have returned to tell the tale. Therefore I would say to you my dear friend, do not make assumptions ... do not judge. The experience of time travel, time zones and time dimensions ... call it what you will ... is a very difficult subject for us in our world to try to explain to you, because your understanding as of yet is not great enough, but it is something that causes great interest in your world, and many are being inspired to understand and to take on board all of the knowledge that is being offered to them."*

Sarah: "My mother once saw something happen in the morning, but in fact the occurrence did not take place until the afternoon. So she had actually entered a different time zone? Was she in an area with a different time zone, or is she capable of doing it herself with a little more knowledge?"

~ *"... There is a difference between entering a time zone physically as the pilot ... that the gentleman spoke about ... and entering a time dimension through the mind. That is the spirit coming to the fore. Not only can you go forwards but you can go backwards in time. There are many who could tell you of this type of situation. Many people are afraid to speak of these things because they are ridiculed ... or they are afraid that their own sanity is at stake. But in the case such as you speak of my dear friend that is the mind of the spirit that at any particular time can be to the forefront of consciousness. That is all."*

The subject of dimensions returned on another occasion when Paul asked a question about Carlos Castaneda and the group with apparent ability to cross over or 'slip' dimensions in order to pass into a spirit world. Salumet was in no way fazed by the question and launched straight into confirmation and proceeded with a degree of explanation:

30th July 2001 ~ "... What I would say to you my dear friend is this: there are those in your world who have the capability of slipping from this

*life to ours. To those people it is a natural process. To others there is, shall
we say, an ego trip to try to develop these powers. I would say about this
group of people that you speak of, that they are in fact no different from
those in your world who commit what you call suicide."*

Paul: "I can't understand the connection…"

~ *"Because they are attempting to come to a dimension to which they
do not belong. It is an analogy. Do you understand?"*

Paul: "Yes, I can see that."

~ *"It is an interference. Perhaps that is a better word…"*

Paul: "A case of learning to run before they can walk…"

~ *"Yes perhaps that is wiser words for your understanding. I would
not say it is wrong in the sense of suicide, but it is something they should
be aware of … if they are not careful, they can go from one dimension
to another too quickly, and in fact they can expel their physical living too
soon."*

A difference seems to be that the dimension slipping described
by Castaneda is consciously attempted while the Bermuda
Triangle disappearances are not. But it is interesting that there
are degrees of similarity between the physical Bermuda triangle
disappearances, the physical Castaneda dimension slipping and
the two-way time slipping in the mind as the spirit comes
forward. It was nearly three months later when I thought to place
another question about dimensions. I had long been aware that
theoretical physicists postulate other universes having different
numbers of dimensions. I sought a possible connection with this
way of thinking but Salumet was encouraging to see the picture
in terms of energy:

*22nd October 2001 ~ "I think that first we must define the word
'dimension' if you are to understand what I am saying to you. What is
dimension? It is nothing but a transmutation of energy. When you speak
of the level that I come from, then all of this energy would become part of
… there is no what you call 'dimension'. We are in a difficult subject here
my friends for your understanding … it is beginning to make sense to you
my friend, I can feel it…"*

George: "It helps to see it more as a transmutation of energy
… thank you for that."

~ *"Again the difficulty comes with the words of your planet. I have to
use words that you are familiar with but the problem is that you do not
understand our world fully enough for the explanation…"*

Sarah had previously mentioned a group who claimed they could travel forwards and backwards in time (in the sense of the H G Wells story 'The Time Machine'). Salumet continued:

~ *"But I will return to the lady (Sarah) and say that whatever group of people you are speaking of, I will say this to you: I have told you that mankind has the capability if he so desires to leave what you call this Earthly dimension, but mankind does not have the capability of going backwards ... and that is what they are saying they are doing. They can only do it (that) in thought. Do you understand? The only way it is possible to return to a former time is through what you call 'mediumship', and (by virtue of) what is spoken through mediumship, by those who exist in our world ... all of you can take yourselves forward, all of you can be aware of other times, but you cannot **physically** return to what has gone before ... again I will say to you that 'dimension' is only energy ... the transmutation of energy."*

Clearly, our teacher feels we are not yet ready for full understanding of slipping dimensions, but he has given some very useful salient facts for us to grasp. Dimension change is a time configuration, and the actual 'dimension' terminology that derives from our scientific endeavours, he prefers to regard as 'energy transmutation'. I would guess this to be a more practical classification. And it would seem that the Bermuda Triangle disappearances have slipped forwards and one cannot slip backwards physically.

Light Signs: During the course of the last fifteen years or so, the presence of unexplained light signs has been reported by news media around the world. Knowing that the symbols are deeply meaningful and seeing a report with photographs in a Sussex newspaper, prompted my question:

"... We have talked about the signs of crop circles but there seem to have been signs in light that have appeared around the world in many countries ... consisting of a circle with a cross in the centre, and the signs in light appear on pavements and on walls. As a symbol, it is very ancient I believe, in which a cross represents humanity and the circle is the universe ... and the four quarters are the four elements or the beings that look after those elements. It is a very ancient symbol that is appearing in many countries at the moment. Would you have anything to say about the significance of the light signs?"

14ᵗʰ July 2003 ~ "I do ... but you have already given what I would have explained to you!"

I think I gulped at that point and was much relieved when Salumet continued:

~ "Therefore for those words I thank you. What I would say to you is this: that light symbols have always existed since mankind has walked the Earth. Light symbols have appeared on storm, mountains, on water, in air ... in fact on all elements of existence. These symbols are not new but have been resurrected, if I may use that phrase at this time ... it has been happening for some considerable time. It is happening at this time because mankind needs to return to the basics of what living is all about. Your explanation explains the symbol. This is what mankind needs to understand."

George: "So the signs at this time would be a reminder for us?"

~ "Yes."

George: "And would the light beings be producing them?"

~ "Always the light beings are the Masters of this universe. You understand? I will speak a little more in detail when I speak to you about the pyramids ... because there my dear friends is a prime example of when these light symbols were used. I will say no more this time but I will elaborate for you when we have the evening about the pyramids. I hope it is enough for you this time. But these signs are not new ... they have been given from times past."

George: "Yes, I didn't realise they went back forever. I thought it was something new. Thank you for that."

~ "They are new to the people of existence now. But 'new' ... what is new?"

What is new indeed! It would seem then that the light signs are another set of signs that have much meaning (as have crop circles). And a connection to the pyramids has come up again. (The Egyptian pyramids are deeply significant in the moderately ancient history of this planet. At this point in time there are many more questions we wish to place with Salumet and an evening has been promised for this subject. This we look forward to. It is my understanding that the timing is important and we must wait a little longer.)

The Football World Cup 2002: It had been a year during which our newspapers and TV screens had been awash with various sporting activities; hence my question:

"Perhaps I could ask a question about our competitive nature. I think competition is something that is a part of evolution and the competitive instinct seems to be still with us. Recently, the nations of the world came together to play football, and one might say: it is much better to compete on the field of sport than the battlefield, and indeed perhaps the conversion of our competitive nature in this way ... to the field of sport ... perhaps this presents a way forward away from war. Do you have words for us about our competitive nature?"

16th September 2002 ~ "Thank you for your question. Of course you realise that what you speak of is the nature of the physical man and not the spiritual being. Man came upon this Earth and he had this ... what you call 'competitiveness' because he needed to survive, and of course, as mankind has evolved ... this spirit of competitiveness has grown to such a degree that mankind now is rather confused by these feelings. What I would say to you is this: rather than using that energy for sport or war, why does mankind not use this energy for the betterment of other people? That is not to say that mankind should not have leisure times. There is nothing wrong with being competitive ... I am not saying that. But in using energy ... let us call it energy ... mankind could use it much more wisely. After all, what is the thought but energy? And you have the thought before you have the action ... would you not agree?"

George: "So it would be good for us to transmute a part of that energy to better purpose?"

~ "Yes, but of course if you ask me ... it is much better that mankind uses this energy for sport rather than to do harm amongst their fellow men."

George: "It did occur to me that our sporting activity is becoming more and more and seems to be quite a considerable preoccupation for the planet at the moment."

*~ "Yes, what we must be careful and aware of is that this energy ... this mass energy cannot erupt into something that is **not** good for mankind. You must be aware of this and therefore I say to you that mankind in general would be much better suited to using all energies in helping one another rather than for the gratification of their own feelings. Do you understand?"*

George: "Yes, that is a very nice message ... thank you."

~ "I do not wish to seem as if I am against all of mankind having some kind of fun ... because that is part of the human nature also. It was given to you that you make laughter and joy in your lives, but I would say

to you that laughter and joy is much greater when it comes from helping others."

It was a carefully phrased reply, decrying neither the principle of having fun nor our competitive natures. But it would be well that we reflect at times on how we direct our energies ... and I think we are aware just how the *'mass energy'* can erupt sometimes into *'something that is not good for mankind'*. But the notion that the competitive instinct that has assisted our evolution has become a little confused is intriguing.

September 11ᵗʰ ... World Trade Centre, New York: I was abroad at the time of the atrocity and missed the Kingsclere Group meeting of 17ᵗʰ September 2001. It was a wonderful meeting and the excerpts that follow will give some indication. Salumet opened with the words:

~ *"Before I speak with you this time, I wish to hold you in love ... I want you to feel that love energy which enfolds you all..."*

There followed a substantial pause before he continued:

~ *"Now, my dear friends, let me say this to you: you know and you feel love which encompasses you all when all around you there is fear and sadness. Therefore my dear friends, I want you to realise that at any given moment in your living, you can seek that peace and love."*

He next referred back to the love and upliftment given at the previous meeting:

~ *"Each one of you present, felt love in some form or another ... you agree ... and I told you that I would explain it to you next time. But what I wish to say to you my dear friends ... since last we met, you must realise why I felt you needed some extra strength. You were unaware at that time but it was given to strengthen and uphold you..."*

He then asked the group to express their feelings about the terrorist attacks:

Sue: (Sue was in deep trance and could not be reached.)

Paul: "I think they're symptoms of the world as it is at the moment ... still out of balance."

Sara: "I tried not to get too involved with it but to send love and light and prayers for the people left behind and those passing on..."

Margaret: "I'm just so sad that people have to do these things because the world is a wonderful place if you are pleasant to everybody. It brought back horrible memories of the last war ...

we have to make people realise this is a wonderful world to live in."

Lilian: "For myself, the immediate reaction was to say a prayer ... to help those who had died or those who were injured ... the helpers ... to say a prayer for those, in whatever way they could be helped. Then, as the days have gone on, I was very touched by the love and prayers from people all around the world. Sorry as we were for the happening, there has been a lot of good response..."

Sarah: "I felt a great sorrow in a way, for the people who did it because I felt that they were misguided, but I also had in the back of my mind your words 'never to judge...'"

~ *"That is what I have waited to hear. Thank you ... all of you know that the happenings within your world will always continue until such times as spirituality touches each one, but until such time, these things will happen on this planet. It gladdens my heart to hear that not only were your prayers and thoughts with those who ... after all, have come home to our world and are perfectly safe ... but it gladdens me to hear that your thoughts have been with those you call 'the perpetrators', because you see my dear friends, they too need help ... there is much sadness, much fear, much anger within your world. But as one of you has said, it has strengthened many of your countries, many of your politicians of like mind. Think for a moment my dear friends, spiritually rather than physically. Remember that I told you, all of life is vibration, that like is attracted to like ... and those people whom you call perpetrators are of like mind. They are the 'dark' seeking the 'light' on the spiritual level. Remember this: they are trying to grow in their own way, for whatever reason is within their thinking. But I can say that the words I have heard from each one of you makes me glad to be amongst you, my dear friends, because I can see you as you truly are. There is much anger in your world from many people. I would say to you my dear friends: think about them. Try to dispel all this hatred, anger and all these negative ways of thinking. Try to bring to your world love in the pure sense, and that love is a love that is given unconditionally to all mankind ... not only to those you consider to be good. After all, no matter what a person has done, no matter how wrong it may seem to you, once more I say to you ... you cannot judge, because you do not have the full picture of life ... we have always needed the interaction with mankind to do the best for, not only this planet but many others. Remember this planet does not stand alone ... it is but a small part of a greater whole. Mankind does not stand alone ... it too is a small part of a greater whole. All of these things, my dear friends, I remind you of because it is important…"*

Two weeks later, Salumet continued to speak of the effect on the world of love, prayer, meditation and the good example. He also referred to the fear that was gripping the planet, and it was plain to all that there was developing at that time, a widespread fear of air travel. He then invited questions and I felt it appropriate to again address the recent act of terrorism, still very much on our minds:

George: "Going on from the destruction of the World Trade Centre and bearing in mind your teaching to us tonight, it appears to me that much good can come of this sad time. It is a time perhaps for the Western World to re-think its standards and its way forward. In our various ways we have probably contributed to this situation. I take your point about not being fearful and this again is a good test … it is important that we go forward without fear … with love instead. As it has been such a traumatic happening, it is perhaps a good time for us to pause and think … and out of this I believe much good could come. Do you agree?"

*1ˢᵗ October 2001 ~ "Yes, I would say this to you: let us not speak of division within your world. Let us not speak of western civilisation, eastern civilisation. Let us speak of the world as a whole … do not separate good and bad … remember that all belongs to the same … that is important. What you can do and what you must understand is that karmic debts can be dissolved. Remember not only do karmic debts belong to human kind but also to the lands without your world … you need to see the wider scheme of life for your understanding to be greater. I can tell you that this is a karmic debt, but you will not understand this unless you look at the wider scheme of life. The positive … the negative … remember all belong to the same vibration. Try my friends to see with spiritual eyes, and of course if you ask me the question: is there good comes from what you call … evil … then of course there must be, because there always has to be balance … but that is why it is imperative for you to use that love which you have … to keep that balance. And yes, many of your countries in the world at this present time have joined together for what they call good … but of course, they have not always been fair in the eyes of this … **our** world. Do you understand?"*

George: "I think we have all had inner feelings that part of the direction of the way we have been going has been questionable.

We have all had these inner doubts I think ... and it is not difficult for us to see that karmic connection."

~ *"Yes, I would say: if you have these inner doubts, then please ... listen to what is being said to you, because that is the spiritual aspect of yourself which is speaking to you. I know it is always difficult when we speak of good and bad, positive and negative, but until you reach that understanding ... of clear seeing ... of further vision ... of being part of the whole cosmos as opposed to part of this planet, you will always struggle with what is truth..."*

We should then simply strive to see the (much) wider picture through spiritual eyes and be accepting of the principle of karmic debt. As to karmic debt, it is clear from other teachings that this extends to our past lives and therefore beyond Earth and into spirit. The wider picture is wide indeed. But first and foremost of course, our love is required ... to embrace all life's pathways of our present knowing.

Before proceeding further it is appropriate that we digress just a little, this on account of a very important scientific advancement that happened around the turn of the century. In a curious way it has spiritual connection with this time. Within our civilisation there has been a long history of gambling and 'games of chance'. In the simple tossing of a coin, many must have at some time wondered if the result really is strictly random, or might it be influenced by mathematical system or focus of mind. Some people certainly seem more habitually 'lucky' than others. A useful device that scientists have built that finds application in a number of fields is the 'electronic coin flipper' more correctly called a 'Random Number Generator' (RNG). The RNG is an electronic binomial machine that produces a series of ones and zeros, by design, as a completely random listing. It was Robert Jahn who later carried out experiments to see if an RNG could be influenced by mind. He brought in strangers from the street and asked them to concentrate mentally on forcing a bias onto the machine's results. He found that a number of individuals, total strangers from the street, were in fact able to influence the machine! It would appear therefore that the delicate workings of the mechanism are sufficiently sensitive to be influenced when it becomes the target of directed thought ... a thought-detector one might say.

A colleague of Jahn, Roger Nelson, had an idea when he heard that a 'global meditation for peace' was being organised. He wondered if such meditation involving thousands of people, all thinking together, would influence a linked system of RNGs positioned around the world. The system was set up and a steady-state graph was observed. The steady state of the graph was interrupted by the event, and the observed peak was seven times greater than anything seen before in earlier work. This time the subjects were not targeting the RNG. The machine network was clearly able to 'eavesdrop' and detect the collective consciousness of the global meditation ... the global thought. His next move was to link together 40 RNGs around the world to his Princetown laboratory computer and keep the system functioning continuously. Many world events both happy and sad, produced peaks on the continuous graph. The worldwide publicised funerals of Princess Diana and Mother Teresa registered on the graph, as did New Year's Eve celebrations for 1998, 1999, 2000 and 2001; this for each time zone around the world. The linked RNGs clearly detect the collective consciousness energy of significant events having many participants.

A huge peak registered on the morning of September 11th when the World Trade Centre was destroyed. It is appropriate that the globally transmitted news of the event, activating a world-shared horror, should yield such a peak. Not only was the world's population utterly horrified at the atrocity ... and one can never express adequately in words the many feelings that will be combined in this ... the RNG system has provided a scientifically recorded proof [33,34] that this was indeed so! The precise shape of the recorded peak has since been the subject of serious debate. The fact is that it begins its rise three hours BEFORE the impact of the first hijacked plane into the building. One part of the debate has centred upon the idea that such a charting system might conceivably be used as a means of predicting disasters. But before this question can be considered, one must of course understand fully why the peak rise precedes the event.

One might possibly surmise that the reason has a connection with premonition. It has since become clear that many people in the vicinity of or connected to the event in some way, had difficult-to-explain feelings, forebodings and premonitions. Some had feelings of depression. Some became preoccupied with something symbolically connected. Some felt inexplicable panic. In fact, it is a feature shared by all major disasters, that they are preceded by premonitions or strange feelings. This has become clearly evident in recent years and the British Premonitions Bureau has made a study of these things. Such premonitions and feelings are likely of course to come to us from spirit. Hence my question to Salumet on the matter:

George: "You told us some time ago about new energies that would be discovered ... and there is a machine that has been developed called a Random Number Generator that seems to pick up energy from the collective consciousness ... and has recorded peaks for events such as the funeral of Diana, the funeral of Mother Teresa and the tragedy of September 11th ... and I think it shows a peak for a mass peace meditation. So I think our science is picking up and measuring the energy of the collective consciousness ... and I think this is leading to one of the energy discoveries that you talked of some time ago Would I be right in thinking that?"

17th February 2002 ~ "I thank you for your question. I have told you your scientists are being impressed ... and so they are. I also wish to say this to you: many, many words are used in descriptive language about energy. This is not new energy ... because it has always been. What is new is the understanding of mankind. I did tell you that machinery in all forms would take part in ... communication with us ... and this applies to what I have always taught you ... that thought is the most powerful energy in existence. This is what these machines are now picking up. It is not new, it is only new to the scientists who hold great store by facts and figures ... do they not?"

George: "What is new is that SCIENCE has discovered the energies..."

~ "But they are being impressed..."

George: "There is one query I would like to put to you: in recording the energy fluctuation associated with that event of September 11th, the energy peak began to rise three hours before the event. Would that be due to those in spirit wanting to influence people concerned and people nearby that event? Would it be their energy being picked up ... three hours before it happened physically?"

~ "Yes ... what you must understand is that these energies exist whether you, mankind, are aware of them or not ... but I understand

your question and I thank you for it. We in our world are constantly influencing many, many people. When there is either negative or positive (we shall use your Earthly words) ... when there is a great surge, it has to be shown and that influence comes most strongly from our world at these particular times."

George: "Yes ... thank you, I thought it must be that."

~ *"Yes ... it applies to both energies. As I said, we will use 'positive' and 'negative' energy for your understanding. It is a little more complex than that ... remember what I have told you: there is nothing that happens on this Earth plane that we are not aware of. What I think perhaps you would find interesting ... these energy surges ... they gather in what you call the 'astral planes' and have the ability to grow and become reality."*

George: "Yes, so it would be those in the astral planes that are endeavouring to influence..."

~ *"Yes ... but of course, remember that those in the astral planes are being influenced from higher vibrations. It is a complex subject..."*

This I felt had been a most significant exchange ... about a most important meeting point of science and spirit. The 'thought' process on such occasion clearly begins in spirit and then emerges into the physical world, where it is detected using scientific equipment. (It is also, of course, felt or detected by those who experience the premonitions and strange feelings.) This represents a physical proof of spiritual existence for any who still require it. Salumet has carefully given the explanation, and how else could such energy be generated three hours in advance of the observed physical happening?

[There are interesting further developments where time and spirit are concerned. In fact, more thought-influence experiments are in progress using the RNG machines. Results appear to indicate that whilst our **examination/perception** of RNG results (either contemporaneous or recorded and seen later), are fixed in linear time, the applied thought is not time-bound. The deep thought that is able to throw the RNG results comes from spirit and that is a non-linear (time-oneness) zone. It therefore matters not whether that thought is applied yesterday, today or tomorrow, the observed result remains the same regardless. It may at first seem odd that a machine's results can be thrown by a thought applied tomorrow or yesterday, but I believe it simply reveals the dual nature of time. It follows that we may have reached the point where time-oneness of spirit is about to be proved scientifically. What a break-through! This and Salumet's input on the matter will be dealt with in more detail in the next book.]

14. TERRORISTS IN SPIRIT

Our meeting of 28th October 2002 took an unexpected turn. Salumet was not with us (sometimes this has been due to difficult ethereal conditions and on rare occasions due to our low numbers for an evening). Another took the opportunity to come through, a most interesting lady who is also a teacher. It seems she often 'sits in' when Salumet is with us and conveys his words to others in spirit. We chatted with her on several topics, including erroneous, deeply embedded, religious beliefs carried by those passing on, and it became clear that this was an advanced one whose job is to teach and encourage those with problems that frustrate their further progress. She had a trite yet most agreeable manner but could also focus onto the deeply serious matter, as required. I had been bothered about what happens to suicide bombers and the like and she was the one to put the question to:

George: "I have another thing on my mind..."

~ *"Just one sir? I'm sure you have more than one..."*

George: "Well yes ... but we have unfortunately, associated with religions ... but away from those religions themselves ... there have been militant groups that indulge in terrorism and they cause many deaths ... not really in the name of religion but they **think** it is, or they use a religious title for their movement. In your teaching work, do these people who come over, present a problem to you?"

~ *"They can do ... they can do ... because you see they have become so engrossed in their way of thinking that they cannot see what is right and what is wrong. Those terms 'right' and 'wrong' are very black and white, and I know I am sure that the teachings you have been given are that black and white is not always just what it should be. Those people come to us with these fixed ideas and sometimes it takes ... many, many of your Earthly years for them to realise that what they have done has not always been the right pathway. But I do have to say ... and I do hope that you can accept this in the way I am telling you ... that those people believe that what they do, in their hearts is right..."*

There was general agreement that we understood, and she continued:

~ *"So there has to be an element of understanding for them ... there has to be a degree of help for them. They are not always the wicked people that you perhaps in your world see them (as), because they genuinely believe that what they are doing is best."*

George: "Yes, I do appreciate that..."

~ *"And it is our task to show them the other way they could have chosen. We have to show them a wider picture, and it is then up to them to accept our teaching. It is then up to them to accept that the spiritual way of life is to allow all people the freedom of thinking, the freedom of bliss. That is what they need to learn."*

George: "Yes, it strikes me that is the more difficult part of your teaching..."

~ *"... I made light of the teaching. It is difficult work at times. It is not just a small growth if you can take just one person and make him see the light. It takes much work. It takes much love and understanding ... and yes ... patience. But that is something that in this world there is a great abundance of. But ... perhaps I can leave you with that thought ... about people who you might say: commit atrocity. I believe that is an expression widely used in this world ... yes? Do not think of people who commit these acts as terrible people. See these people as lost souls..."*

George: "Who need praying for?"

~ *"... To help themselves ...help their understanding, hope that they too will feel life so strongly that they could not harm another human being. That is what we are teaching them ... that every single individual could not utter a single word or a deed against another human being, with either malice or hatred ... but with gentleness and with love."*

George: "Yes, that's very good to hear."

~ *"Something to think of when you feel strongly ... I do not say anger ...because I know ... because of the teaching you've had, that you must not make judgement on others ... but still you do don't you?"*

And there followed a general agreement to that! But how good it is to know that there are those on the other side who lovingly and dedicatedly work to restore a feeling for love of life to those unfortunates who have for a while at least, lost it.

15. 'RESCUE' OF AN UNNAMED GUNMAN

It is true that not everyone departing this life has a smooth passage in spirit. A number of possible factors may restrict progress ... lack of belief, inability to forgive themselves for some bad deed, an irrational attachment etc. Some form of help is always available however, and quite regularly, those who need a helping hand will be brought along to our meeting by helpers in spirit, for counselling or for whatever is required. They are slipped into a medium/instrument and talked to, usually by Leslie or Lilian until their problem is sorted. These happenings are known generally as 'rescues'. Many are considered 'ordinary' rescues, especially those relating to a disbelief regarding life after physical death. Disbelief may relate simply to non-recognition of life continuing after physical death or to non-recognition of own death. (Because awareness continues, they assume physical life also continues ... yet something is not quite right.) It is a matter of educating and convincing the one in spirit. Following this, that one in spirit is then able to move on. There have also been rescue evenings that can only be classed as 'extraordinary'.

In recent years, there have been a number of terrible shootings in the towns of several countries, involving armed individuals that have seemingly gone berserk, shooting people around them before turning the gun on themselves. These happenings have been shocking and have received much media coverage. It would be wrong (in respect of both spirit and relatives), to publicly name the one brought through to us or to give details that could lead to naming. Nevertheless, it would I think be of value to make known that one of the several assassins of recent years has been brought to our group to receive guidance, and then to say something about that guidance process. This particular rescue was arranged and 'overseen' by Salumet who remained with his instrument Eileen during the session. The medium receiving 'X' was asked to sit at the centre of our circle and we were asked to direct our love energy to that centre. X felt the love and he began by thanking us for it. Leslie counselled. Our visitor was slow to

begin but gave his name and details of the shooting. He repented
… he could not say why it happened, could not forgive himself
and had remained in a self-imposed darkness since.

Leslie:"Many who come to us have had to wait many, many of
our years before they've received forgiveness…"

At this, he replied that he had been with us previously. In
fact it had been four weeks earlier. On that occasion he (and
instrument) had knelt before Salumet to beg forgiveness for his
transgression. We had no knowledge of his name or the deed at
that time. It had been a brief visit at the end of a session but it had
clearly been a firm step forward for him. And now he was again
with us on his knees. He needed coaxing from the self-imposed
darkness. Leslie's counsel centred on this (for which, as was usual,
Leslie received guidance from spirit). It was clear that X very
much wanted to make amends and was being led by Leslie in
what he could do for others. But first he must extricate himself
from the blackness so that he would be in a position to use his
mind to help others … to make amends. It was made clear to him
that there are a number in the same state as he. He would be able
to help them also to come to terms.

Leslie was saying: "… You can turn that mind to helping
others, in order to compensate for what you did. There are many
in your world in a similar state to what you were in … did you
know that?"

X: ~ *"No."*

Leslie:"There are. Would you like to help **them** to come out
of the darkness, and to make amends for what **they** did?"

X: ~ *"Yes."*

Leslie:"That could be available to you if you wish. Look upon
it, if you will, as a duty you now have to do, for your own internal
forgiveness, if you wish to forgive yourself. Do you understand?"

X: ~ *"Yes."*

Leslie:"Will you do that then?"

X: ~ *"I will … I will."*

Leslie:"Will you say that so that everybody can hear you?"

X, more emphatically: ~ *"I will do that."*

Leslie: "Good. That's fine. Anything else you would like to
say? You have learned tonight what the power of love can do for
you."

X: ~ *"Yes."*

Leslie: "You can give that power of love to others, you know"

X: ~ *"I want to … to the ones I took."*

Leslie: "You can do. You can be shown how to contact them … and if it is important to you, you can go and ask them for their forgiveness for what you did. That's been troubling you, hasn't it?"

X: ~ *"Yes."*

Leslie: "Well you can do it. You can be shown how to contact them, and to ask each individually for their forgiveness. Does that make you feel any happier about it?"

X: ~ *"Yes."*

Leslie: "Good. That's fine…"

Clearly this was no ordinary rescue. It concerned a gunman … a murderer in spirit, being helped in working out a pathway of redemption. The chosen pathway would help in his recovery, and would also help others in similar plight. In fact it is true to say that it is a general principle to be observed in rescue work, however serious or trivial the matter might be, that helping the one has a 'knock-on' effect. Many are so often helped as the result of helping the one.

16. MOSES, LOVE AND THE HEAVEN ON EARTH

It was during one of our very early meetings, when we were still cautiously feeling our way, that Sara had asked a question about heaven.

Sara: "Can I assume that it's possible to create a heaven on Earth with the power of positive thought and service?"

4th July 1994 ~ "You are quite correct. 'Heaven' can be here on Earth. That is what we are all striving for. You are quite right young lady."

Leslie had then observed that it would have to be a tremendous amount of positive thought, emanating from everyone, and I had followed with a question about 'love' that I felt must come into the equation somewhere.

George: "I think 'love' is the most important factor on Earth. Sometimes we feel that, as a whole, we're just not generating enough of it. Would you care to comment on that?"

~ "I will. Love is the most important thing not only on your Earth but in everything. You speak of 'God'. Who or what is God, if it is not the universal power of love? Love is indeed the most powerful thing that anyone can possess. It is that element of spirit that shines forth from each and every one of you to varying degrees. Love ... love is what you are about."

They were apt and accurate replies to our simple questions. Now, we have moved on a decade and the world is a different place. We have had the benefit of Salumet's further teaching and you have had the benefit of reading his words as printed thus far. Our awareness has grown, your awareness has grown and more can now be said on these matters. So let us now look to Salumet's more recent words.

24th March 2003 ~ "... I feel each one of you is now beginning to understand the energy behind a word. Would you agree with me? ... As your awareness grows so too will your understanding of your own lives. You will not doubt my words when I say to you my dear friends that what you call 'heaven' is also part of your existence here and not something that you should strive for outwardly. Do you understand my words?"

George: "I think your meaning might be: living with a strong soul-connection?"

~ *"Yes, because with the all-knowing comes the pathway that is indeed 'heaven' as you call it ... and that is your Earthly word for God-connection. Yes, heaven already exists, but it is up to each one of you to become aware of it here and now. After all, I will use an Earthly word again ... that is what you 'strive' for. May I say this to you: Why strive when you already have the knowledge? I pause there in order for you to digest the meaning of those two words. Would anyone like to comment?"*

Paul: "I think where some of us fall down is in thinking that heaven can be achieved with certain material things, whereas it is a state of mind, I think..."

~ *"It is not just a state of mind. It is the all-knowing part of you that already exists. Do you see the difference? Each one of you on this Earth, except for the ones you call 'Masters', strive for what you call spirituality ... or searching for the God-energy. What I tell you this time my dear friends ... there is no need to strive, because you already have that knowledge within ... I say to you my dear friends that each one of you has this awareness but it is up to you to bring it forth in order that it may be used. This inner knowing continues throughout all of your existence. It is this all-knowing that you need to find whilst on this Earth ... you are seekers of the one truth. Perhaps I could compare you to one in your religious book known to most people and his name was 'Moses'. He was but a seeker of truth. He was the one that introduced in that religious book what you term 'commandments'. I would like to say to you this time, and it may surprise you or at this time in your growth it may not, that as a seeker of truth, he brought many words to many people ... but I would say to you my dear friends that the words that he brought to this world were not 'commandments'. That Great Creative Force does not command but issued forth words that should have been 'commitments'. I would like you to ponder those words this time, and perhaps when next we meet, we will discuss what you think I mean. Would anyone like to comment briefly?"*

George: "So we are thinking of what we might call 'the ten commitments' as a pattern for living?"

~ *"I would feel more comfortable with that ... yes. Of course, ten is but a number. There were many words given that were to enable mankind to seek out the truth; the truth that already existed but which mankind at that time in your history, needed to hear."*

George: "It is just that ten of those commitments were written into the book as commandments..."

~ *"And named as 'commandments'. I would say but one thing: why would the Creative Force who is all-knowing ... and we are part of that Creative Force ... why would he need to command part of himself? That is what I wish you to think about. That is what I wish you to ponder."*

We pondered. We turned up Deuteronomy ... the fifth book of Moses ... chapter V and refreshed our memories on that teaching of old. Some 'commandments' still remain as clearly in focus today. 'Thou shalt not kill', remains sharply clear and in keeping with the peaceful Earth that we should all be striving for. But as to coveting a neighbour's 'ass' ... well perhaps in today's world, if we covet our neighbour's 'Aston Martin', then that might be closer to the meaning intended. Some of the ideas of that earlier time are now outdated.

The following week, we assured Salumet that the term 'commitment' felt comfortable. Sarah pointed out that in loving your neighbour, you are having no bad thoughts, in keeping with the general teaching. And Salumet responded:

7th April 2003 ~ *"It is not only the thought that is important ... in loving your neighbour you are loving yourself, and in loving yourself you are expressing that God-force which is all-loving."*

George: "Of course, the overriding one is, I think: 'love your God with all your heart, with all your soul and with all your mind'. I think if one lives to this, then everything else follows... (In fact this is the revised presentation of that commandment given by Jesus according to Matthew XXII).

~ *"Of course, because ... we will use the word 'God' for your convenience but you know it is a much wider picture ... yes. If your awareness is such that you love that God-force, then what you are doing is saying; 'I am aware of who and what I am' and if that awareness is there, then of course you must understand that you are part of the greater picture of life."*

George: "And other commandments such as 'Thou shalt not kill'... they seem to be, or that particular commandment seems ... a mere detail embraced within the love principle..."

~ *"All are embraced in the love principle because, if you are love itself, there would be no need to harm anyone; so the important word for these commitments is 'love' ... awareness, thankfulness of beginning to know yourselves. Each one of you has the responsibility of taking those commitments and working through them, seeking, searching, in order that you may know yourselves. It all sounds so simple does it not? But full well you know, that as you tread each step in life, that sometimes it seems more difficult. The more awareness you gain, the more difficult life seems to be at times. Remember what I told you: you have to experience life. That is the secret … but in gaining the experience, then you have that fuller awareness. Do you understand?"*

Lilian: "The harder times … make us more aware of…"

~ *"It should make you more aware of who and what you are and that you are that all-knowing, all-knowingness that is part of the fuller picture. It is not easy my friends … but if we return to what we call 'The Ten Commandments' … they were given to those people of that time whose minds were not completely open to the truths. Therefore, to be commanded … to them (it) was a natural progression. It was much easier for them to take those words of truth and to use them for the betterment of mankind … for that particular time. As in all cases with other nations … they have their own Masters if you wish to call them that … who came at specific times onto this Earth in order that the people would accept what was truth. Truth has never altered but men have, and in this time of your evolution on this planet, and especially in groups such as this, mankind is beginning to awaken once more. Mankind for too long has existed in quite a great deal of darkness … because they have not accepted truth. Would you have any comments?"*

George: "Yes, I can see the consistent truth as received from Silver Birch and White Eagle and from yourself, to name three recent teachers of truth (all 20th/21st century). I would comment that you are able to talk to us about certain items that previous Masters have not mentioned, such as UFOs and space travel and corn circles, and these are all very modern things. And so I can see the present teaching embraces extra details of knowledge, I would say."

~ *"Each one who has come to this planet teaches to the ability of the pupil. You must know and understand that throughout your Earthly history mankind has varied so much. There have been many civilisations, as I have told you previously, whose knowledge was far greater but in the course of time, for whatever reason, (each) has been extinguished. There also has been on this planet many people who have been simple in their life styles but who have had great knowledge and truth … but each one of us who has come to this planet for the betterment of mankind has always taught to the ability of those to whom we speak. And yes, my dear friend, you mentioned the modern areas of living which is of interest to man and this is as it should be. When I came to you, I came to you in the knowledge that each step we took would be a single, simple step ... that my teaching to each of you, each of you in your various degrees of understanding would be simple, my words would be simple and my teaching would be understandable. I know that my approach to you my dear friends has been the right one. I have seen you grow ... I have seen the hearts of each one of you shine forth ... I have seen my teachings to you come to fruition through your very words to others. I could say that each one of you within this room now knows and understands that life is a great responsibility upon this planet ... that each one of you accepts not only for yourselves but for the whole of the planet, that man has a great responsibility. In accepting that responsibility, what you are doing is accepting that you are part of creation. That is profound my dear friends."*

And a little further into the evening, Salumet was saying:

~ *"This planet at this time my dear friends, although you feel it is troubled, this planet is growing. This planet has much to give. The people of this planet are being bombarded with the truth. So never despair: there is no room now for such emotion in your lives ... you are part of the Creative Force. You have responsibilities and you are going forward with all that I give to you. Therefore again, this time I would say: look to those words given as 'The Ten Commandments'; look to them with new eyes and see how you are committed to them ... it is not necessary to speak more words to you. These commitments of life should to each one of you possibly have different meaning, but to each one of you these commitments are the next step forward in our growth together."*

Once again we have the connection to ancient Egypt. The name 'Moses' is Egyptian because he was brought up in that country. He lived in the 13th century BC and the stories of his leading the exodus out of Egypt and his receipt of the 'commandments' on Mount Sinai are well known. The Torah, or first five books of the 'Old Testament', also comes to us via Moses. He was of course a truly great man of that time with strong God-connection. The Torah too, has a very special place within the scriptures, and contains 'sealed within itself', an encoded record to which there are several references within the Holy Bible, for example the following passage from Daniel 12, 4:

"... And seal the record, until the fixed period, when many will travel and knowledge will be increased."

Now is that fixed period of widespread travel and rapidly increasing knowledge (including that of the developing and especially relevant computer science). It is now that the seal is being removed and the encoded information is being made known. This contained information has become popularly known as 'The Bible Code'. This and its implications are reported quite fully elsewhere[3, 35, 36, 37]. I mention these matters briefly here to highlight the very special significance of Moses, both in his time as well as in ours. He was indeed a truly historic figure of very marked influence. His soul-connection whilst on Earth would undoubtedly have been strong indeed.

Salumet's teaching is that heaven relates to our God-connection, that we experience via our soul-connection, and a result of regular meditation is that these links are strengthened. We have also learned that knowledge is innate within soul, so that the state of all-knowing would seem to be intimately bound with what we term 'heaven'.

17. THE BIBLE CODE

It was towards the end of 1997 and following publication of Michael Drosnin's book The Bible Code that we first sought Salumet's confirmation of the book within the book, and we received at that time some account of its value and its connection to computer science from one who helped create that hidden record [3]. The account received on that occasion had made it a truly mind-blowing evening. Now, following publication of Drosnin's second book on the subject, it seemed appropriate to refer to the subject again.

George: "... there have been other influences that are all contributing to this road to a better planet. Would I be right in thinking that the Bible Code of which we know a little more now ... would I be right in thinking that our understanding of that would also make a contribution to the way forward?"

3rd November 2003 ~ "Yes, why my dear friend do you suppose that these things surface at a particular time? It is not by accident."

George: "That one indeed has surfaced at a particular time ... as was prophesied."

~ "All I would say to you ... all things of knowledge have their time. It has not been by accident that these things have been made known..."

It was good to have the note on timeliness. There then followed some advice concerning how we should seek within for answers to questions and there was some talk on how the ever-growing love energy within our meeting place was assisting Salumet's visits. And there had been mention of the challenges being met by science and by world religions. Following this, our further questions were invited, whereupon I sought permission to again pursue the subject of the Bible Code, declaring that I had in fact written to Drosnin concerning specific data.

George: "... He is very knowledgeable amongst the people who know something of this. The code itself (according to his publication), indicates that there is a key to further unlock the book that is sealed within the book, and this key seems to be in the form of a stone obelisk now submerged beneath the land;

also there is mention of a steel container, and these are on the shore of the Dead Sea near a village called Mazra. He was talking of using scientific equipment to locate this key. I suggested it might be better to endeavour to locate it through either spirit communication or dowsing. I wonder if I have given him a reasonable suggestion?"

~ *"I will say this to you my dear friend: there will be communication between you, that is for sure. There is a purpose in not finding the key that you speak of. Again I will say: there is a time for all things. It will happen, but I tell you: not yet. I would say to you that your suggestion to him ... those would have been my words. If he needs the answer, then he must approach it from the spiritual aspect. You can spend much time, much energy (and) much money in your world, but until the time is right for you and for us in spirit, it will not happen. But I would say that he is being influenced."*

George: "This particular one seems to me, very well motivated to help the world as much as he possibly can..."

~ *"He has a good heart, but sometimes the thinking interferes ... but he is being influenced, because these things must be known ... but at a time that is right for all people."*

George: "Could I also mention the scientist Dr Eliyahu Rips who has worked out the computer programme for seeking out the code? I am sure he has been very much influenced from spirit..."

~ *"That is almost like the challenges I speak of. Do you understand? These challenges ... although it is of the Earth, it also comes from spirit ... all who are chosen to bring forth the wonders of our world to mankind are being influenced in many ways. That is what matters ... that is why so often they seem committed individuals, because they are being influenced from our world to do the work they feel is of the Earth, but indeed (it) is of (a) spiritual nature ... because these thoughts are necessary for humankind to understand what is about to take place. It (the Bible Code) is a knowledge that has been kept from you for very good reasons because mankind, to put it simply, has not been ready for these revelations."*

George: "Yes, I appreciate that we must be ready to handle whatever knowledge comes to us."

~ *"If it comes too soon then mankind would deny or ridicule, because those feelings are also within the human nature. So the time must be right for them to be acceptable. Do you understand?"*

George: "Yes, yes … I see that."

~ *"But it matters not whether the individual believes or does not believe as long as the purpose of the work is taken up and done with dedication and that the wider knowledge be given to all … and that is what is happening here…"*

This is, as I think all will agree, a very clear statement on the code. It and its value to humanity are plainly acknowledged and the timing of its fuller revelation is of utmost importance. The 'key' exists but its detection and use must wait a little while yet. But without doubt its existence is acknowledged. There is an emphasis that all is subject to influence from spirit … including the dedication of individuals and the timing. I am very taken with the phrase: *to bring forth the wonders of our world to mankind.* These words are carefully chosen! The Bible Code is without doubt a wonder of spirit world implanted within the Torah and it is soon to be brought forth when the time is precisely right. The wording is perfect! One might also observe that it (information from the code), is at this instant in time, partly emerged. Many are sceptical and a few of those sufficiently informed will ridicule. Mathematicians are subjecting the code to rigorous statistical analysis. Not all of us have the intellectual ability to make assessment of their findings. And there are political matters to be resolved in the Dead Sea region.

One might also say that the very nature of the Bible Code itself (encoded accurate historic facts relating to a time-span of 3,200 years), presents ample further proof that true prophecy is indeed possible and can no longer be denied.

PART III
IN CONCLUSION

During the course of our evenings so much ground has been covered, and so many sorties have been made into unknown or little-thought-about territory that there may be some difficulty for mere Earthly minds to encompass all. Some of the material presented, if considered in isolation, may appear odd, bizarre or perhaps simply not of Earthly thinking. Yet, if one can just grasp for one moment the whole picture, it will be seen that its parts fit together extremely well. The pattern of existence that has been given is indeed a pattern. As such, it has a remarkable cohesion. It is not a disjointed higgledy-piggledy collection of unrelated ideas. (Similarly, each piece of a jigsaw puzzle has small meaning but the completed picture says all.) The whole may be seen as a living tapestry with threads running in all directions without dislocation. It is a smoothly connected schematic presentation that unites all things ... humanity, nature, consciousness, life throughout the universe, folklore, legend, planets, galaxies, spirit, soul, angels, elementals, teaching missions of Masters, world religions and a Creative Principle known to many as God. Such coordination of pattern spells TRUTH.

In view of the sheer complexity of this presentation from ten years of the teachings, it seems appropriate to lightly skim through the sections, picking out particular salient factors. In part this might be seen as a refresher course, in part a brief list of definitions as they emerge, in part glossary, and in part it highlights connections within the wider scheme. And since we have now come thus far, perhaps we might begin this brief overview by first mentioning the elusive 'time':

Time: It appears linear in our everyday living but is 'as one' in spirit. It is well that we recognise both forms because the duality of time is the basis of true prophecy, and after all, theoretical physicists are also committed to time's non-linearity as well as its more familiar linear form. Our science

therefore endorses the need for us to accept both linear and non-
linear time. It might even be said that proof of time's non-linear
form lies equally at the heart of theoretical physics and in the
prophecy made by a true seer.

Prophecy: Quite simply, shamans, seers and 'advanced ones'
have the ability to go into trance and see in the way of spirit.
Seeing time-as-one facilitates their gaining knowledge of future
events, to be recounted to those on the physical Earth. Glimpsing
the future in this way happens not only in trance but also
sometimes in dream-state.

Soul: As part of spirit, soul has always been and remains
immortal, as does that tiny aspect of soul that is part of each one's
Earthly existence. That tiny aspect is forever connected to the
parent soul. There are vast interconnected systems of soul, some
being much advanced in the heavenly order.

Incarnation/reincarnation: Planetary physical life for
aspects of soul is a valuable process for soul progression. One
aspect may have repeated Earthly life or different aspects of
the same soul may follow one another (There are different
kinds of reincarnation). Recognition of reincarnation has been
a difficulty for some within modern world religions. It has to
be acknowledged, however, that on a worldwide consideration,
acceptance of the principle is the majority view.

Masters: 'Advanced ones' in spirit, as part of general
progression, continue to provide wonderful missions to Earth and
elsewhere in the cosmos. Sometimes they choose to incarnate,
sometimes not. Sometimes religions have resulted following a
particular Master's teaching. Each mission to Earth is of course
designed to suit the people/awareness of that particular time. The
central core of the teaching (peace, love and reality of spirit) has
always been consistent. Isolationism or that religions should vie
with one another was never intended and results solely from our
own erroneous thinking. That the details of a teaching become
dated must be accepted if we are to accept progression and that
our awareness increases.

Nuclear holocaust: One of Salumet's two objectives has
been to avert nuclear oblivion and we are assured that this cannot
now happen. This result follows the wider mission to Earth of
which Salumet's teaching forms a valuable part, and this result has
already been signalled by a change in the planetary etheric.

Ancient civilisations: Some have achieved much advancement. They leave behind a wealth of residues to be accessed and marvelled at. On the Earth: stone edifices, inscriptions and legends. In spirit: souls, karma and innate knowledge abound. Some cultures have received 'space travellers' and some have themselves aspired to space travel. Their very existence, in fact, continues in spirit, so that they are 'ancient' only as contemplated by those upon the physical Earth.

Space travel/space exploration: Rocketry made media headlines and caught the imagination during the latter 20th century. But space travel is in no way new, either to the cosmos or to this Earth, and the methods currently sought by our science must in the general scheme be seen as primitive. Methods based on the belching of hot gases are far too severely limiting in both speed and distance of travel. Even with really vast expenditure of funds and resources, exploration in this way will remain confined to local planets in our own system. Dematerialisation, which is a spiritual attribute, must first be mastered before we can exceed the speed of light. Then, and only then, shall we be in a position to explore the galaxy. This format would appear to be the time-honoured cosmic approach to successful space travel.

Creative Principle: All galaxies, all planets, all cultures answer to the one Divinity. All evolution is part of the Grand Design overseen by the one Creative Principle. Within this awesome pattern, individual planets have, through 'chain of command/influence', their own individual guidance. The Earthly guidance has been illustrated through angelic vision to Saint John who has placed that record in 'Revelation'.

Human brain function: Brain function is of course of utmost importance and our understanding of it requires revision from time to time. The brain must now be seen as our connection to all that is, has been and will be. It is much more a processor than a generator. As generator it produces physical thinking, calculation, evaluation, organisation and controls body function. As processor it has soul-connection, receives visions, inspiration and guidance, part of which may be referred to as conscience. Great artists, writers and composers rely heavily on the brain's receiving facility. It is our connection to God, Heaven and innate knowledge. The connection to soul-body can be much strengthened through regular meditation. Brain activity continues during sleep-state and the spirit ventures out-of-body each night.

Innate knowledge: Spirit/soul has always been and contains all-knowledge (past, present and future). This may be accessed or accessed in part, especially if soul-connection is strengthened through daily meditation. The soul-connection of a Master such as Jesus will be strong indeed and all will be known to his Earthly aspect. Such philosophers as Immanuel Kant and Samuel Alexander were able to intuit the innate nature of knowledge.

Angels: There are many kinds of being throughout the universe. All are comprised of energy in a variety of forms and that includes our selves. (A proportion of our own energy is in the form of physical matter). Angelic beings are pure energy with no physical counterpart (usually unseen and not subject to gravity). There are many angels. All are light-beings. In the higher order, angels are wondrous purity of light and even Salumet feels awe in their presence. The higher order watch over and guide planetary evolution and we each of us have one guardian angel whose concern is consciousness. They are probably the best acknowledged of the pure energy entities often referred to in our literature, art and everyday expressions.

Elementals: These are energy beings within the 'ethers' of the four elements: earth, air, fire and water. They are named: gnomes, fairies, salamanders and undines, and since they have mention in multi-national folklore in the widest sense, they are also known by many other names. They respond to our emotions and deserve our respect and they deserve that farming practice acknowledges their presence and value. Without them, neither the natural order nor farming would exist.

Ancient site guardians: These are energy beings that attend the Earth for the duration of its existence. They are as yet little known but a few gifted people are able to channel their speech so that there has been communication with them. Their purpose is planetary protection and they work with ley line energies..

Idyllic farming system: This has due regard for elementals and is essentially an organic system. There are islands in Indonesia and a few places in other countries where an essentially organic agriculture system still remains. Much of the world needs to revise its agriculture. In the UK, the labour-intensive mixed farming system of the 1930s and earlier was much closer to an idyllic system than exists today, as was evidenced by beauty in the natural order in the shape of bird, butterfly and bee populations. But there are some successful organic farms currently in operation and perhaps this marks the beginning of much needed reform.

Diet and food resources: Much has been said on this. Although not seen as essential, vegetarian regime has to be the ideal with regard to both our spiritual progression and good health. It is an essential factor in health to include fresh raw food in diet. This would seem to indicate that good farming methods, short-haul transportation and garden produce are important criteria in food production. Drinking and smoking are viewed as 'crutches' and we should take care not to violate the body-temple by overdoing these. We are reassured that population will never outgrow the potential to feed all.

Disease: Much has also been said on the matter of disease. Through our thinking, lifestyle and misdirection of free will, we are architects of our own diseases; usually in this life, but emotional blockages may spring from the past lives that we have lived. Disease begins in spirit/energy body before it manifests in the physical. Modern medicines frequently treat just the physical symptoms that are clearly visible to us. Where cancerous growth is concerned, surgery may be helpful but the root cause lies not within the physical body. The cause is likely to be stress and cure will result from loss of the stress. 'Miraculous' remissions of tumours that are sometimes reported relate to release of stress … through deeply moving music, altered lifestyle, love realisation etc. It is said that for healing to take place, the (stressed) spirit must be touched.

Spontaneous combustion: As with disease, the cause of this extremely rare phenomenon lies with the energy body that can become distorted to such a degree that there is sudden destruction of the physical being. An important aspect of this is demonstration and proof of the enormous power that normally resides within us. When Salumet refers to the tremendous power of thought/spirit/energy within, it should be an easy matter in the light of this knowledge, to believe implicitly that such enormous power is indeed available from within.

Healing: Taking heed of the guidelines arising from data in the above four paragraphs should in general lead to health

improvement. Notwithstanding this, methods of healing that are available to us are:
- Healing (spiritual healing)
- Absent healing (as above but at undefined distance)
- Prayer
- Psychic surgery
- Regression therapy
- Dr Bach flower remedies
- Homeopathy
- Herbal remedies
- Manufactured medicines/chemicals/drugs
- Surgery

The first seven methods act on the spirit/energy body where the causative factors reside. The last three listed categories work on the physical body that shows the physical symptoms or deformity. Sceptics who think only in physical terms view the first seven methods as dubious because they do not see a direct impact on the physical body. To promote harmonious life and health, spirit should be to the fore and beyond disturbance by emotion. Wrong thinking/emotion that causes illness may be corrected by right thinking. Deep thought that springs from the spirit is all-powerful. Hence there is the facility to self-heal. One should not overlook the fact that many doctors and medical practitioners are (spiritual) healers without necessarily being aware of that fact, so that in the course of physical treatment, the spirit may be touched and complete healing follow. The teaching is that the key to longevity lies in the thinking. Finally, there are two simple rules in healing:

1. The spirit must be touched.

2. The karma of any karma-related condition must be recognised/released.

Both conditions must be satisfied, for healing to take place.

Earthly events: It is both wonderful as well as a great privilege that we have been able to put questions and receive answers confirming happenings that have sometimes been viewed as uncertain by many of us; also some clarification has been given for a number of more recent occurrences. Events that are confirmed and/or clarified are:
- Extinction of the dinosaurs,
- The continued existence of Noah' ark,

- Jesus walking on water, the crucifixion and his materialisation,
- Mary's mission at Fatima 1917,
- Saint Stephen's return/teaching in New Zealand,
- Spencer Perceval's vision in dream-state,
- Mary Stuart's return/teaching,
- Saint Columba's Iona mission,
- Tunguska Event does not relate to a comet,
- Bermuda Triangle is subject to time/dimension slip,
- Carlos Castaneda/Don Juan and dimension slipping,
- Light signs,
- Football World Cup and energies devoted to sport.
- September 11th as evidence of spirit existence,
- Terrorists and gunmen in spirit domain,
- Moses/Exodus/10 Commandments/Encoded Torah,
- The Bible Code.

There is no doubt that these things have happened and now make their contribution to the present day reality. This is a truly wonderful world, but also, what a wonderful world in past times it has been!

Credibility versus ridicule: Things and events considered to be above or beyond 'nature' are often labelled 'supernatural'. Things and events considered to be outside the normal range of scientific investigation are usually termed 'paranormal'. And things and happenings from within both of these categories are frequently ridiculed. I would suggest that ridicule in this application is a kind of defence mechanism. It is an attempt to keep that which is not fully understood and which is possibly rather frightening, outside the cosy world of full familiarity. It is a simple matter to say that something does not exist or is absurd. But one has to nevertheless observe in all this, one strictly logical change-factor: as our knowledge of things and events grows and as scientific investigation spreads, both the supernatural and the paranormal must diminish. This simply is progress. It is implausible to say that the change-factor, or indeed progress itself, does not exist. And Salumet's very words from his teaching of 10th March 1997 are:

~ *"...No longer will there be the fear and ... the distrust shall I say ... over all things termed 'supernatural'. They will become known and 'natural' to mankind."*

In this century, these domains of distrust are shrinking rapidly and as this process continues, it follows that we must learn to embrace new facts and ideas previously not allowed into consciousness.

There has been much ridicule in recent years of such items as crop circles, UFOs, 'aliens', fairies, prophecy and psychic surgery; even reincarnation and karma have been sadly misrepresented by media. Yet all of these things form part of our rich Earthly reality. They will not go away. It is now time to put aside ridicule and to open our minds to the wider, wonderful reality that has long been with us, and has been acknowledged by so many in those, in many ways advanced, past civilisations that once adorned our planet. And perhaps we shall even be able to talk to our children at bedtime about REAL fairy stories instead of contrived make-believe ones that often have the right idea but sadly veer away from informed truth.

Salumet's teaching, when accepted and taken to heart will take us forward on the crest of a wave with the rest of the galaxy. In taking this step we shall find that, in so doing, we revolutionise health, medicine, religion, farming, space travel and perception of our selves. What a truly majestic thought!

PART IV
FURTHER WORDS FROM LESLIE

I subscribe to the idea that a book should always be finished well and I had been turning over in my mind for several weeks how best to do this. Then, as if in answer to my thought, it happened. Just six of us had managed to get to the Monday meeting of 25th August 2003, including Eileen, and it was one of those rare occasions when Salumet was unavailable. Leslie was around and saw his chance to drop in for a chat. Perfect! What could be better than for he whose endeavours have contributed so much to make it all possible, to have the final word?

We became aware that one was with Eileen and, as is our usual formality, Lilian leaned forward and welcomed the visiting guest. It is almost unheard-of that there should be any mention of names at this stage of course. This is something that does not generally happen, but it was not so on this occasion:

~ *"You don't have to welcome **me**, Lilian…"*

Lilian (much surprised): "It's lovely to have you here anyway!"

~ *"As you can see, I am still being taught that dratted 'patience' issue…"*

Lilian (midst general laughter): "It's lovely to hear from you."

~ *"Yes … it's good to be with you all. I've worked hard on the emotion and on this dratted breathing, that always caused me a problem as you know full well."*

(On returning to the Earth in this way, as has been intimated in earlier pages, the old physical difficulties such as laboured breathing get temporarily revived as memory of it continues to prevail. The problem would no longer exist in spirit … only at the start of a visit to the physical world).

Lilian: "You sound fine now…"

~ *"I'm well."*

Lilian: "Good!"

~ *"You wouldn't believe how well … of course you do … of course you know how well I am!"*

Lilian: "Yes."

~ *"I took this opportunity, because I don't feel that I thanked everybody for all their good work and I know it still continues, and I don't come back as often as I thought I might, because … you'll enjoy this George … there's plenty to do, plenty to read … I'm always in the 'halls of learning'."*

George: "We all thank you of course … we are very much indebted to you, for the work that you initiated here."

(There followed spontaneous and enthusiastic agreement to this from all.)

Sarah: "I was only thinking the other day, if it hadn't been for you Leslie, none of us would be sitting here now."

~ *"Not at all … without all of you, the work wouldn't have continued. Remember that … it's the work that's important. We're just individuals, so remember that friends … that at every opportunity you are doing good work."*

Lilian: "Do you have a chance to listen to people like Salumet, where you are now?"

~ *"There's great teachers here, who come every so often. I unfortunately haven't had that pleasure yet, but I'm sure the day will come. I'm so involved in these halls of learning that it takes all of my time. And, as you can imagine, there were many people to talk to, to greet and remember old times. It was a wonderful experience and still is."*

George: "And these would all be friends and acquaintances from the past?"

~ *"Exactly … and more … and all the helpers and the people that we spoke about at the meetings. All those people are available if you so desire … and knowing me, I so desired!"*

(Indeed we all know him and our knowing laughter intervened for a spell.)

~ *"I've been and watched you all for little whiles at a time … I don't know if you have been aware of me around, but it's been good to see how your lives have been progressing."*

George: "Your name comes up from time to time."

~ *"Yes, and I'm aware of it … each thought of a name is collected, so we are aware. There's no need to tell me … or to tell you rather … I see my words still get confused at times. I don't need to tell you that all these thoughts get collected, and we know what's going on."*

George: "Speaking for myself, I get along better with the hearing aids now ... there was quite a serious problem with my hearing at one time and I was missing some things ... but it's improved. (I had wanted to say this to Leslie for quite some time ... the fact is that I would have liked to have contributed more during that awkward period when I was learning to cope with deafness and Leslie was moving house. But at least, my present words now gave Leslie the opportunity for one of those jokes that we know to be so typical of his brand of humour...)"

~ *"I could offer you the solution George, but I don't think you're ready yet   ..."*

(General laughter ... the solution of course being death, after which there is no hearing problem once in spirit!)

~ *"I don't think you would appreciate the suggestion..."*

George: "It's nice to be reminded there is a long-term solution!"

~ *"Yes."*

Sarah: "It's good you started the typing of the scripts Leslie, because that's been a boon for all of us."

~ *"Yes, it was a good idea wasn't it?"*

Sarah: "A very good idea..."

Lilian: "It's amazing. I was going through some earlier ones tonight..."

~ *"It's strange when tapes are played and you're listening (from spirit!), to yourself talking; quite strange I can tell you, but at the same time it's very touching that these memories can be brought to mind."*

Lilian: "Do you ever drop in on the Wednesday Group (a further spirit communication group of Leslie's initiation)?"

~ *"I have done, but as I say, I haven't returned too often, because there's so much for me to be doing."*

George: "And have you awareness that another book is in preparation?"

~ *"Well let me say this to you George ... I probably know more than you think!"*

(General laughter.)

~ *"And if I might say, there's been the odd tap on the shoulder, just to help you along."*

Sarah: "I was wondering if you'd had a little input Leslie?"

George: "I'm getting help I know, from a number..."

~ *"From a number of sources ... yes, you'd be right ... yes. It's not down to one. This work here goes on and on and it's a joint effort."*

George: "I thought you would be aware ... because there are no flies on Leslie!"

(General laughter.)

~ *"I'll accept that as a compliment George ... thank you very much ... yes."*

Lilian: "Can you give our love to Ruth and Roy ... Graham? ..."

~ *"They're aware of you all, don't you worry ... yes, you don't forget old friends ... yes. Oh, I'm so pleased that I've managed this time without the emotion!"*

Sarah: "So it's easier to come through this time is it?"

~ *"I've been working hard ... it's not easy. I understand now exactly why there are difficulties in communication."*

George: "Well, it's wonderful to have a cosy chat ... yes, I've no idea how easy or difficult it is for you ... but it seems to be a cosy chat to us."

~ *"Yes, we always assumed that having a bit of knowledge would make things easier; let me tell you, that's not the case. There's much that goes on behind the scenes and of course it helps when the energy is good and people are open ... and of course, to come back to friends makes it much, much easier. But what blocked me last time was the emotion that I was feeling. But I know you knew it was me and I tried hard this time, not to give the breathing problem."*

Sarah: "You sound fine."

~ *"Yes."*

Margaret: "It's lovely to hear your voice."

~ *"It's the result of hard work I assure you. Anyway, I won't keep talking ... I'm sure you've heard my voice often enough."*

George: "We don't hear it often enough these days."

Margaret: "No ... come again."

Lilian: "But we do think about you..."

(General concurrence.)

~ *"I know you do and I do as well. You were all a great part of my later years, for which I was really, really grateful to you all."*

All: "Thank you!"

George: "The feeling's mutual."

~ *"Well, I won't take up much more of your time, because there might be others wishing to come…"*

Margaret: "You've made my life a lot happier…"

Sarah: "Do you want us to pass any messages on to anyone Leslie?"

~ *"No … all I can say is, I'm around my own family quite often, which is natural … and unfortunately, I can now see that I was quite harsh at times, in my words … in my thinking. That may surprise you? It was a surprise to me. But I feel that I've helped since … in many ways, to make things right."*

George: "We're all human … we make our little changes here and there."

~ *"Yes, that was one of my favourite sayings, wasn't it George? 'We're all human' … and I still stand by those words."*

(Much laughter.)

George: "Yes, that's the saying of which Salumet once said: I don't want to hear!"

~ *"Yes, I know."*

Lilian: "I was talking to Vic … you know, your old neighbour … and he said, did we hear from you? So now I can say: yes, we've had a good long chat!"

~ *"You can tell him I'm still Leslie … still haven't changed too much … but improving…"*

George: "And do you look in on your daughter in Canada?"

~ *"Yes, my family are well looked after by me. It's one of the things that I am able to do from here, that I wasn't able to do when I was with you … because she was too far away."*

George: "Yes, it's an easier journey for you these days…"

~ *"Easier! It's the click of a finger George!"*

George: "Wonderful!"

~ *"Yes, I won't even begin to describe what it's like, because it's almost impossible. All your imaginings … all your thinking … under-rated! You have to come to discover what it really is … it's a wonderful life!"*

George: "We will, we will!"

Lilian: "And you can help show us the right way to go…"

~ *"Yes … now, although I'd like to stay and share a cup of tea…"*

(More laughs.)

~ *"… At least I don't have to **make** it any more … so that's a consolation if nothing else…"*

George: "One question that comes to mind … are you aware of the politics in the world and the problems in Iraq, or has that all become more dimmed?"

~ *"We have an awareness. If you are interested, then of course you have much more detail, but of course, you have to be interested in what's happening … and do you know … lots of people just want to move forward. So always remember that all of the information is available, but not necessarily known. So that would explain why sometimes people who come through to you, seem vague on all these issues."*

George: "Ah yes … thank you! So that which is not interesting (to the person), is conversely almost boring and becomes dimmed…"

~ *"Yes."*

George: "Thank you, that's nice to know."

~ *"But we have awareness of all things, if you wish. I wish I could take you George, to these books … you would have a whale of a time!"*

George: "Yes, I'm sure. I guess it will happen eventually."

Sarah: "So I suppose as you don't need any sleep, you are there all the time, are you Leslie?"

~ *"No, not all the time. I'm involved in healing on this side … I'm involved in many things … but now I'm being shown the clock…"*

(More laughs.)

~ *"I've been told I've spoken enough for one time, so that information might come next time."*

All then expressed their delight at Leslie's visit and asked that he come again.

~ *"I'm sure the opportunity will come. I am aware of you all and ever grateful. And again I want to say: thanks and love to you all … oh, and I don't like what they've done to my bungalow!"*

George, midst much laughter at Leslie's parting quip: "Now that's a very Leslie remark!"

And so, our dear friend of so many shared evenings withdrew on that high note of his very typical humour, and we were left chatting excitedly for quite some time. As to his reference to the help received from several sources in compiling this book, it is good to have Leslie's confirmation of this. In fact I have been aware of and much value the help received from several. I can mention one, who managed to come through in séance: an uncle, Christian Moss, who fell at the Somme in 1916 (and so we never met). We do in fact appear to have a bond, and I know of his Earthly letters, diaries and of his interest in writing that continues.

EPILOGUE

The following exchanges with Salumet relate to dispensation of the material presented here and to the way in which it is written down. Firstly there is part of a transcript from the meeting of 14th August 1995.

Leslie:"… We are collecting, as you know, all the information, and that which comes from your colleagues. I'm hoping that it's not going to remain tucked away somewhere, but that it will eventually … be published for the benefit of others. Whether I do the publishing or not is immaterial … I can't see myself getting time to do it, but I'm hoping that all that you've told us will be made public. Are you able to confirm that for me?"

~ *"Let me speak upon this matter. It is not so important that my words are put upon the paper, but let me say: I do understand the desire that the words spoken here should travel further afield. When first I came to you, I told you that information given by me, would be received by many others throughout your Earthly world … that all that would be given would be clarified by others. But we know that it is important for others to see and hear the words spoken within these selected groups. Therefore the time will come, the opportunity will be placed, whereby the information will be put down, will be gathered and will be distributed."*

Leslie: "Thank you. That's all I wanted to know. Thank you very much indeed. I should hate to have thought it just remaining stagnant."

~ *"All truth is never stagnant. It must go forward. It must travel from person to person, in order that what we say (is known) … and this time it cannot be dismissed as in times gone by. We have come to an age when the truth is here to stay."*

Later during that same evening, Salumet invited each in turn to come forward and place a hand upon his for just a few seconds (the physical hand of Eileen aligned of course to Salumet). We each reported on what was felt. It was Leslie who had the vision.

Leslie:"… As I sat down, I had a magnificent picture of a tall-ship fully rigged, gorgeous white sails and a wonderfully blue sea. I don't know the significance of the symbol, but I can only assume that it means that everything is sailing along splendidly."

And then as an afterthought:

"Incidentally, if any of you get a vision like that, which you can relate to something … if it is heading towards your right, it indicates the future; if it is heading towards the left, it indicates the past. My ship was heading towards the right."

It was thus stated during that evening of 1995, in answer to Leslie's question, that the words given would be clarified by others, be put down, gathered and distributed. The time would come and the opportunity would be placed. I see this book as the beginning of that process. In pursuance of that, on 1st December 2003 I spoke with Salumet, seeking his agreement to the very occasional, small adjustment to text that has been made in the interest of good grammatical presentation and flow of phrase. I felt touched and reassured by his reply:

~ *"My good friend, let me say: I trust you completely that my words be known. It matters not that there are slight adjustments provided the content of the truth be known."*

After stating that that had indeed been my feeling, I then added lightly that whilst at the computer keyboard I was not aware of any raps on the knuckles, to which he replied:

~ *"But there has been breath on your shoulder. It is well known what you have written…"*

Indeed, in accord with that oneness of time that prevails in spirit, the words would already be known (to our physical way of thinking at least), before they assemble onto the pages. And I feel wonderfully privileged to have been able to make my small contribution in putting it all together for we who currently dwell physically in the linear time reality.

REFERENCES

1 *The Divine Pymander of Hermes Trismegistus,* The Shrine of Wisdom, Fintry Brook, 1978, p. 9.

2 Timothy Freke & Peter Gandy, *The Hermetica, The Lost Wisdom of the Pharaohs,* Piatkus, London, 1997.

3 George E Moss, *A Smudge in Time,* Gemma Books, E. Wittering, 2000; prophecy 107-147, 348-355, crop circles 256-269, 278, 330-332, a being of light 343-347, health enhancement 295-296, Marian visions 107-119, Mary Stewart 311-315, Bible Code 348-355.

4 Erika Cheetham, *The Prophecies of Nostradamus,* Corgi Books, London, 1982, Quatrain X-72, p. 468.

5 Ivan Cooke, *Arthur Conan Doyle's Book of the Beyond,* The White Eagle Publishing Trust, Liss, 1994, p.102.

6 The Holy Bible, John 1, 1.

7 Robert Bauval & Graham Hancock, *Keeper of Genesis, A Quest for the Hidden Legacy of Mankind,* BCA, London, 1996. p. 64.

8 Graham Hancock, *Fingerprints of the Gods, A Quest for the Beginning and the End,* BCA, London, 1995.

9 Akbar-Ezzeman MS, *Abu'l Hassan Ma'sudi,* Bodleiean Library, Oxford.

10 The history of Herodotus, Book II – Euterpé 142-144; also included in: Great Books of the Western World Vol. 5, Ed. Mortimer J Adler, Encyclopaedia Britannica Inc., 1990, p. 79-80.

11 Plato, The dialogues of: *Timaeus* and *Critias;* also included in: Great Books of the Western World Vol. 6, Ed. Mortimer J Adler, Encyclopaedia Britannica Inc., 1990, p. 442-485.

12 Edgar Evans Cayce, *Edgar Cayce on Atlantis,* Ed. Hugh Lynn Cayce, Warner Books, New York, 1988.

13 Andy Thomas, *Vital Signs,* S. B. Publications, Seaford, 2002.

14 The Holy Bible, *Revelation,* Chapters 5-22.

15 White Eagle, *Spiritual Unfoldment 2,* The White Eagle Publishing Trust, Liss, Hampshire, 1969.

16 Sir James Jeans, *Physics & Philosophy,* Cambridge, London, 1943, p. 32-42.

17 John G. Fuller, *Arigo: Surgeon of the Rusty Knife,* Hart-Davis, MacGibbon, London, 1975.

18 Linda Chard, *Dr Kahn:The Spirit Surgeon,* Elmore – Chard, London, 1992.

19 Swami Rama, *Living with the Himalayan Masters,* Himalayan International Institute of Yoga Science and Philosophy of the USA, Honesdale, Pennsylvania, 1980.

20 Roger Woolger, *Other Lives Other Selves,* HarperCollins Publishers Ltd., London, 1999.

21 Paramahansa Yogananda, *Autobiography of a Yogi,* Crystal & Clarity Publishers, Nevada City, 1995, p. 331.

22 Tenzin Gyatso - The Fourteenth Dalai Lama, *The Meaning of Life,* Wisdom Publications, Boston, 2000, p.14.

23 Sheila Ostrander & Lynn Schroeder, *Handbook of PSI Discoveries,* Sphere Books Ltd, London, 1977.

24 Edited by: Geoff Tansey and Joyce D'Silva, *The Meat Business, Devouring a Hungry Planet,* Earthscan Publications, London, 1999, p. 9.

25 Lord Avebury, *British Wild Flowers Considered in Relation to Insects,* Macmillan & Co, London, 1875.

26 Dorothy Hodges, *The Pollen Loads of the Honey Bee,* Bee Research Association, London, 1952.

27 Paul Bura, *Stepping to the Drummer, The Extraordinary Tales of a Psychic Man,* Honeytone Promotions, Newstead, 2000, p. 99-143.

28 David Fasold, *The Discovery of Noah's Ark,* Sidgwick & Jackson, London, 1990.

29 Desmond Seward, *The Dancing Sun, Journeys to the Miracle Shrines,* MacMillan, London, 1993.

30 The Holy Bible, Acts of the Apostles, Chapter 7, 54-60.

31 Michael Cocks, *The Stephen Experience, The Christ of the Space Between,* Kelso, Auckland, NZ, 2001.

32 Leo Hobbis, *Seminar on 'The Stephen Experience' with Rev Michael Cocks.* Network, **85,** 30-31, 2004.

33 Roger D Nelson, *Correlation of Global Events with REG Data, An Internet-based nonlocal anomalies experiment,* Journal of Parapsychology, **65,** 247-271, 2001.

34 Dean Radin, *Seeking for Whom the Bell Tolls: Exploring Mind-Matter Interactions on a Global Scale*, Network, **79**, 12–15, 2002.

35 Michael Drosnin, *The Bible Code*, Weidenfeld & Nicolson, London, 1997.

36 Michael Drosnin, The *Bible Code 2, The Countdown*, Weidenfeld & Nicolson, London, 2002.

37 Jeffrey Satinover, *The Truth Behind the Bible Code*, Sidgwick & Jackson, London, 1997.

Copies of *A Smudge in Time* are available from Gemma Books. Full details from:

George E. Moss
geo 'Ruyton', Charlmead, E. Wittering
Chichester, W. Sussex PO20 8DN
Tel: 01243 673805
Email: georgemoss@talktalk.net

Gemma Books
Ruyton, E Wittering
Chichester, W Sussex PO20 8DN

PLEASE VISIT THE TRUTH CHANNEL
www.salumet.net
LOVE • LAUGHS • EXISTENCE • PAST LIVES
CROP CIRCLES • UFOs • ANGELS • HEALTH
INTERPLANETARY COMMUNICATIONS

ABOUT THE AUTHORS

Salumet: The principal author of this work is the one we know as Salumet. He is a Master who comes to us from the further domains of spirit to teach the cosmic truth and to uplift. He is of that same divine essence as Jesus, Krishna, Buddha and other Masters whose missions have made their mark in times past. He is of all-knowledge and can work what we would term 'miracles'. His words will revolutionise our thoughts and living. Humanity's awareness need have no bounds and our world-view will extend until we know our place in the galaxy and beyond.

George E Moss: As co-author and editor I take Earthly responsibility for presenting the inspirational teachings. I do not work alone. I feel the guidance of many in spirit and I have my companions who are the Kingsclere Group and they all contribute enormously.

As to personal life, I experience much happiness with my wife Ann, four children and their families. That includes the enjoyment of grandchildren, one of whom plays a fair game of scrabble! I am now retired from being a scientific consultant with laboratories in Reading but the knowledge of that discipline has helped in placing meaningful questions to Salumet. I am a member of the worldwide organisation: The Scientific and Medical Network, that has within its structure, a Science and Consciousness Group.

Also by George E Moss: *A Smudge in Time* ... An odyssey that charts Earthly progress through the last two million years. Its four parts account tribal origins, belief and prophecy, the impact of science and materialism, and the surge of spiritual awareness as we now move into a new millennium. Published 2000.

Also by Salumet: *Evenings with 'Salumet'* ... a chapter of the above work, plus various entries through Part 4 with appendix updates.

Further note: A Salumet website is planned. This will feature transcripts of the Kingsclere Group meetings that may be freely downloaded. These are all dated so that it should be possible to cross-reference them to book entries.

ISBN 141202661-X